Skoki Lodge, Banff National Park, Alberta, Canada

To Steve Williams, my valued colleague and friend these past four decades, in business and on the trail

Contents

Preface

It should come as no surprise that John Muir is my idol. After all, we share some striking commonalities. Though not born in Scotland like Muir, my grandfather was Scotch-Irish. Growing up, I was fascinated by the outdoors and adventure as was Muir. My father would let me plan our annual three week auto trips, often to the American West. Muir was raised in a Presbyterian family in which his father was a minister. I have been Presbyterian for many years. Muir attended the University of Wisconsin in Madison, Wisconsin. I received my two degrees from there. Muir found his way to make the West his home as I did. Since then, I have enjoyed hiking on the John Muir Trail in California, and with my wife, Lori, becoming a member of the Sierra Club that Muir co-founded in 1892. Even with the similarities though, I could not hold a candle to all that John Muir was, and to all that he accomplished in honoring the natural world.

I was ready for a career change in 1977. My wife, Lori (Loretta), and I were both weary from having struggled through yet another severe winter in the Chicago area. Along with over 54 inches of snow, the winter of 1976-77 tallied 43 days of continuous sub-freezing weather, the longest such stretch in Chicago history. So it was, in December 1977, ironically in the midst of a snow storm, that we packed up our car and headed west to Southern California, never looking back.

The adjustment to the sunny, warm clime and the potential it held were vividly accentuated one February day a couple months after our arrival. The day before had brought a considerable amount of rain, not unusual during the brief season that contrasted with the many drier months. But now the bright blue sky was clear. As I peered out in the near distance, I was awestruck by the glistening white snow on the mountains, gleaming from the radiance of the sun's rays. In that moment of intense natural beauty, I could relate to John Muir's reaction to one of countless moments he treasured. As recalled by his traveling companion, Stephen Young, in Glacier Bay, Alaska, after a rainy night, Muir's gaze upon a mountain brought this breathless exclamation: "'God Almighty!' he said. Following his gaze...I saw the summit highest of all crowned with glory indeed...As we looked in ecstatic silence we saw the light creep down the mountain...Our minds cleared with the landscape...But there was no profanity in Muir's exclamation, 'We have met with God.' A lifelong devoutness of gratitude filled us, to think that we were guided into this most wonderful room of God's great gallery...'We saw it! We saw it. He sent us to his most glorious exhibition. Praise God from whom all blessings flow.'"

Our first summer in California found us driving up the east side of the magnificent Sierra Nevada Mountains to Yosemite National Park for our first visit. On the way, we could see the pinnacles of Mount Whitney as we passed near by. Mt. Whitney is North America's highest peak, south of Alaska. I was reminded of a summer as a teenager, when I traveled with a group to Rocky Mountain National Park, where we hiked to the top of Long's Peak, the highest in that park. I wondered how Mt. Whitney would compare.

Though my desire to spend time in the mountains had already been established, I had a healthy respect for the challenges of high altitudes. Though not afraid of heights as long as there was an established trail of adequate width, I was not the type that had a stomach for technical climbing. That characteristic would become strikingly clear years later when my Firm's annual "Death March" took place in Zion National Park. We were contemplating a hike to the top of Angels Landing, an incredibly sheer, narrow rock tower rising 1,500 feet from the valley floor. We asked a ranger before starting whether we could go all the way to the top. She replied, "When you get to Scout Lookout, you will know if you can make it to the top." She was right. Once at Scout's Lookout, I knew there was no way I could go any further. At points, the steep, narrow, gravelly trail dropped off straight down on both sides for a thousand feet or more. Though physically possible, nerves of cold steel would be required to avoid freaking out with fright beyond that point. Frozen in fear when two teenagers in our group scampered on ahead, I vowed that no future hike would pose such a risk.

The good news is that America's west offers countless trails, mountains, canyons, rivers and lakes to explore without the need for technical climbing. I am grateful that the past four decades have provided a wide variety of opportunities for my colleagues and me to experience the indescribable splendor that abounds in the country that we love. Through it all, we have developed mutual bonds of caring and respect for one another and the natural environment.

From the start, I recorded rough trail notes for each death march along the way. These trail notes are reproduced chronologically in Appendix B just as they were originally written.

The main text of the book is organized in parts, generally by geographic areas. For each part, a chapter first recounts the various visits to that area. Then other stories follow. Midway through the past forty years, I began to write stories of some of the death marches. A couple of these stories were published in newspapers. All of these stories make up the chapters in the respective parts.

The High Sierra on the way to Mt. Whitney on Death March 1

Introduction

Traumatic beginnings gave birth to the "Annual Death March," a weekend backpacking adventure eagerly awaited by members and friends of HMWC CPAs & Business Advisors, a seemingly all-business bunch of Certified Public Accountants. In 1979, several of them thought it would be fun to drive to the Sierra Nevada Mountains and then walk to the summit of Mt. Whitney, the highest peak in California. A whole weekend would be spent to make the hike especially easy. Obviously knowing nothing of backpacking in the rugged mountains at high altitudes, these fellows were lucky to survive this misadventure. Typical of their naiveté, they discovered at the last moment that a wilderness permit was needed. When none was available for the popular direct route to Mt. Whitney, they were not the least bit suspicious at the ease with which they were able to get a pass for an alternate route that turned what was to be a 20 mile hike into a 45 mile "Death March!" The rest is history.

Death March Veterans

Gerry, Steve & George on Death March 3

Steve, Gerry & George on Death March 28-Mineral King, CA

Part 1

Looking Forward, Looking Back

Death March 20 – Kalalau Trail, Kauai, Hawaii

Death March 25 – Yosemite High Sierra Camps

Death Marches 30 & 35 – Banff National Park, Alberta, Canada

Chapter 1

Milestones Past and Future

Unique adventures to mark special years

As I write these opening pages, fans of the HMWC Death March are eagerly preparing for the 40th annual edition of this historic event. Earlier milestones were marked with unparalleled journeys.

For the 20th, the Kalalau Trail on the Hawaiian Island of Kauai was the dramatic choice. Chapter 12 recounts that sojourn in paradise.

For the 25th, we took a week, led by a National Park Ranger, to revisit each of the High Sierra Camps in Yosemite National Park, all of which we had individually tackled over the years. Chapter 4 tells the story.

Then on the 30th and 35th we set our sights further north to lodges high in the Canadian Rockies of Banff National Park. While picking a clear favorite Death March from all the spectacular places we have been would be difficult, the Canadian Rockies are at or near the top of the list. Chapters 2 and 3 touch on these two enchanting escapes.

To commemorate the unique accomplishment of a 40 year tradition would require a truly exceptional setting that typified the essence of the natural wonders and experiences that the prior four decades had held. The destination became obvious as Steve Williams and I contemplated the momentous decision. We would lift our glasses in celebration at Grand Teton and Yellowstone National Parks. With canyons, rivers, lakes with expansive shorelines, volcanic action, and, of course, arguably the most striking mountain range in North America, this superlative choice displays what the Death March is all about.

Steve on Ball Pass at Banff National Park, Alberta, Canada

Chapter 2

From Ledgers to Ledges

A retrospective of the first thirty years

"Our 'Leading the Firm to New Heights Award' goes to our new Managing Partner, Steve Williams," I proudly announced to the rousing applause of HMWC's forty employees and partners gathered at Disney's Grand Californian Hotel for the annual firm breakfast in September, 2008. This event gave us the opportunity each year to share our Tustin, California CPA firm's accomplishments and goals, while enjoying a weekend at the Magic Kingdom.

The award mug I held up bore Steve's likeness standing at the top of Ball Pass, near Shadow Lake Lodge, in Banff National Park, Canada. There twenty firm members, family, friends and clients had converged that July for the thirtieth rendition of a tradition ironically named "The Death March." More award mugs were given out for fun aspects of this adventure, such as "Swiss Family Robinson," "Stop and Smell the Roses" and "No Stone Left Unturned." These provided a fitting counterpoint to the impressive staff productivity awards that accompanied record results for the firm's fortieth year.

As the breakfast festivities continued, my mind wandered, contemplating what was the glue that held the firm and its members together with such a loyal bond. A major factor had to be the many special times like this that we spent together relishing triumphs and enduring challenges; the long hours during winter months sharing dinners and weekends working together, diligently serving our clients; bi-weekly Partner Meetings; Annual Planning Retreats, all assured that we had ample time together. But along with those was the firm's unique team building experience that we celebrated this morning: "The Death March."

It all started more than thirty years ago, as recorded in my journal...

Hail pelted my brow, icy winds chafed my cheeks, yet with chest heaving, I staggered the final gut wrenching steps to the majestic, 13,700 foot summit of Trail Crest. Rain soaked through my clothes as it had all day. A day where the impact of fifteen miles of trekking across the barren rocks of the High Sierra, burned into shoulders that grudgingly supported my forty pound pack. "All we wanted to do was climb Mt. Whitney," I pondered. "This has become a death march." I surveyed the breathtaking panorama spreading out below in all directions, as the deepening shadows raced across the landscape. I shook my head, wondering how I would manage to complete the final ten miles to Whitney Portals. My fellow backpackers had gone ahead hours ago. Would they wait for me? The prospect of hypothermia loomed closer with every step. It would be dark before long. How would they find me...? How would anyone find me...? What would they find...?

Somehow I made it out to the trailhead in the pitch blackness of that moonless night so long ago. No one was there. Totally exhausted, I collapsed into a ditch, vaguely thinking as I started to doze off, that dealing with the predicament of how to get home from this wilderness would have to wait until my weary body rested.

Ten minutes later, lights pierced the darkness. Before my half-open eyes could focus, colleagues were out of the car gathering me up along with my pack. In my weakened state, I had forgotten that they would need to drive to the beginning trailhead miles away to pick up the other car we had left at the outset. Since our hiking route was one way, cars had to be left at both ends.

Little did we know at the time, but important team building lessons were being learned, even then. Among them were the importance of proper preparation (or lack thereof), and that all members of the team mattered and needed to be accounted for.

Arriving safely home well past midnight, we swore we would never do that again. Funny how the mind works. Several months later, the hardships and misery we felt on the trip had faded, while the thrill and adventure of the mountains called again. We eagerly started planning the newly named Second Annual Death March.

This time we would do it right. We lowered our sights to more realistic levels. Again our objective would be the High Sierra, just not quite so high. And our packs would be not quite so heavy. No more cans of tuna or baked beans. Freeze dried meals and Gore-Tex gear would lighten the load. Getting in better shape was in order, also.

In mid-June we set out from Onion Valley trail head, on the east side of California's Sierra Nevada mountain range. Before long we were trudging through increasingly deeper snow covering the trail. At one point a colleague started slipping on the icy path through the collapsing snow. He headed uncontrollably toward the edge, just barely gaining a foothold at the brink of a sharp slope. Another step would have launched him down a thousand foot vertical slide. That was it for him. Regaining his composure, he turned around and headed back to the trailhead, never to join us again.

I was further along the trail with my newly hired staff accountant, Steve Williams. We were oblivious to our colleague's predicament and pushed on. We would be pushing on together on the trail and in the firm for many years to come. Later, as we looked out from atop 11,723 foot high Kearsarge Pass, we could not even have dreamed that twenty-nine years later, I would be passing on the mantle of Managing Partner to Steve.

However, dreaming was not an option as we surveyed the frozen landscape before us. We had anticipated deep blue hued lakes surrounded by bright green meadows welcoming us. But all we saw were ice-covered ponds amidst a dull white backdrop of snow covered trees and rocks. The view sapped what little resolve we had left. There was no use pressing on. But the snow-slowed climb left us with little energy for hiking back. We had no choice but to make

Gerry on top of Kearsarge Pass – Death March 2

camp here on the icy pass, bracing ourselves against the constant stinging wind. Fortunately, we had no appetite, since at this altitude our stove took forever to melt snow into a warm enough liquid for soup.

Hiking back down the next morning, we hoped we would glean from this experience the importance of learning all we could about the factors that can impact an anticipated endeavor, before forging ahead.

The third year would be the charm, we told ourselves. We would surely get it right this time. We decided to return to the same High Sierra locale as the prior year. We would be familiar with the terrain and know to go a month later, giving the area time to thaw out. The shift in tactics rewarded us. Peering over Kearsarge Pass after a grueling but dry climb, we saw the vibrant color of the previously frozen lakes: deep green at the centers, translucent near the shallow edges; snow only in the highest mountain crevices; a stream rippling vigorously through the valley.

Exhilarated, we hiked into the wilderness, accompanied by elusive marmots along forested slopes, moving confidently like the bighorn sheep that paralleled our route high above. On the next day, fascination with this remote back country captured our spirits so thoroughly that we had gone three miles out of our way before realizing a trail junction had been missed. The miscue and backtracking cost valuable time, causing us to fall short of the day's destination, and requiring the makeshift clearing of a campsite after dark. The lessons learned this year were the need to have well delineated trail maps and the sense to follow them closely. Back at the office we also found that thoroughly developed plans, that were well monitored, succeeded best.

Having conquered the High Sierra, we were ready to broaden our horizons the following year. The Grand Canyon beckoned us. Traversing the twenty-four miles from the North Rim to the South Rim would require the support of an additional team member. George's wife, Kay, once an HMWC employee before she married George, agreed to drive the car around to the South Rim after dropping us off at the North Rim. The arid terrain of the canyon contrasted sharply with the verdant slopes we remembered of the Sierras. After two days of smothering heat and blistered feet, tramping through the canyon's steep, rugged grandeur, we arrived to rejoin a relieved Kay at the South Rim. She got a little too anxious driving us home, drawing the attention of an Arizona highway patrolman, who promptly issued her a speeding ticket. That trip, Kay learned both the key role and the personal responsibility that a team member shoulders.

With mountain and canyon adventures behind us, we proceeded to river rafting, selecting the Kings River for the Fifth Annual Death March. Over the next twenty-five years, we would tackle four more river rafting trips, three island adventures, treks on horseback and sea-going vessels, through volcanic terrain, desert and seaside, along with several sojourns crisscrossing the farthest reaches of Yosemite

National Park. We endured hot and cold, wet and dry, high and low, bears, rattlesnakes, a mountain lion, and scorpions, a helicopter rescue, and a near fall from a cliff.

Along the way, we shared stories with fellow adventurers at remote wilderness lodges. We hiked with rangers, one of whom helped us to slow down, while showing us how to match up our diverse personalities to distinct tree groups such as quaking aspen and lodgepole pine. We paddled with river guides who deciphered mysteries for us, like that of the multi-hued layers of rock spanning billions of years of time on canyon walls. Most of all, we learned to revere nature. Each experience taught us new ways to work together, depend on one another and value the special bond that deepened with each passing year.

A round of applause brought me back to the present. With the annual firm breakfast nearing completion, Steve energized the audience with challenging new goals for the year ahead, along with poignant quotes, such as "We must risk going too far to discover just how far we can go." (Jim Rohn).

A feeling of satisfaction filled me, knowing that our firm had reached record results without the highly aggressive, hard charging marketing strategy that had seemed the norm in the profession for a long time. Over the years, our approach contended that an insightful attention to the development of people and sound management practices shared equal importance with, if not more, than the ongoing push for new business. I was pleased at recent industry conferences to hear methods like ours gaining more prominence. We also surrounded our efforts with an affirming sense of mutual respect, which had been a key to our success.

It finally struck me that the glue holding these factors together was brought home at our Partner retreat early in that summer, when facilitator Steve Erickson reported the results of a survey he had given to each Partner independently. On the question that asked what the trust level was within the firm, all Partners had given the highest rating. Erickson was duly impressed. Considering the many firms he'd worked with through the years, this was the first time he'd seen such consensus. We had not fully grasped the rarity of the special camaraderie the Partners shared. An added vote of confidence in our practices came that October, when the industry publication, Inside Public Accounting, named HMWC one of the 25 best managed accounting firms in the United States.

While many factors go into building a successful team, the confidence that comes from trusting relationships forged on jointly shared wilderness adventures, can have a lasting impact. Looking back thirty years, one of the reasons these adventures succeeded in building our team was that we didn't look at them as such. For us, they were merely a means to share a mutual love for nature and adventure. That they did, along with so much more.

Death March 30 Group at Sperry Chalet Trailhead-Glacier N. P.

Esther approaching Skoki Lodge on Death March 35

Chapter 3

Splendor and Solitude in the Canadian Rockies

The relaxed enchantment of Skoki Lodge

Unless you're a prince or princess, reaching Skoki Lodge requires a challenging, yet inspiring hike of seven miles. Nestled high among the Canadian Rockies in Banff National Park, the lodge and its surroundings have offered solitude and breathtaking natural vistas to hearty travelers since 1931.

Just days before a trek to Skoki, I had hiked to a waterfall in Johnston Canyon, located on the popular Bow Valley Parkway, just a few miles south of the Skoki trailhead. Though skies were overcast and rainy, hundreds of park visitors descended on the limestone-walled canyon, often impatient with the pace of others on the narrow walkway. Normally an enchanting diversion, the gridlocked gorge was now a victim of its own allure and accessibility.

I observed a similar result a few miles north at Lake Louise, where I spent the night at the renowned Chateau before striking out for Skoki. The stunning uniqueness of the lake, whose turquoise waters shimmer, gemlike within a setting of sheer, glacier-clad peaks, was dulled by the daily horde of 16,000 partakers, crowding in for a look. The broad lakeside path became a congested freeway of humanity, with anxious vacationers darting and weaving as they went.

By now I knew that any chance of gaining even a hint of the tranquility and solitude the early explorers sensed, would first entail an extended hike on a mountain trail, leaving comforts and crowds behind. That was reason enough. On a sunny August morning, seven colleagues and I set out. Once on the trail, we spotted a grizzly bear, deer and several hoary marmots, but only a handful of humans.

Nevertheless, each new turn in our path revealed yet more spectacular vistas, evoking spontaneous wows from group members.

Crossing Boulder and Deception Passes gave us a thousand foot elevation gain prior to reaching Skoki. Along the way, snow-speckled peaks with names like Wall of Jericho and Fossil Mountain mesmerized our senses, as did the emerald green lakes with their glacial fed streams and waterfalls. Wildflowers of yellow, blue, lavender, white and red covered the alpine meadows.

At Skoki, a friendly staff from Australia and New Zealand greeted us warmly, with lemonade and an array of cheese, crackers, pumpkin bread and cheesecake. At dinner, we met Leo Mitzel, the manager of ten years, who shared the Skoki spirit with us. Raised in a family that led horseback tours in the area, Leo exuded the mellow lifestyle that typified the Skoki legacy.

Leo related the story of Prince William and Catherine, Duchess of Cambridge, who he and his wife, Katie, hosted on the royals' honeymoon trip in 2011. Though protocol required running water and toilet facilities, features non-existent before and after the visit, Leo sensed that England's future king and queen would have been just as happy without.

The next morning as we shared a cup of coffee by the fire before others arose, Leo asked me: "You're from Chicago. Why do you come to places like this?" I responded: "I feel closer to God here. It's a spiritual experience for me." Leo replied that it was spiritual for him as well. When he needed spiritual help, he told me he climbed to a mountain top, where he felt God's presence. He didn't need organized religion.

Leo enjoyed meeting guests with the diverse backgrounds that arrive at Skoki from all corners of the world. He observed that usually the hike in to Skoki changed peoples' perspective. Having endured the exhausting hike myself the prior day, I could relate to what he was saying. The effort tended to show the commonality of our human limitations, resulting in a relaxed atmosphere where mutual respect flowed effortlessly.

Following breakfast, Leo sat at our table with a folder of maps and a marker, to lay out the day's hikes for us. We selected Merlin Lake, which the royal couple had tackled on their visit. After marking the way, Leo handed the map to me, "Here, this is yours. Use it to guide the way."

On the trail an hour later, I had developed a new found respect for the pluck of the Prince and Princess. A boulder field and steep rocky scramble near the top caused some anxious moments. Hand holds in narrow crevices for lifting, coordinated with careful foot placement, were called for to negotiate the final few steps.

The brotherly perspective Leo had mentioned became apparent, when my hiking companion and I noticed a woman afraid to proceed. "Let us help. You can make it," I said. Though we were strangers, she willingly trusted our guidance and outstretched hands to bring her through the most precarious section. At this moment, we were fellow seekers on a common journey.

The demanding effort proved worthwhile when, at the top we viewed the placid grandeur of Merlin Lake filling the valley below us. A restful lunch at the serene lakeshore followed, beneath the purview of a hoary marmot peering boldly from atop a nearby boulder.

The longer we stayed at Skoki the closer the bond grew with the other guests at the lodge, who came to feel more like family. There was no other choice, since we found ourselves in the back country together, in close quarters with nowhere else to go. Happily, Skoki has welcomed no more than 24 guests at a time since opening in 1931, a far cry from the crowds down below.

We all gathered around two tables to feast on the cuisine, which displayed a level of sophistication not expected with accommodations that lacked running water or electricity. The dinner menu boasted New Zealand lamb, organic rice & quinoa, roasted beets, corn medley and apple caramel cake. Second helpings were welcome and taken gladly. Dining in candlelight transformed the atmosphere of the rustic room into that of a secluded romantic hideaway.

The scenic splendor of the area coupled with the gracious ambiance, softened the harsh realities of existence taken for granted back home. Crave a shower? A bowl of warm water and a rag will have to do. Feet sore from hiking over rough terrain? Soothe them in the cold, rushing water of the nearby stream. Need to answer nature's call during the night? Bundle up and grab a flashlight before venturing to the outhouse a dozen steps away from the lodge.

Did you bring a good book to wile away the quiet hours? The gift of time was my most cherished gift at Skoki. Though modern daily life has a way of consuming every moment, up there unfettered time flowed abundantly: early in the morning, after a day hike, and in the evening hours. Some napped, while others enjoyed games. I prized the freedom to just sit and contemplate; to reflect; to find myself.

The prince and princess chose Skoki Lodge as a honeymoon stop for two reasons: its remoteness and its reputation for friendly hospitality. Having been the benefactor of Leo and the staff's care and kindness, I am confident the royal couple was not disappointed in that regard. Even so, with the constant exposure that defines their existence, I can only hope that the special quality of Skoki's remoteness brought a brief taste of the solitude they sought.

Yosemite Valley and Falls (above) and Half Dome (below)

Part II

Yosemite National Park

Lake high in Yosemite (above) and Tuolumne Meadows (below)

Chapter 4

Yosemite National Park

It is by far the grandest of all the special temples of Nature I was ever permitted to enter.-John Muir

Though our first visit to Yosemite National Park did not come until the sixth Death March in 1984, it soon became our most popular. Over the next thirty years, we explored some aspect of this monumental national park nine different times. We began there with a backpack trip in 1984, starting in Tuolumne Meadows, after overnighting at the Upper Pines Campground in Yosemite Valley. Crossing the green, stream-covered alpine meadow, we passed the angelic Cathedral Rock, first climbed by John Muir in 1869, during his initial summer in Yosemite.

From there, our hike took us to the expansive meadow-side campground, known as Sunrise, where we pitched our tents for the night. Located on the side of a mountain, the site gave us a panoramic view of Long Meadow, with its meandering streams and mountains on the far side. Sunrise also exposed us, as onlookers, for the first time to a High Sierra Camp, a luxury heretofore unknown to us. Situated next to our campground, the High Sierra Camp came complete with tent cabins, dining hall, solar heated showers, wash tub, flush toilets, and water. When no one was looking, we took advantage of the showers and toilets, meant only for paying High Sierra Camp guests. Later, while tantalizing aromas wafted our way from the dining hall, we fired up the camp stove and 'feasted' on freeze dried turkey tetrazzini and cup-o-noodles.

The next morning, after freeze dried granola and blueberries (my breakfast tradition on all the back-packing Death Marches), we completed a glorious 14-mile hike, around the backside of Half Dome, and on down the Mist Trail, past gorgeous Nevada and Vernal Falls, finally arriving in Yosemite Valley at the Happy Isles

Trailhead. Happy Isles would be the welcome finish to several of our Yosemite Death Marches, thanks especially to the ice cream stand awaiting us there.

Other memorable events from this Sixth Annual Death March included the first one for Scott Williams, all of five years old. Scott would not miss a Death March for the next fifteen years. Though Scott was unable to make a few during college and early marriage years, when he brought one-year-old son, Jonah, on the 34th Annual Death March to Yosemite in 2014, by then he was only the third youngest to join us. Five years after young Scott Williams made his inaugural hike, his sister, Monica, at six months of age, broke the youngest age record, as her dad, Steve, carried her on his back across Catalina Island, on Death March 11 in 1989.

Scott & Steve   **Scott & Jonah**

Monica also became a regular Death Marcher over the years, and now even holds the title of proud mom to our second youngest Death Marcher, her daughter Brooke. At ten months of age, Brooke completed the 36th Annual Death March in Sequoia National Park, on, you guessed it, the back of Grandpa Steve Williams.

One not so pleasant memory from that initial Yosemite Death March was the first casualty, not counting the numerous bruises and blisters suffered by all. The mother of one of the marchers had graciously driven us all up to the Tuolumne Meadows trail head, and then drove her van back to the Valley campground to stay while we hiked. The plan was for her to prepare a celebratory steak dinner for us upon our return.

When we arrived back at the Valley campground, tired and weary, she was no where to be found. Turns out, that while out for a ride, she was thrown by a horse, crushing two vertebrae, and landing herself in the park hospital. She eventually recovered, but her husband had to drive up and bring her home. All that and she didn't even hike.

Four years later, we were ready to return to Yosemite. Seasoned and experienced, and also tiring of sleeping on the ground, we planned ahead, and embarked on the first of several Death Marches staying at the various High Sierra Camps. The 10th Annual Death March took in Glen Aulin and May Lake, while the 12th went to Merced Lake and the 16th to high altitude Vogelsang. We would return to May Lake in 2000, and made the circuit of all five High Sierra Camps on our 25th anniversary Death March. But in between, we explored Yosemite in different ways as well, including on horseback and on river rafts.

The 10th Death March was a milestone, with a record 21 participants. Though the inaugural Death March included 5 participants, by the 3rd we were down to only a hearty three: Steve, George and me. Not discouraged in the least (though arguably a little nuts), we keep selling the unparalleled rewards to be gained from these outdoor adventures. Our perseverance paid off, and not only with males. Ten women were among the 21 who left the comforts of Yosemite Lodge in the valley back in 1988 to hike first the six miles to Glen Aulin High Sierra Camp, and then eight more miles to May Lake the next day.

Each High Sierra Camp has its own unique charm, in addition to the dramatic scenery of granite cliffs and outcroppings, interspersed with lush meadows that are found on the trails connecting the camps. Glen Aulin sits beside the Tuolumne River with the White Cascade waterfall providing a striking backdrop.

The home style meals at the High Sierra Camps were always substantial and tasty. That night at Glen Aulin was a good example, with cream of celery soup, Austrian-Hungarian goulash, pasta, stir-fried vegetables, and topped off with a delicious apple crisp. The following night even topped that with steak and chocolate cake. College students spent the summer making meals and maintaining the camps.

The four-bed tent cabins had warm wool blankets plus a wood stove to ward off the coldness of the night. The filling breakfast the next morning was also typical, with hot cereal, bacon, eggs scrambled with vegetables, potatoes, juice and coffee. We already knew there would be no turning back to the days of camping in a tent and dining on freeze-dried food.

The hike to May Lake was grueling, through forests and over granite-faced mountains, with spectacular vistas of lakes and the Sierras. The reward however was the clear, pristine May Lake, reflecting the towering white granite of Mount Hoffman, rising from the far side. Worn out from the eight mile trek, and hearing the rumbling of a thunderstorm closing in, we easily decided that an ascent of Mount Hoffman could wait until a future Death March.

May Lake's location, only 1.2 miles from the trailhead and parking lot, was a blessing and a curse. Upon hearing a report that bears had broken into some cars there, Marley rushed down the trail to check, since food had been left inside her car. Though finding no damage, she got soaked from the storm on her way back, while the rest of us enjoyed the spectacle of nature while safe and warm in the dining hall. Later, when the storm had passed, a gorgeous sunset and a view of Half Dome were enjoyed from a nearby bluff.

Loretta on trail from Glen Aulin to May Lake

Completing the 10th Annual Death March, we were pleased that we had finally found a more "civilized" way to experience the challenges and adventures of the great outdoors, while still enjoying some creature comforts along the way. There was just one minor disappointment. Though hearing of numerous sightings and assurances that they were around, no time in the first ten years of Death Marches had a bear been encountered on the trail. Though some of the group were glad of that, the day would eventually come when the record would be broken.

Though the High Sierra Camps made the hiking treks more pleasant, they did not provide immunity from the occasional mishap. The 12th Death March to Merced Lake proved the most dramatic by way of misfortune for one unlucky participant.

On the first night at Merced Lake, having completed a strenuous thirteen mile hike up and over the spectacular Mist Trail, we were all relaxing by the campfire, with slippers or flip flops replacing hiking boots on our tired feet. All at once someone came into camp reporting a bear nearby. Anxious for the first bear sighting on any Death March, everyone raced over to the area of the report. We looked high and low, but alas, no bear.

However, on the way back, Julia slipped on the rocky path and severely strained her ankle and leg. She was in much pain. We carried her back to camp and put her to bed with ice on the injured limb. The next day we put her in the stream to soak the leg with the cold flowing mountain water.

Finally in the afternoon a ranger arrived. After examining Julia, he decided she should be taken out by helicopter. Her ankle and leg were swollen and stiff by that point. Julia was embarrassed and disappointed, but knew she could not hike out. The ranger would have put her on a horse, but he felt the pain would be unbearable, and further injury could occur.

Fortunately, there was a wide flat rock formation near camp. After improvising a stretcher from a canvas tarp, eight of us moved Julia to the landing zone. Though the chopper ride to the Valley would take only five minutes, Julia had to wait until 4 pm to get lifted off, due to other more pressing emergencies in other parts of the Park. Meanwhile, Ranger Bob placed an inflatable plastic splint on the injured leg.

When the chopper eventually arrived, with the blades blowing dust all around, the crew transferred Julia to a real stretcher and loaded her into the rear of the aircraft. The chopper then slowly lifted off the ground a foot or two, before dropping back to earth. It was too heavy. One of the crew had to hop off and stay behind, while Julia was whisked off to the Park clinic.

The next day, after we had finished the hike back out to the Valley, Julia was waiting for us, with a cast stretching from knee to toe. With the limited facilities at the Park, clinic staff were unable to

Julia sprains her ankle badly on Death March 12 and gets airlifted out from Merced Lake

determine if bones had been broken. That would have to wait until she got home. As bad luck would have it, the first bear sighting would also have to wait for a Death March yet to come.

Paul fishing in Merced Lake on Death March 12

But the next Death March to Virginia Lakes brought an even scarier animal sighting. We had packed in by horseback the day before to a remote area near the far north east boundary of Yosemite National Park. All were glad to be on foot after a full day on horseback, which included riding past several lakes, then up and over a steep pass.

Karen, Mark, Jeff and Gerry hiked for two hours, reaching further into the back country, up toward Shepherd Lake, where spectacular views of Shepherd's Crest were the reward. Gerry had gotten far ahead of the rest when he spotted an inviting rock outcropping fifty yards ahead. About to climb up and explore the formation, he suddenly froze in his tracks. For a split second he glimpsed the form of a mountain lion, just as it moved behind the rocks, out of sight. Cautiously, he started to slowly backpedal a few steps, not taking his eyes off the spot where the lion was last seen. Then he turned and ran at full speed back to the others. Upon hearing Gerry's report,

Riding in to Virginia Lake on Death March 13

they all turned and ran without hesitation, anxious to get out of range from the lion. Fortunately, the lion was not seen again. But the episode made for excited talk around the campfire that night.

By the campfire near Virginia Lake

Steve on horseback heading to Virginia Lake

Gerry by Mono Lake calcite deposits on death March 13

May Lake and Mt Hoffman (above) and May Lake Cabins
(below) on Death March 22

Chapter 5

Discovering Yosemite's High Sierra in Comfort

A short hike leads to peaceful, alpine lake at the Park's center

On separate occasions over the past fifteen years, my colleagues and I had hiked to all of the five High Sierra Camps in Yosemite National Park. But this was our first visit since the lottery system was put in place. We picked May Lake, above Tuolumne Meadows in the northern section of the park, because of its easy accessibility and the possibility of a variety of challenging day hikes.

The High Sierra Camps provide a means of experiencing the backcountry grandeur of Yosemite without having to "rough it." Each consists of tent cabins with beds (usually 4 singles to a cabin), showers, pit toilets, and best of all, hot meals prepared by the college age staff that run the Camp. Getting to the Camps requires a hike of from two to ten miles. Guided saddle trips also bring in small groups on mules.

The lottery system required that an application be submitted between October 15 and November 30 requesting specific camps and dates within the short July through mid-September season. Snow and weather conditions keep the camps closed the rest of the year. A maximum of eight spaces can be requested on the application. Twelve years ago we had brought twenty-one co-workers and friends through two of the Camps, so making do with eight would be difficult.

My colleague, Steve and I decided to apply independently, hoping to increase the total number. The drawing was held in mid-December and notification came in mid-February. We were both successful at getting eight spots, but for different weekends. We settled on the last weekend in August, and put into motion our second plan for securing more. For the next several months, we called at least weekly hoping to pick up cancellations.

Finally as summer approached, we succeeded in obtaining the four additional reservations we needed, for our group that now totaled twelve. As a backup strategy, I had obtained a Wilderness Permit that would allow us to stay with our own tents in a nearby campground. For those backpackers lucky enough, a limited number (six) of meals-only passes could be reserved at the High Sierra Camp.

Though I had been to Yosemite many times, I was again left breathless by the first view of Yosemite Valley that dramatically appeared when the car emerged from a tunnel as we approached from the south. Accented by a few billowy clouds and deep blue sky, the massive stone face of 3,000 foot El Capitan rose majestically before us, while the equally imposing Half Dome loomed in the distance.

We were headed to Curry Village in the Valley for the first night, having driven up from our homes in Southern California. Curry Village, with its motel units and numerous tent cabins, was not as crowded as I expected on this Saturday. Nearby Yosemite Village, however, was bustling and parking difficult to find as we stopped there to check out weather and trail conditions in the Wilderness Center.

The next morning, a little acclimated after a night's sleep at the 4,000-foot altitude of the Valley, we started with breakfast at the Curry Village buffet. I was puzzled why the check-in cashier asked who was President the year I was born. My friend, Carl, clued me in. That was her discreet way of determining if I qualified for the seniors' discount (I did). We departed Curry Village at 9 AM and drove north along the Tioga Pass Road. By the time we reached the trailhead to May Lake an hour later, we were well over 8,000 feet above sea level. After a group photo we embarked on the short 1.2-

mile trial. Though uphill and rocky most of the way, we arrived at the Camp in a half-hour, with little effort.

This High Sierra Camp is favorably situated on the wooded south shore of serene May Lake. Across the half-mile circumference of this circular body of water, Mount Hoffman's barren white slopes rose sharply over 1,500 feet.

Having arrived before 11:00 AM, the tent cabins were still being cleaned from the night before. We unloaded all but the water and box lunches from our packs, and seven of us decided to continue on to the day's hiking objective: the summit of 10,850 foot Mount Hoffman. One of the staff pointed us to the trail along the left side of the lake.

Before long, we realized that the easy, well-marked path we just completed to the Camp, had given us a false sense of confidence. Soon we were huffing and puffing in the thin air and hot sun, up a steep, unmaintained trail that was hard to follow, and often broke into several alternative routes. Small mounds of rocks placed by earlier trailblazers were often all that kept us from getting lost or off into dead ends, as we staggered ahead. Though the distance to the peak was barely two miles, the altitude and heat were taking their toll as we neared the summit.

The final challenge was a harrowing scramble up a difficult rock face where hand and foot holds were hard to find. Reaching the top just behind me was my friend, Curtis, looking a bit harried and weary. This was his first time hiking in the mountains with us. He remarked: "If this is what you consider fun, don't invite me if you plan something that's not considered fun." After catching his breath for a moment however, he agreed with me that the spectacular 360-degree view of the whole of Yosemite made the struggle worth it.

Madison scrambling up Mt Hoffman

Mount Hoffman is near the geographical center of the Park.
From here the churning landscape of alternating mountain peaks and
valleys unfurled before us, dotted with evergreen trees that thickened

to a forest on the lower reaches. Half Dome and the rest of Yosemite Valley were an outlying ripple amidst this geologic blend. Contemplating this expansive scene along with a little anxiety about the descent to come, we took a break with our box lunches on the confined boulder strewn crest that we shared with a few other hikers.

Surprisingly, the hike down was less fearful than anticipated. We quickly retraced our footsteps and were back in camp by 2:00 PM. Grateful that we were not "roughing it," we indulged in refreshing showers and spent the remainder of the afternoon perched on the lakeshore, reading and absorbing the quiet beauty of the high country. Almost. Half of our group was in the dining hall engaged in a raucous game of cards.

Dinner that night was family style with the thirty-six guests sharing four tables in the tent covered dining room that adjoined the permanent rock-walled kitchen structure. Servings were ample with roast turkey, mashed potatoes, zucchini, soup, salad, and soda bread, topped off with apple cobbler. The camaraderie generated among guests during dinner carried over to the campfire later that topped off a fulfilling day. Even so, everyone was ready to call it a night by 9:30.

Monday morning came early, with most of us up already by 6 AM. Though I found the comforter and blankets more than adequate against the chill night air, smoke billowed from the small stack of the next tent cabin. Wood burning stoves are provided to warm the tent cabins as needed. Coffee and hot chocolate were welcomed at 7, followed by a hearty breakfast of tomato and cheese omelets at 7:30.

Fully rested and much better acclimated to the 9,270-foot altitude of May Lake, we were ready for another adventure. Taking the lead from a Yosemite trail journal, we decided on an ambitious twelve-mile trek to North Dome, for a not often seen view of Yosemite Valley from the north side. From our camp, this hike first required a 1.2 mile hike back to the May Lake Trail Head, followed by a two mile drive to Porcupine Flat and the North Dome Trail Head. All in our group were game except for George, a former colleague, and his son Gene. They were enjoying the relaxing solitude of the Camp and had little desire to venture off.

Despite the long distance of Monday's hike, everyone was more appreciative now of a well-maintained trail and the gentler inclines than had strained our leg muscles and lungs the day before. Also, the route was filled with diversity, some up, some down, in and out of the woods for awhile, then across an exposed rockscape.

At the midpoint, we were rewarded with an unusual rock formation rising above us, called Indian Rock. As we approached, a beautiful delicate arch came into view high on the Rock. Anxious to get our pictures taken on the arch, we waited patiently while a trio of young people from England and Germany struck a precarious pose, their feet dangling above the long drop-off as they sat on the front of the arch.

Toward the end of the final two miles, we started to walk onto the white rock of the bald dome. With the edge looming ever nearer with each step, we could sense that we were approaching a profoundly moving experience. The far walls of Yosemite Valley started to slowly emerge before us. Then we were there, standing as though on a pedestal, with this awe inspiring natural cathedral enveloping us on three sides.

Across the way were Glacier Point and the smooth, white surface of Cloud's Rest. Far below, Yosemite Village nestled on the Valley floor. But the most impressive sight was Half Dome. So close and immense, I felt I could almost reach out and touch the sheer 2,000-foot granite face. An igneous dome, carved by exfoliation and glacial movement, Half Dome rose 8,842 feet above sea level, with almost 5,000 feet of that total extending above the Valley.

We hated to leave this unique treasure. But we knew the sense of overpowering awe would stay with us long after this special moment passed. We returned to camp instilled with a humbling gratitude for this rare, weekend sojourn.

Arriving back at the North Dome Trail Head, a light rain had started to fall. Not wanting to get wet hiking the final mile back to May Lake, we hopped in the cars and drove a few miles further to Tuolumne Meadows and the General Store there for ice cream and cold sodas. Unfortunately, the rain continued, so we got wet anyway. Of course, our ponchos were up at the camp, none of us thinking the sunny day this morning would turn to rain later. The rain actually felt good. Dry clothes and a campfire when the rain stopped warmed us up.

After dinner that night, we walked up the nearby ridge to see a final glowing crimson sunset; a fitting conclusion to a wondrous adventure.

Ranger Steve serenading the group in camp

Chapter 6

Connecting With the Yosemite Wilderness

A Park Ranger leads a week-long nature bonding trek

"I could tell this was going to be a good group when I saw the campfire burning as I approached," exclaimed Ranger Steve Schwarz to the partakers gathered around the fire ring.

Three singles, two couples and a group of six comprised the hearty contingent assembled at the Tuolumne Meadows Lodge (elevation 8,600 feet) the eve before a seven day, 50 mile, hiking loop to all five of the High Sierra Camps, in the northern climes of Yosemite National Park. When Steve, a National Park Service Ranger Naturalist, was late in arriving, group members took it upon themselves to start the fire that would fight off the cold of a dissipating rain.

Steve welcomed us for the journey together, passing out journals for recording our personal impressions. Yosemite offers the most comprehensive set of backcountry camps of all the National Parks in the United States. Situated seven to ten miles apart and connected by trails traversable only on foot or on horseback, the camps provide beds in tent cabins, toilets, showers (in some), and hot meals prepared by a staff that spends the short summer season serving guests who pass through.

But aside from these basics, each camp takes on its own personality, at times in spectacular ways from unique natural settings, and at other times in more subtle ways, stemming from the quirky character of the facility and staff.

Our group was diverse, with some who were venturing off the main road for the first time. Others, like my party of six, had been doing this type of adventure for twenty-five years. In fact, this trip was, for us, a commemoration of that milestone.

To set the tone for the week, Steve shared a poem by John Muir:

Climb the mountains and get their good tidings.

Nature's peace will flow into you as sunshine flows into the trees.

The winds will blow their own freshness into you,

and the storms their energy,

while cares will drop off like autumn leaves.

Crossing a bridge on the Tuolumne River the next day, I felt those "leaves of cares" dropping off behind. After a downhill hike of seven miles, we had arrived at Glen Aulin High Sierra Camp (elevation 7,800 feet) in the early afternoon, to the sounds of a twenty-foot high waterfall and cascade that bordered one side. Camp manager, Thom Dodd, welcomed us in the combination store and dining hall, with a glass of lemonade and a briefing of camp policies. "There are no showers here," he sadly announced, but then softened the blow by adding, "Bathing suits are optional if you wish to cool off in the river. It won't bother me if you don't have one."

After a skinny dip, nap and some reading in our four-bed tent, we felt renewed and ravished with hunger as the time for our first backcountry dinner approached.

At 6:00 PM, a loud clanging sound announced coffee and cocoa, to be followed by the meal at 6:30. "It's Sunday, so that means Thanksgiving dinner at the High Sierra Camps," Steve informed us. All the camps have the same menu on any given night of the week, so hikers can go from camp to camp, assured of variety.

Following a meal of turkey with all the trimmings, Steve took us to the top of a dramatic ridge to present the first of nightly nature talks. Looking behind us in the distance, we watched a turbulent wall of white water drop straight down from a cliff high on the mountain, then tumble across outcrops, forming a lengthy series of cascades and waterfalls before reaching the lower elevation of the camp area. To our front, the U-shaped beginning of the Grand Canyon of the

Tuolumne spread out below us. The river wound through the evergreen lined gorge's smooth granite walls, as it journeyed toward the sun, descending on the horizon.

The HMWC group at dinner at the High Sierra Camp

Not wanting to distract from the sunset, Steve promised, "I'll cover 500 million years of geologic history in five minutes." And he did! When he was done, we could identify the minute, like the potassium feldspar phenocrysts (crystals protruding from granite boulders, locally known as "chicken heads"), to the massive, like the glacially created valleys. When the sunset finally culminated, the enchanting orange hues filled any remaining nooks and crannies of our contented souls.

Returning to camp tired but exhilarated, we were ready for bed at 9:00 pm. The tent cabins came well equipped for the cold nights. Several blankets and a comforter topped the beds, while a bucket of wood stood ready by a little stove.

The next morning, we gorged ourselves with the first of daily breakfasts that contained various forms of eggs scrambled with veggies, bacon and fruit, along with muffins, scones, or pancakes and cereals hot and cold. The hearty meals proved invaluable, sustaining us through the long days of hiking over rough terrain and high altitudes.

Prior to departure, Steve asked that we come up with a song each day to sing as a thank you to the camp staff. Group member Sean displayed a creative knack for quickly composing the needed verses. Gathering around the staff, our voices added a simple melody to the words: "O, Glen Aulin staff. We thank you for the food. We ate so much, we ate so fast, we hope you did not think us rude."

Amidst appreciative laughter, we donned our packs, picked up box lunches, and headed out. The trail proved more challenging this Monday, with two tough uphill stretches over eight miles. The terrain alternated between shaded, evergreen forests and open, granite shelves. On one smooth outcropping overlooking a mountain vista, we rested while wolfing down sandwiches, along with fruit, cookies and juice.

By mid-afternoon, we walked into May Lake High Sierra Camp (elevation 9,270 feet). The lake is bounded on the far side by rock-strewn Mount Hoffman, which rises up sharply from the bank to its 10,280-foot peak. A smiling Brian Shoor greeted us warmly.

May Lake turned out to be the best-run camp. Brian's wife, Jennifer was the cook, and his five-year-old daughter Riley acted as the self-appointed greeter and jokester. That evening while we feasted on a dinner of Chicken Orange with brown rice, Riley stopped by our table and asked, "Why didn't the teddy bear eat dinner?" To our puzzled looks she gushed, "Because he was stuffed."

Brian Shoor, Camp Manager, welcomes us to May Lake

From their pleasant manner and capable efforts, the Shoor's exuded a special pride in their Camp. Here there were flush toilets that actually worked, an inviting shower, and a large sink complete with a wringer for washing out clothes, grubby from the trail. Meals and early morning coffee were right on time, if not early.

For tonight's talk, Ranger Steve again took us up on a ridge for another spectacular sunset, accompanied by a history of Yosemite. Not your typical dry retelling of events, though. Steve pointed our gaze across the broad valley to the distant mountains, and as he named each of the numerous peaks, he told us the story behind the name.

Names, such as Mount Conness, mysteriously peering through wispy clouds, honored the Senator who introduced the bill in Congress, first preserving Yosemite for the State of California. Mount Clark and the Clark Range paid tribute to Galen Clark, the Park's first appointed guardian. Even May Lake and the protective Mount Hoffman bore romantically appropriate monikers. The mountain's namesake, Charles Hoffman, topographer for the first geological survey of the Park in 1863, dubbed the lake, May, for the sweetheart who became his bride in 1870. Steve related how each of the designees had "followed their dream," and encouraged us to follow our dreams as well.

The third day's hike to Sunrise High Sierra Camp (elevation 9,400 feet) would net only a hundred foot elevation gain, but to get there first required a descent of over 1,000 feet followed by a steep climb up a series of switchbacks. Along the way, we passed by the picturesque lake named for Chief Tenaya, leader of the Ahwanachee tribe that occupied Yosemite Valley for hundreds of years until rousted by the Mariposa Battalion in 1851.

Ranger Steve proved his worth daily, tipping us off of breathtaking vantage points just off the trail. At lunchtime, we found the knoll he described, opening up an expansive vista down mysterious Tenaya Canyon, all the way to Yosemite Valley, with a side view of stately Half Dome rising 4,737 feet straight up. The National Park map describes "hiking in Tenaya Canyon is dangerous and strongly discouraged." Steve recounted a story of a hiker entering the canyon and never returning, his body remains found many years later propped against a tree. Fortunately for us, our trail skirted around this enchanting, yet forbidding place.

Sunrise High Sierra Camp, perched on a rise overlooking lush Long Meadow, left a totally different impression than the other camps. Here, one gained a sense of Yosemite's boundless space, with its sweeping alpine meadows, connecting lofty mountain ranges with deep canyons. Meandering streams crisscrossed the green, grassy length of the aptly named Long Meadow.

Though sunny and clear for the third consecutive day, the temperature had been dropping rapidly since mid-afternoon. We dreaded going outside in the cold after dinner, for the ranger lesson. Steve sensed our concern and canceled his talk. We all raced for our tent cabins and hopped under the covers, after lighting the stoves. Even with three blankets and a comforter, I never felt warm that night.

On Wednesday, we endured our longest hike at ten miles, following Echo Creek and then the Merced River. However, the trail was downhill all the way, a welcome break from the prior two days. As we passed two symmetrical twin peaks, everyone understood why, when Steve divulged that they were locally known as the "Jayne Mansfield Points."

Merced Lake High Sierra Camp (elevation 7,150 feet) was an especially welcome sight, since here we would stay two nights and have a layover day to rest our weary bodies. The largest of the camps, Merced Lake occupied a wooded area and held a maximum of fifty-nine campers in nineteen tents, forming a large rectangle with a campfire ring in the center. The site boasted eight toilets, though by nightfall all were clogged. After showers and a nap, we dined on halibut and enjoyed a campfire quiz about the National Parks, led by Ranger Steve.

Thursday morning brought the most unique experience of the week. Ranger Steve gathered us together for a tree walk. Knowing Steve as we did now, we knew this would be no ordinary tree walk. "I want you not only to identify the trees, but to identify *with* the trees," he implored. Steve felt this was the only way to really get to know them. "If you introduce yourself to someone, but then walk away, you don't know that person. I am going to take you to *your* tree!"

First, he asked us a series of questions: "Do you like sun or shade? Do you prefer to be alone or in a group? Are you a Type A or Type B personality? Do you prefer berries or nuts? Are you a complex or simple person?" After each question, he had us separate into groups based on our answers. When done, there were six distinct groups. Then he led us to six different trees and explained how each one matched the personalities of a particular group.

A young, attractive, red-head, Stephanie, preferred the sun, being alone, and liked berries. Stopping by a juniper tree, Steve motioned to Stephanie, "This is your tree. Come and give it a hug!"

Ranger Steve explaining the trees

My friend, Carl, a Type A personality, preferred the sun and being in a group. His tree was the quaking aspen, whose leaves constantly flutter in the wind. I initially thought I belonged with the huckleberry oak, known for its complexity and fondness for shade. After further reflection, I realized, like Stephanie, I belonged with the juniper, by myself in the sunlight. Others found their trees, Jeffrey pine, white fir, and lodgepole pine, close by.

The rest of the day was spent relaxing by the lake with a book, writing in our journals, and watching the camp crew frolic in the river with boogie board and inner tube. All the while, everyone mulled over their expected participation in the evening's talent show that Steve had announced.

At 5:30 PM, we were all gathered around the fire ring sharing the day's experiences, but also curious as to why Ranger Steve had called for a group meeting at this time. Then he walked up with pack in hand and a twinkle in his eye. Out came a plastic bottle filled with a clear liquid. Indicating this was a good opportunity to celebrate our time together, he announced that for the past five days, he had carried this bottle, containing Bombay Sapphire Gin, for all to share now. With little hesitation, we gratefully imbibed, emptying the bottle in no time.

Steve also shared some exciting news. While hiking in a remote area of the park, he had stumbled across a two-foot long pine cone. Knowing it was larger than any he had ever seen, Steve submitted details to the Guinness Book of Records. Just before our trip, he received a certificate in the mail, acknowledging his find as the world's largest pine cone. Steve hoped the cone would remain in Yosemite on display for all to see.

That night at dinner, the creative spirit of the Merced Lake staff, led by manager Sean Lassiter, delighted our senses as well as our palettes. The menu included Brazilian roast pork loin with Grandma Jeanne's ratatouille and polenta drizzled in olive oil and Bleu cheese. When the main course was ready, the staff appeared in brightly colored costumes and hats, singing and dancing as they served up the succulent dishes. Later, during the talent show, Ranger Steve amazed the group with a fire-lit baton juggling act. Others joined in with humorous stories, camp songs and poems.

That the next day's hike to Vogelsang High Sierra Camp was saved for the end of the week was no accident. To get there, we would first have to ascend 3,600 over Vogelsang Pass (elevation 11,000 feet), before arriving for our final night's camp at an elevation of 10, 180 feet. By now, all were used to the thin air and rocky trails.

While traversing a lateral stretch in a narrow canyon above Lewis Creek, we spotted a young black bear lumbering along at a slightly higher level, a hundred feet away. Ranger Steve remarked that this was a rare sighting of a bear in its natural habitat. We were thirteen miles from the nearest road and miles from a camp. In recent years, the Park has been successful in removing temptations that attract the bears to populated areas. Gone are the days when bears would prowl popular campgrounds looking for food. This bear paid no attention to us, continuing to forage within our sight for the next ten minutes.

As the day progressed, the hike was strenuous and tiring, but everyone made camp by late afternoon. Even Carol and Linda, who had brought up the rear most days, arrived in good shape and high spirits.

Situated in a pristine meadow beside a creek, with the stark white, fractured granite face of Fletcher Peak cradling a rock glacier at its base, we felt close to heaven. Manager Chrissy Kochakji checked us in to camp with a cheerful smile. We followed our routine of napping and reading, while reflecting on mixed feelings of returning to civilization tomorrow. We longed for creature comforts that were missed, but knew the special bond with nature would be left behind.

Sitting under a boulder that night after our final dinner together, Ranger Steve imparted to us his deep concern for the importance of preserving the precious wilderness. He noted that "we all care *about* a lot of things. But we all don't care *for* many things. Find things to care for," he urged us.

As we said our heartfelt goodbyes, Steve passed out certificates of achievement, personally inscribed with a unique contribution each of us had made that week. We gave Steve a card all had signed with words of appreciation. Departing, we did not yet fully grasp the long lasting impact Steve's presence with us would make, each time we recalled our bonding experience at Yosemite.

Steve, Gerry & Carl arrive at Vogelsang High Sierra Camp

Death March 29 Group atop Dam at Hetch Hetchy Valley

Hetch Hetchy Valley and Reservoir

Chapter 7

Hetch Hetchy's Timeless Grandeur?

Dam Hetch Hetchy! As well dam for water-tanks the people's cathedrals and churches, for no holier temple has ever been consecrated by the heart of man.-John Muir

"Why would they want to drain the reservoir?" my colleague Steve pondered. "This would just be another Yosemite Valley with all the crowds."

"They would do it differently," I replied wistfully, as we downed sack lunches, while resting on a log at serene Rancheria Falls Campsite. We had just hiked 6-1/2 miles from O' Shaughnessy Dam, which gave birth to the reservoir in the early twentieth century. Ever since, the reservoir has supplied drinking water to distant San Francisco.

I envisioned in my mind how a restored Hetch Hetchy Valley could be, a century from now. With the three hundred plus feet of water gone and the dam removed, there would be time for the valley floor to heal, and for the native black oak trees, plants and other wildlife to return. As they do today, future tourists by the thousands will still marvel at the towering sheer walls of Yosemite Valley with its abundance of waterfalls, from delicate Bridal Veil, to majestic Yosemite, and powerful Vernal and Nevada Falls.

However, those wanting to experience how Yosemite Valley might have looked, before the wearing impact of civilization took its toll, could travel a few miles north to Hetch Hetchy Valley. Access would be restricted to shuttles carrying foot travelers, with all motor vehicles left behind. This valley would be preserved in its natural state, only for hikers, campers and wildlife. One could just imagine John Muir's spirit smiling proudly at the valley he once tried to save.

But Steve's question made me wonder. Is that how it would be? Knowing the vagaries of politics and changing priorities over time, who is to say that it would be better and not far worse than it is today? Even before that, the question of San Francisco's water supply would need to be resolved.

Returning to the present, I eyed my weary companions. Nine of us made the journey this far, through the Hetch Hetchy Valley on a bright sunny July day, where temperatures crossed the one hundred degree level. Others had cooled off by the sporadic spray of Wapama Falls, 2-1/5 miles from the trailhead, before turning back. We were part of a group of 28, co-workers, family, friends and clients, all enjoying an annual tradition my CPA firm started twenty-eight years ago. Sharing a love of nature and a spirit of adventure, each summer we sought a weekend escape from the tedium at work, somewhere special within reach of our Orange County, California offices.

Over the years, Yosemite National Park was often that place. We had packed into the northern reaches of the park on horseback from Virginia Lakes. Another year found us white water rafting the Tuolumne River just outside the western boundary. Then were the numerous times we crisscrossed the interior, at first backpacking, later tramping to the High Sierra Camps, where warm meals and soft beds rewarded the wilderness hiker.

Through all those ramblings, Hetch Hetchy was not even in our vocabulary. A hidden gem, just thirty miles north of popular Yosemite Valley, Hetch Hetchy received a mere trickle of visitors. But when California Governor Arnold Schwarzenegger announced a study that confirmed the feasibility of restoring Hetch Hetchy, we took notice. How could we have missed this part of Yosemite National Park all these years? The time had come to see it for ourselves.

On the drive up here, the reasons for Hetch Hetchy's lack of sightseers became clearer. Despite the closeness to Yosemite Valley, the trip took almost another hour on a winding mountain road. Once at the dam where the road ends, a scarcity of facilities deters the casual visitor. Since a typical tourist may drive into Yosemite Valley for a couple hours and then move on, the likelihood of a side trip to Hetch Hetchy, though well worth the time, is remote.

For those willing to go the extra distance, another pleasant surprise awaits. Eight miles from the dam, and just a mile outside the park entrance, historic Evergreen Lodge welcomes vacationers. The lodge was originally built in 1921 to support construction of the dam. However, a major upgrade and expansion launched in 2001, when resourceful new owners took over, transformed the lodge into an inviting destination from which to explore the area. Though 50 new cabins were added to the previous 18, the owners were careful to preserve the rustic feel of a forested mountain retreat, complete with comfortable beds, a well-stocked tavern and gourmet meals.

We arrived on a Saturday afternoon and checked in to several one and two bedroom cabins. To our amazement, the staff were busily preparing for a wedding reception later in the day, on the open-air plaza between the restaurant and recreation center. Our waiter that night informed us that they handled about thirty weddings a year. Obviously word had gotten out that Evergreen Lodge made a unique setting for nuptials.

Surprises continued that evening as our group dined on such gourmet treats as wild Alaskan salmon and blackened rib-eye steak, topped off with home made tiramisu and chocolate lava cake. The restaurant's outdoor dining area, appointed with nine picnic tables, was just the right size for our gathering, which consisted of three families, a couple, and several diverse parties of men and women. Clad in shorts and t-shirts, we relaxed to the sounds of the band playing for the more nattily attired wedding party, happily dancing away next to us.

Anticipating the long Hetch Hetchy Valley trek on Monday, we planned two easy three-mile hikes on Sunday. That would give the group a chance to acclimatize to the 4,500-foot altitude at the lodge, as well as test the state of their conditioning.

Just a couple miles away, next to the national park entrance station, the trail to Lookout Point began. Suggested by the guidebook as a good morning hike before the heat of the day, the trail rose in elevation only about 600 feet over a mile and a half, providing a good initial workout. Some of the younger kids got a little antsy along the way. But when they spotted the large boulders and rock faces near the top, they become virtual mountain goats scampering around the natural playground, while nervous parents watched.

The summit was a broad granite knob offering clear views over a 360-degree range. Here we caught our first glimpse of Hetch Hetchy Valley to the north, with the deep blue of the reservoir stretching out from the dam. The scene was idyllic and peaceful from this distance. The dam appeared miniscule from our vantage point, while Wapama Falls was a barely visible sliver of white against a granite precipice, midway through the valley.

Retracing our steps, we were back at the lodge in time for lunch. We indulged on a variety of burgers, including turkey and buffalo, and Caesar salads, and then were off to the Carlon Day Use area, a former campground seven miles from the lodge, for a hike to Carlon Falls. This trail, punctuated by several fallen logs, proceeded mostly through the dense woods, affording welcome shade from the sun. The falls, in three stages, were delightful, each sporting an inviting pool beneath cascades ranging up to twenty feet high. Adults and children alike stripped down to swimsuits or shorts for a refreshing dip in the clear, cool waters. Jumping off from smooth narrow ledges, swimmers would splash over to the falls for a shower.

Later at the lodge's tavern, my friend, Carl, and I unwound while savoring the highlights of the day. Our toughest decision now was which of the ten beers on tap to choose from. Moose Drool, a tasty brown brew, was my favorite, while Carl opted for Sierra Nevada. A large black and white photo over the bar depicted Hetch Hetchy Valley around the beginning of the twentieth century, before the dam was built. The tranquil scene evoked images of a simpler, more natural time. We were anxious to see how we would react to the current Valley condition tomorrow.

The evening meal was quieter without the wedding to entertain us. After feasting on the special of Orange Roughy stuffed with lump crab, we sauntered over to the Recreation Building where computers were connected to the internet, and free phone calls were offered on the Lodge's WATS line, since cell phone access was not available.

In the morning, anticipating a hot day, the group met at 8 am for the drive to the dam. Once there, a man in a Hetch Hetchy Water Supply uniform greeted us. "Are there any questions I can answer?" Ken Brewer proceeded to give us an informed history of the dam project. "It amazes me how a guy could ride a horse all the way out here from San Francisco and back, and tell them they could get the water they need from here." Ken added that the dam structure had been expanded once, and that another twenty feet could still be added to the top.

We thanked Ken for the helpful introduction, and then started our exploration of the valley by walking across the dam. The still waters of the reservoir mirrored the valley walls, brightly reflecting the morning sun on south facing cliffs, while casting eerie blue gray shadows on monolithic Hetch Hetchy Dome and the towering Kolana Rock, rising 1800 feet from the shore across the lake. A 500-foot long construction era tunnel through the granite mountain led from the far side of the dam to the trailhead on the north side of the valley. The tunnel, with a temperature some twenty degrees lower than outside, would provide a welcome respite from the hot sun on the way back.

A sense of solitude surrounded us from the start. That we were alone was evident early on as Jeff and his son, Ryan, in the lead, twice startled rattlesnakes sunning on the trail. Fortunately, the venomous reptiles wanted nothing to do with us and quickly slithered into the underbrush. Snakes were not the only motivator for watching where we stepped. Though the colorful wildflowers of spring were long gone, red-hued poison oak blanketed the trailside in spots.

A downside of visiting the park later in summer of the driest year in recent history is the impact on the waterfalls. Tueeulala Falls, with its normally gossamer –like, eight hundred foot, early spring free fall, was no where to be found. However, a little further on, powerful Wapama Falls still flowed steadily, cascading over 1300 feet in three stages. Wooden bridges skirt the base. Despite the fact that these bridges have to be closed in spring due to the tumultuous torrent, we crossed without feeling a drop.

From here, the trail paralleled the side of the valley for four miles leading to more diminutive Rancheria Falls, a creek cascading over shelves of broad granite, smoothed over by ancient glaciations. The intense sun provided a changing array of perspectives as the day progressed, radiating sharp shafts of afternoon light on previously shaded valley walls.

Three hours after departing the dam, we reached the Rancheria Falls Campsite, ready for a rest and lunch. Now that we had traversed the length of Hetch Hetchy Valley, there was time to stop and reflect on what we had observed. Steve and I had compared viewpoints on the future of this special place.

I envied the early Miwok Native Americans, who in prior centuries roamed the pristine valley gathering the grass with edible seed, hatchatchie, from which the current name came from. I recalled the extraordinary painting with the Tuolumne River meandering through the valley floor that Albert Bierstadt created after a journey in 1873. And I remembered John Muir's characterization in a 1908 essay, as he unsuccessfully tried to preserve the valley, "I have always called it the Tuolumne Yosemite, for it is a wonderfully exact counterpart of the great Yosemite, not only in its crystal river and sublime rocks and waterfalls, but in the gardens, groves, and meadows of its flower park-like floor."

Hiking back, my body was tired and thirsty, but my spirit was refreshed again by the peacefulness of this place. I knew that Hetch Hetchy would never look like it once did, in my lifetime. If restoration could one day return it to the rarified state that the

Miwok's, Bierstadt, Muir and others cherished, I would encourage a move in that direction. But for now, for those who take the time to walk the trails through this valley, the quiet, timeless grandeur that is Hetch Hetchy today can evoke a sense of tranquility that richly nourishes the soul.

Cooling off with a swim at Carlon Falls

Gerry, Mel and Karen tackle a Kern River rapid on Death March 14

In memory of Jerry Higashi on Tuolumne River Death March 15

Part III

River Rafting

In memory of Tom Ahling and Mark Carter on Death March 15

Loretta and Gerry in King's River rapid on Death March 5

Chapter 8

River Rafting

Six wild rivers in three states

Death March 5, the first whitewater river rafting adventure, took place on the King's River in King's Canyon National Park. My trail notes characterized it well: "In a major departure from the first four death marches, this was not to be a march, but a 'death cruise,' rafting along the treacherous, icy cold waters of the King's River." That was followed years later by Death March 14 along central California's Kern River, Death March 15 on the Tuolumne River by Yosemite National Park, and Death March 19 up in Oregon on the Rogue and North Umpqua Rivers.

The first three raft trips employed six person inflatable rafts, while the Oregon trip involved individual, bright orange kayaks, also of the blow-up variety. Those were tiny in comparison to the 20 person motorized pontoon rafts that powered us through the breathtaking Grand Canyon on the Colorado River in Death Marches 27 and 32.

By the time the fifth Death March came about, a tradition had been established that each Death March must include an element of hiking. So as we prepared for our initial raft trip, the first night was spent camping in tents at nearby Sequoia National Park. Special features of the park would draw us back several times in future years. For now, we marveled at the huge Sequoia trees along the Congress Trail, highlighted by the General Sherman Tree, largest in the world at 275 feet tall and 36 feet in diameter at the base. After an evening ranger talk and securing our food from reported bears in the area, we spent a restful and uneventful night.

The next day, after a two-hour drive along the windy, mountain roads of Sequoia, we reached the King's River, and our guides with the King's River Expeditions rafting company. During the briefing, wetsuits were offered to shield from the cold water. However, as described in the Trail Notes, attempting to get in one can bring unexpected results: "Loretta is practically launched into space attempting to don hers. With one fellow holding each side as she steps into the tight, stretchable rubber leg, they lift upward as she steps down, sending her heavenward." Fortunately, no harm was done, and the incident was soon forgotten, as we proceeded to endure a harrowing white-knuckle ride in a World War I bus "along a cliff on the side of the river canyon, along what must have been a pioneer's trail, about half a lane wide and impassable. I think they took us that way so the river wouldn't seem so treacherous by the time we got there."

The King's River is considered Class III on the whitewater rating system, which goes from Class I, the easiest, to Class VI, which is unpassable. That was a good level for beginners like us, though after "crossing several challenging rapids, holding on for dear life, and getting thoroughly drenched," we felt like we had gotten our money's worth. The eight of us had a great time and then felt like experts, ready to tackle higher class rapids the next time we rafted.

Two things that were consistent on all our raft trips were great food and talented guides. On the King's River, we had steak kabobs for dinner, a hearty breakfast, and sandwiches for lunch along the river, all prepared by the guides, who also entertained us with singing and skits by the campfire in the evening. The guides were also safety conscious and careful, making our well-being their top priority.

Though we all thoroughly enjoyed our first rafting adventure, the second would not occur until Death March 14, nine years later. After a variety of Death Marches to places like Mammoth Lakes, Catalina, Grand Canyon, Sequoia, and several visits to Yosemite, we were ready for the Kern River, east of Bakersfield and south of Sequoia National Park. With Class IV and V rapids, this river would be a step up in difficulty, which by that time we considered well within our reach.

With our group of twelve filling the bulk of three rafts, we reveled in excitement, running several rapids, including a Class IV, in short order. That all changed at White Maiden Falls. There, George bounced out into the river just as his raft went over the falls. He floundered, bobbing up and down in front of and under the raft for 100 feet down the rapids. It looked like he was doomed to smash against a massive rock. Mercifully he missed it. Then much to his relief, the guide on his raft, a pretty, tanned young girl, was there at the ready, and pulled him out before anything other than his male pride could be hurt.

Though several more colorful rapids with names like Deadman's Curve and the Staircase were tackled, no further mishaps occurred. Even so, the guides were not about to let us attempt the Class V Royal Flush. Instead, we portaged about 100 hundred yards around, carrying the rafts up and over a rock face and dropping them back in down stream.

Not wanting to wait another nine years for so much fun and excitement, we decided on our third raft trip the very next year, for Death March 15. The Tuolumne River, famed waterway flowing through the Hetch Hetchy Valley in the northern reaches of Yosemite National Park, was our challenge. The stretch we would traverse, however, was just outside of the National Park below the controversial O'Shaugnessey Dam, which we explored much later during Death March 29, as described in a previous chapter titled "Hetch Hetchy's Timeless Grandeur."

Taking advantage of our proximity to the National Park, we spent the first two nights at Yosemite Lodge in breathtaking Yosemite Valley. On our first foray into Yosemite on Death March 6, some of us had toyed with climbing Half Dome in route from Tuolumne Meadows to Yosemite Valley. Wisely, we passed at that time, the result of sore feet from over twenty miles of hiking over two days.

But now our time had come. Three of us hiked the gorgeous, but steep and aptly named Mist Trail, up past Vernal and Nevada Falls.

The last mile was especially strenuous, first with stairs starting up the expansive rock and then dual cables 3-4 feet apart for the final 500 foot elevation gain up the sheer side of the rock face to the summit. Every ten feet along that part, a wood two by four spanned the path to provide a foothold. We held tightly onto the cables, praying that we would not pass out, since there was nothing to stop a fall almost straight down the smooth granite side of the dome.

The view on top was indescribably spectacular in all directions. But peering over the 4,000 cliff face was so scary, we had to crawl there on our stomachs, not trusting our balance at the perilous edge.

The next morning, we drove to Groveland to meet the rafting company. Another rickety bus ride on a narrow, dirt road brought us down the five hundred foot canyon side to the river. On this trip, we would camp along the river on the way, so three supply rafts were needed to accompany the three paddle rats.

We did not have to question for long why they gave us helmets, when the Class IV Rock Garden rapids appeared. The powerful whitewater arose so quickly that Jerry Higashi went flying out before he could secure his grip. Fortunately, he got hauled back in safely before too long in the cold water. However, a little later we are surprised to encounter our first Class V rapids, Clavey Falls. Gratefully our guides did not fool around with what could have been a dangerous passage. They had us get out for a thorough briefing and viewing of what was in store, complete with all contingencies. That careful preparation proved fortuitous, as we flew through the foamy torrent like pros, without a hitch.

Even with the constant roar of the river near our feet, camping along the bank that night, far from civilization was surprisingly serene and peaceful. That is, until the morning.

While preparing to embark, Jerry twisted his back and could barely move without excruciating pain. Having no contact with the outside world, we had no choice but to prop him up on one of the supply rafts for the trip out. We proceeded cautiously down river, even negotiating several more Class IV rapids. "After a while, Jerry is feeling a little better, and rides sitting up on the cushioned back of the raft. It is fitting. He looks like an ancient monarch perched on his throne, as his subjects row him down the river."

The narrow river canyon was exceedingly scenic, with steep sloping walls rising five hundred feet above, and California's golden hills dotted with green bushes and trees stretching out beyond.

That night, our celebration dinner was held at the historic, colonial Wawona Hotel in the southern end of the National Park, where we spent our final night before heading home.

Our final wilderness river rafting trip was Death March 19, when we went further north to Merlin, Oregon, to tackle the Rogue River and the infamous single person inflatable orange kayaks. At 775 miles, Oregon was the most distant Death March yet. On our earliest Death Marches, we would form car caravans to transport everyone to the starting point. While this practice gradually faded away, the custom was practically not feasible this time. Most participants, like my wife, sister and I, drove, taking two days to enjoy California scenery along the way. Others flew into Medford, Oregon, about 40 miles away, or Redding, California.

Our base of operations was Morrison's Rogue River Lodge, with rustic cabins in a beautiful wooded setting right on the Rogue River. Our warm, friendly hosts for the three nights served some of the best meals ever on Death Marches, with main dinner dishes such as salmon, roast pork, beef tenderloin, and halibut, finished off with desserts of Swiss walnut torte, blueberry cheesecake, and blackberry cobbler ala mode, complete with berries fresh picked from their own bushes.

Steve and his family enjoyed Morrison's so much that twenty years later they returned prior to the start of Death March 39 at Crater Lake National Park. They especially looked forward to feasting on the unforgettably tasty orange rolls served at breakfast.

After a good night's sleep followed by a hearty breakfast complete with the aforementioned rolls, all were ready for the new adventure. All that is, except for a few who found contentment just relaxing by the Lodge. The rest of us had two options. Nine elected to take on the kayaks, while seven opted for regular rafts.

Since individual kayaks pose completely different dynamics than six-person rafts, the guides took special precautions to prepare us for the river. For one thing, on the Rogue River, we would only tackle Class II rapids, so that there would be plenty of time in relatively calm waters to adapt to fending for ourselves. Even so, on the very first rapids, Bernie pops out of his kayak. But by the end of the day, he is out paddling everyone, as we glide past the green forested banks and rock outcroppings of Hellgate Canyon. We even raft past the Lodge, where the stay behinds on the beach wave to us from afar.

The next day is on the "treacherous" and swift North Umqua River. Over confident and cocky, with a day of kayaking experience behind us, all but one of us go flying into the river at the first Class III rapids: Right Creek. Only afterwards did the guides tell us that Right Creek was practically Class IV and the toughest rapids of the trip.

The North Umpqua was equally scenic, but narrower and more remote than the Rogue, with deer, heron, osprey and hawks spotted along the way. By the end of the day, we were all worn out. Though great fun and incredibly exciting, one-man kayaks were HARD work. No one seemed anxious to try one again any time soon. We now had an unwavering appreciation for the difference that joint efforts made in the six-man version.

Even better would be a twenty person, motorized raft. But that we would not know until eight years later. Our two Death Marches on the Colorado River, through the Grand Canyon, are covered next in the chapter on that most amazing natural wonder of the world.

Rogue River kayaking and Williams' family at breakfast

Don scopes out the trail on Death March 18

Part IV

Grand Canyon National Park

Chapter 9

Grand Canyon

Into the depths for a timeless journey

My fascination with the Grand Canyon began at age 17. My parents and I were enroute from our suburban Chicago home to check out New Mexico State University, where my high school gymnastics coach had just accepted a position as Head Coach of the gymnastics team. We stopped at the Grand Canyon for a couple days to break up the long drive.

From the first moment I encountered the majestically mystic immensity and strength exuding from the Canyon's depths, I was captivated. I knew I had to experience the embrace of the warm red walls around me.

The plan was set. Mom and dad would spend the next day driving the rim after dropping me off at the Kaibab Trailhead. Starting down the trail at 9:00 AM, I was ecstatic, skipping along, even jogging through the steepest sections. The deeper I went, the stronger grew the sense of this unique creation and how its power, while so much greater then mine, welcomed and sheltered me within its grasp.

By 11:30 AM, with eight miles of trail behind and having descended 5,000 feet, I arrived at historic Phantom Ranch, set amidst an oasis of trees beside Bright Angel Creek. Walking by the scattered cabins in the quiet of the noonday heat, I came upon the welcome sight of a small swimming pool. Wondering only briefly what might lurk beneath the murkily opaque green water, I plunged right in, relishing the refreshing coolness on my sweaty skin. At that moment, it couldn't get any better than that.

Fully refreshed, I emerged and relaxed for a few moments with my sack lunch. By noon, I was ready for the return journey back to the rim. I would take the Bright Angel Trail this time, for variety and a gentler inclining trail.

Then reality set in.

With a 100+ degree temperature, and a blazing sun bearing down, my prior energy quickly melted away. For the first couple miles, I was surprised to discover that I could barely take ten steps before needing to stop and rest. The Bright Angel Trail, which I highly recommend, is magnificently beautiful. But the gentler incline of the trail on the ascent, compared to the Kaibab Trail, came at a price: two extra miles in length. However, though both trails were relentlessly exposed to the direct rays of the sun, Indian Garden provided a tree-covered oasis half way up the Bright Angel Trail, if only you got that far. Also, beyond that point, water and restrooms were strategically located in two places between Indian Garden and the rim.

The prospect of those respites ahead, and my constant mantra, "one step in front of the other" propelled me forward. With each frequent stop to rest, I hoped for a bit of shade. On rare occasions, the backside of a large boulder cast a cooling slice of shadow.

Thankfully, my energy gradually revived and I was able to maintain a steady, if slow, pace for the rest of the trek to the surface. I emerged six hours later at 6 PM to the relieved looks on the faces of my parents.

A couple days later, upon arriving at New Mexico State University in Lac Cruces, my coach excitedly informed me that he had arranged for me to give an exhibition at his summer gymnastics camp the next day. My specialty was the pommel horse (back then we called it the side horse). When the time came, as I did more bouncing on the horse than spinning around it, the lesson learned was to not expect to be in top form shortly after a grueling one day hike to the bottom of the Grand Canyon. Sadly, a few months later, I would have to tell my old coach that I had chosen the University of Wisconsin over New Mexico State. Two years later, we were reunited briefly when we met at the NCAA National Collegiate Gymnastics Championships.

Having grown up in the far-off Midwest, I would have to wait thirty years before the opportunity came to return to the Grand Canyon in 1992 for Death March 4. This time, Steve, George and I would make the ultimate journey, traversing from the North Rim to the South Rim, 24 miles in total. Having been in the mountains for the first three Death Marches, we were still not fully prepared for the rigors of backpacking, especially now in the totally different desert canyon environment. As I recall, Steve wore tennis shoes, and both he and George carried canned food in their packs, weighing them down.

At 14 miles, the trail to Phantom Ranch campground was much longer than the trails down from the South Rim. At one point, Steve and I would have to employ all our skills at psychology to get George the full distance. About halfway down, George sat on a boulder and announced that he was not moving any further. His feet were killing him. The problem was that there was nothing for seven miles either way but cactus and desert creatures, not all of which were friendly.

Steve and I were dreading that we might have to prop George up between us and drag him the rest of the way. Starting with humorous pleas that gradually evolved into stern commands, we finally cajoled him onto his feet and moving forward, albeit with a limp and somewhat bent over. Time spent soaking his feet in Bright Angel Creek helped as well.

Along the final stretch, our spirits were buoyed by the sight of Ribbon Falls, where the "unique, feather of water drops 30 feet to [a] cone-like pedestal and flows down all sides like ribbons" as described in the Trail Notes. Arriving at Phantom Ranch at 5 p.m., our weary bodies were refreshed with several glasses of ice-cold lemonade from the snack bar.

Fortunately, we had planned two nights at the bottom. The next day George and Steve spent the day in Bright Angel Creek, with George resting his feet, while Steve swam. I hiked the Clear Creek inner canyon trail for the first time. From the Phantom Overlook, the views of the South Rim, multi-hued Zoroaster temple, the Colorado River and our camp far below were spectacular.

Steve and Gerry cool sore feet in Bright Angel Creek on Death March 4

Later at dinner in camp, George had a request regarding our hike back out in the morning. He had been scared to death crossing the Colorado River on the silver suspension bridge on the hike down. The bridge sways and has a floor of steel mesh that you can see through to the river 60 feet below. The experience walking over it can be exhilarating or frightening, depending on your temperament. George asked that we plan our departure so that we would cross the bridge in the dark, so that he couldn't see down.

Just glad that George was ready to tackle the ascent, we happily agreed, even though that meant rising at 3:40 AM. By 4:30 that morning, we were on the trail, flashlights in hand. Though we could hear the roar of the river, the canyon was pitch black as we crossed the bridge without incident, and proceeded upward. Another advantage of the early start was the cooler canyon air at this hour. Though the sun and heat would find us before reaching the summit, we were far along by then. With only a long breakfast stop at Indian Garden, Steve and I arrived at the top by 10 AM, with George eventually making it out at 1 PM.

Kay welcomes George to the rim

Our return to the Grand Canyon on Death March 9 was a completely different experience. This time we moved to the far west end, north of Peach Springs, to hike down the Havasupai Canyon trail, part of the Havasupai Indian Reservation. Along with our trek through a Native American domain, this adventure would include waterfalls cascading into turquoise blue pools, accommodations other than tents, riding out on horseback, and a record up to that point of eighteen participants.

Havasupai Canyon

Riding out   **Mooney Falls**

The trail began with steep switchbacks for a mile, followed by a largely level streambed within narrow red rock canyon walls reaching up as far as several hundred feet on either side for the rest of the eight miles. At the end we reached the Indian village of Supai, complete with store, café, school, clinic, and a lodge which was to be our home for two nights.

The highlight came the next day which was spent at the magnificent waterfalls. We focused on two of the five unique falls: Havasu and Mooney. After a two mile hike from the village, passing Navaho Falls on the way, we reached majestic Havasu Falls. Plunging down clearly and forcefully for one hundred feet from a travertine overhang, the translucent blue-green water filled delicate limestone pools, then flowed gently outward over the step-stone terraces into Havasu. Creek. The pleasantly cool water made for great swimming among the terraced pools.

Bathing in the travertine pools

Mooney Falls, a mile further down the trail, and at two hundred feet high, posed an even more dramatic and challenging encounter. Reaching the pool at the bottom required climbing down a treacherous cliff face, while holding onto chains pounded into the rock wall with spikes. Once there, we swam beneath the mesmerizing torrent to feel its energy pulsating directly on us. However, as the Trail Notes recounted, "the intensity of the pounding water is like a hurricane, with the mist blasting us in the face. We can only take the power of it for a few moments, and then swim back."

The trek out the next day provided yet another new experience for some of us. While part of the group departed early, hoping to complete the hike before the heat and sun became oppressive, several of us headed out on horseback, led by an Indian guide. Feeling like cowboys, we gained a whole new perspective, and got to the top with a lot less wear and tear.

The lure of the Grand Canyon drew us back nine years later for Death March 18. The itinerary followed in similar fashion to my initial hike at age seventeen, with two notable exceptions. This time we spent two nights in the cabins of Phantom ranch, and the pool I found refreshing so long ago, had since been filled in with dirt and vegetation, having succumbed to overuse and pollution. The rustic charms of Phantom Ranch would be enjoyed two more times on future Death Marches, and are described more fully in the next chapter.

Though not directly a part of the Grand Canyon, Zion National Park makes up one segment of the triumvirate, also including Bryce Canyon National Park and the Grand Canyon's north rim, that travelers in the past century would include in a grand circle tour of the southwest. On a visit during my teenage trip to the Grand Canyon, I considered Zion the least of the three as to scenic merit. Only upon returning for Death March 26 did I discover the stunning landscape that I had missed before. One of the many lessons learned through the Death Marches, was the necessity for getting out of the car, as well as off the beaten path, in order to uncover the true depth of natural beauty and phenomenon just beyond the surface. Zion was a pleasant surprise in that regard.

We had arranged for a three night stay at Zion Lodge in the heart of the park. The plan was to hike the Narrows one day and Angels Landing the next. The two destinations could not be more different. The Narrows followed a tight stretch along the river through the canyon, while Angels Landing involved a climb high up a 1,500 foot tall red sandstone tower. Each had its unique appeal and corresponding danger.

The Narrows hike required some advanced planning. The hikers would need to be dropped off at Chamberlain's Ranch where the trailhead was located in the north, above the park, an hour and a half drive away. From there, the trail dropped into the canyon by, and ultimately in, the Virgin River.

Because of the narrow width and steep walls, the canyon was subject to sudden flash floods when rain fell, even if a storm appeared distant. Hikers finding themselves in these circumstances could be caught in a death trap.

Consequently, a stop at the ranger station beforehand to check weather conditions was a must, as well as to get a hiking permit.

That's when we got the bad news. Rain was expected. The ranger strongly recommended against hiking through from the top. A safer bet was to enter the Narrows at the bottom, hiking in for an hour or two, while watching the weather. In that section, higher ground was within reach if rushing waters were to come.

We started up the Narrows trail, which begins where the road ends, early Sunday morning. Before long, we were hiking in the river itself, since the sheer walls allowed no room for a trail. Fortunately, we all had walking sticks to steady us. Even so, Gerry took a spill as his feet slid out from the slippery rock-covered bottom. Though soaked, Gerry was refreshed by the cold water, cooling him off as it quickly dried in the August heat.

Hiking the Narrows of Zion Canyon on Death March 26

We had never experienced a hike quite like this one. The spectacular multi-hued canyon walls reaching high to the rim, gave the closed in channel an eerie claustrophobic feel. We were in the canyon's clutches for sure.

After a couple hours of splendid hiking, escape routes up the sides became sparse, as clouds grew thicker. So we turned around and retraced our steps, now adept at negotiating the slick stones under our feet.

The next day, majestic Angels Landing beckoned. No need to worry about flash floods on this day, as the trail climbed high above the canyon floor, rising about 1,500 feet in elevation over 2-1/2 miles. A fascinating stretch of 21 tightly packed switchbacks had been named Walter's Wiggles for the first park superintendent, Walter Ruesch, who constructed them in 1926. The Wiggles began almost two miles into the hike, after which we arrived at Scout Lookout.

This was the spot we had been briefed on earlier that morning by a park ranger. We had wanted to know if she thought we would be able to go all the way to the top. She related to us that we would know without question whether we could make it, once we set foot on Scout Lookout.

Angels Landing and view from Scout Lookout

She was right! Looking on ahead, we knew instantly that there was no way we would continue upward. At this point, the narrow, gravelly trail wound steeply up and around the conical spire. The problem was the sheer drop off, over a thousand feet on each side of the trail in spots. Nerves of steel and sure footing were mandatory.

However, while we were shaking our heads "No way!" to each other, teens Madison and Tom scurried on ahead, fearless as they sped along, soon out of sight. We were petrified at their lack of concern. The next half hour was spent with an impending sense of dread, until they finally reappeared, wondering what all the fuss was about. Theirs had been the ultimate adventure, taking in 360° views from the top.

Relieved as I was that they had returned safely, I vowed never again to take the group on a trail that portended life endangering risk of this magnitude.

With ample challenges behind us on this trip, some in the group ventured to nearby Bryce National Park for sights and hikes of a mellower nature, but filled with even more intense colors and views. All in all, Death March 26 had more than lived up to expectations, and everyone arrived home in one piece.

The following year, now that we had traversed the Grand Canyon from the north rim to the south rim, hiked the length of the Kaibab and Bright Angel Trails, gone down and up the Havasupai Trail, and explored nearby national parks, we were ready for the ultimate Grand Canyon adventure: rafting the mighty Colorado River. Considering the time required to navigate through the whole Canyon via the river, we decided to cover the distance on two separate Death Marches. Death March 27 started on the still waters of the Colorado at Lee's Ferry in Utah, and finished up two days later at Phantom Ranch, followed by a hike out the Bright Angel Trail. Death March 32 picked up where 27 left off, starting with a hike down the Bright Angel Trail to meet the rafts for four days on the river, finishing up at Lake Mead in Nevada.

Rafting the Grand Canyon was like no other raft trip we had taken. For starters, the rating system of 1 to 6 for the difficulty of the rapids used on other rivers was tossed out the window. On the mighty Colorado, the difficulty rating went all the way to 10, a scary thought for sure. Just thinking about the prospect of getting thrown into the tumultuous rapids of that magnitude sent chills up our spines.

Fortunately, our able guides, including the captain who had been running groups through the Canyon for 28 years, had no intention of letting any of us land in the river. The one exception was when we were settled in camp on a wide sand bar, and a quiet eddy there formed a safe swimming hole for a refreshing dip at the end of the day.

The 17,000 pound, 20 person motorized rafts, had huge white pontoons on each side, with parallel benches in the center. During stretches of calm weather, we would sit straddling the pontoons. But when thunderous rapids approached, we were ordered down low on the center benches and told to get a solid hand grip and hold on tight. That position gave a sense of security, possibly akin to the feeling of being safely within the bowels of a great whale.

Along the river and in the rapids

In any event, it worked. The raft pounded wildly over the tumult, sending thrills and ice cold water over and through our bodies, but leaving us laughing and shivering, and most importantly still in place. That is, except for one huge wave that we encountered on Death March 32. Infamous Lava Falls, the most treacherous rapid on the river, washed forcefully across the raft, pushing Esther powerfully from her seat in front of me directly onto my lap. I held her tight with my free arm and we rode out together, exhilarated but breathless, and most of all thankful that we were still in the raft.

Thinking back, especially considering Lava Falls, doing the upper part of the river through the Canyon first was a good decision, since it was shorter and most rapids had lower ratings than those in the lower section. The upper stretch covered about 89 miles, while the lower was more than double that at 208 miles long. Also, the tough rapids came quickly at the start of Death March 32, including several ranking 7-10. Of those, the Trail Notes indicated that "Hermit is the toughest with a big hole and wall of water high over the raft, pelting everyone mercilessly, as we hold on for dear life. Water up nose and everywhere."

Group in the raft   **Lunch on the river**

Starting out at Lee's Ferry on Death March 27, the Colorado River was a muddy olive green, but before long took on its reddish brown namesake color, owing to the sand and dirt that was carried through the Canyon.

Curtis "Lawrence of Arabia" Campbell by river cave

On both regions of the river, aspects of the Canyon were accessible that could be seen no other way. Side canyon hikes revealed prehistoric fossils in rock surfaces, remnants of age-old Indian cliff dwellings, Anasazi painted hand outlines on walls, and several delicate waterfalls. Wildlife spotted at varying intervals included deer, beaver, blue herons, and bighorn sheep moving along the ledges. A huge scorpion even crawled into camp during one breakfast.

Floating along the River would have made a geologist gaze in wonder. Our well-versed guides gave lessons, explaining the history of the various bands of color on the canyon walls, including the mysterious case of the Great Unconformity, a missing billion years between two adjacent layers of stone. The age of Grand Canyon formations ranges from a couple hundred million years old at top to over a couple billions years old at the bottom.

The kids enjoying a break on a sand bar along the river

Our guides on both parts of the river were clearly multi-talented. An all female guide crew on the lower section was as seasoned and capable, if not more so, then the men on the upper section. Besides being experts at bringing groups safely through the Canyon, and readily conversant on the geology, wildlife, ancient and recent history, both sets of guides could set up and take down a camp in record time, all the while preparing delicious, gourmet meals, even including rib-eye steak one evening.

Fortunately, the participants on both of the Colorado River Death Marches all completed the journeys without major mishaps. That was good, since there was only one realistic way out when in the depths of the canyon with walls rising thousands of feet above: going down the river to the end.

Actually, there was one minor injury. The side hike to Ladder Falls in Elf Chasm required scaling the rock wall employing two ropes and two ladders. All who tried made their way up and marveled at the spectacular waterfall. However, one person got too anxious on the way down. As the Trail Notes report: "On way down second ladder, rappelling, Gerry's foot slips on wet, slippery rock wall, & he slams into wall, twisting & hurting back. – burning stabs of pain. Amity, Rachel & Carolyn check it out & help. I can still move everything, just get stabs of pain in moving right upper back. Manage to get back to raft. Marc examines me & determines that spine & shoulder blade are OK. Appears to be bruised muscle between them. Take 3 Advil." The females, of course, were our reassuring guides, while Marc was one of two doctors taking part in the trip.

That incident occurred on the final day of Death March 32. Other than wounded pride and embarrassment, I incurred no lasting damage. The next day was mostly calm floating out the end of the Canyon gorge on to the pickup point at Pearce Ferry on Lake Mead.

Gerry rappelling down just before his mishap

Five years later, we decided that we needed one more opportunity to revisit and reminisce at the wondrous Grand Canyon. Death March 37 took place in the year 2015 and is recaptured in the next chapter.

Curtis at the El Tovar Suite and on the trail down

Chapter 10

From Grand to Grandeur in the Canyon

A fond farewell to the world's greatest natural wonder

"Throw us a rope," a loud voice called from the rim walkway below. Stirred from our reverie on our second floor balcony at the historic El Tovar Hotel, Curtis and I saw our friends, Huw and Rachel gazing up in amused wonder.

"Come on up. The view's great," I called back as I motioned to them.

Curtis and I had just settled into cushioned chairs, looking out at the Grand Canyon, after checking into the Fred Harvey Suite, mere steps from the Canyon's South Rim.

Far below, we could see the thread-like Bright Angel Trail disappear into the massive depths of the sun-drenched chasm. Tomorrow, along with the seventeen others in our group, we would be descending on that trail eight miles to the Canyon floor, then along the Colorado River another two miles to rustic Phantom Ranch, for a two-night stay.

But for now we were ensconced in the luxury of one of the El Tovar Hotel's best kept secrets. Only four suites in the hotel have expansive balconies facing the Canyon. Here I felt like a king surveying his boundless realm.

For thirty-six years, friends and colleagues from our CPA firm in Orange County, California, had been taking annual hikes to places of natural beauty in the West. In the early days, they were backpacking treks. But as the years went by, and bodies aged, creature comforts often replaced tents and sleeping bags. Even so, though several of our earlier hikes had included the Grand Canyon, the likes of an El Tovar suite were not typical.

This trip was our fifth to the Grand Canyon. We had originally hiked from the north rim to the south, camping at the bottom. We had rafted though the length of the Canyon on two visits, sleeping on sandbars along the way. Now we were reprising an earlier stay at Phantom Ranch.

On those past occasions I had noticed people peering out from balconies at the El Tovar, and found myself wondering how they got there. When planning return travels to the Grand Canyon, I would go online earlier each time, hoping to snag a suite. But no luck, until this past year, when I unraveled the mystery: the suites are never offered online. Only by calling very far ahead, and perhaps by divine providence, can a treasured suite be booked.

We heard Huw and Rachel's knock on the door. This was their first time joining us on one of these adventures. Entering the bedroom, they gushed at the plushly pillowed king bed and rich, dark wood furnishings, highlighted by an elegant portrait of Fred Harvey.

Between the bedroom and sitting room, the marble-clad bath and a refreshment nook separated the two living areas. The Keurig coffeemaker came stocked with a variety of blends and teas.

The sitting room was ample with soft leather chairs and loveseat. The cot we ordered filled the center of the room, converting the area into a second bedroom. A door on the far end of the room led to the expansive balcony which covered more floor space than the whole rest of the suite.

More glowing words of amazement flowed as Huw and Rachel stepped onto the balcony. The exclamations were repeated by our other guests as each arrived. The balcony was the perfect setting for our group to meet and toast the hike to come, as we looked out at the Canyon in deep purple shadows as the sun receded in the west.

Later, we soaked up the relaxed elegance of the El Tovar Dining Room. Solid pine wood logs formed the ceiling and walls, set off by brightly colored murals portraying Native Americans of bygone days. A sizable fireplace of rough white stone evoked a sense of the sandstone Canyon walls that loomed through the broad windows on either side. We indulged on specialties with both a Southwestern and European flair, such as Sustainable Salmon Tostada on Organic Greens and Pork Chops with Braised Apples & Sauerkraut. Lingering over coffee, comfortably full, we savored the moment, one that would have to last us the next couple nights, when our cuisine and accommodations promised to be much more rustic.

A short jaunt to the Maswik Foodcourt helped us walk off the dinner. There we bought muffins and bagels for the next morning's breakfast, as well as sack lunches for the trail. Back at our suite afterward, we soaked up the quiet solitude on the balcony, with a sky full of stars casting silvery reflections on the endless depths below.

A few hours later, we woke with the dawn breaking over the horizon. Moment by moment the Canyon's splendor intensified, then stood out dramatically as the sun's rays slowly spread, sharpening the colors of the contrasting strata.

"How can it get any better than this? Why don't we just spend the next two days here, drinking our coffee and taking in this spectacle of nature?" I yawned quietly while stretching my arms and looking over at my contented friend.

Curtis didn't need to answer. We knew from past travels that even this moment of wonder could not compare with the breathtaking feeling we would sense along the trail, enveloped by the boundless intensity of beauty and strength exuded by these timeless canyon walls.

A few moments later, with one last, lingering look, we checked out and headed west on the rim walk toward the Bright Angel trailhead. When almost there, we noticed a parked car with two women fast asleep in the front seat. I gave Curtis a knowing smile, contemplating how different their night must have been from ours. Looking twice, I realized they were Michaele and Aileen, part of our group. They had left home after work yesterday, arriving well after mid-night.

Sensing our presence, they awoke. Before long, they joined us at the trailhead as the other group members gradually converged from various points, two by two.

While waiting, we chatted with a cowboy who was preparing his guests for their mule ride down the canyon. We listened to him tell them: "If you are afraid of heights, this will be a very long day." Though the trail is generally wide and safe, the experience can be scary when one is sitting on top of a mule, as it goes around steep switchbacks that have long drop-offs. The cowboy assured them that the mules were surefooted veterans, and there was nothing to worry about as long as guests followed his instructions closely. "If you lose something, let it go. If you lean over, you may end up in the canyon. Tell us. We'll retrieve it for you." I was glad to be on my own two feet for the descent.

After a group photo, we started down the trail at 7:10 AM on a beautiful day, with just enough clouds in the sky to offer welcome shade from the sun for a while, keeping the temperature cool, initially. Within an hour the sun fully rose, its rays reflecting vibrantly off the red canyon walls and quickly warming things up. The views got more and more spectacular and the heat more penetrating as we descended, with shadows and perspectives constantly changing the further we went.

The teenagers in our group, Nick and Lauren, quickly moved out ahead, with their parents, Jodi and Joe, soon chasing after them. Before long, our whole group was spread out along the well trod, rocky dirt trail, all progressing steadily down the winding footpath, albeit at varied paces.

By 10 AM, most of us reached the halfway point, oasis-like Indian Garden. A welcome respite from the rapidly warming sun, Indian Garden offered picnic tables, water, toilets, and shade from an abundance of cottonwood trees, planted by an early developer over a hundred years ago. As the name implies, Indian Garden had been farmed for many centuries before that by the native Pueblo Indians.

After a restful lunch, we trudged onward, following tree-lined Garden Creek out of Indian Garden, as it gurgled along by our side down the trail. The slope for the next mile was gentle, a stretch I knew we would welcome when making the trek back out of the canyon, especially considering what came next. Known as the Devil's Corkscrew for obvious reasons, the trail now descended steeply down a series of switchbacks that followed Pipe Creek to the inner canyon.

Then we were at the Colorado River, much more large and powerful, than its ribbon-like appearance as viewed from the rim. But our work was not done, since the River trail required a climb back up a couple hundred feet while paralleling the channel below for the next mile or so.

The silver suspension bridge finally came into view. A welcome site it was at this point, since we knew that Phantom Ranch was just a half mile further. An adventure in itself, the bridge had open wire mesh floor and sides, so when looking straight down past their feet, hikers were gaping through the grate directly at the roaring river some 60 feet below. An unnerving sensation for some, along with the slight sway of the bridge, I recalled a time when a companion on a previous hike convinced us to cross the bridge in the pre-dawn darkness to avoid having to peer down at the ominous river.

Safely across the 300 foot expanse, our pace quickened along the now level path for the final push to Phantom Ranch. Nearing the Cottonwood-lined compound, we were greeted by Jodi and Lauren, looking relaxed sitting in Bright Angel Creek, cooling their travel weary feet. Eager now, we headed directly to the multi-purpose dining hall/general store/lounge, where our first priority was a large glass of cold lemonade, which we had been obsessing about in the sun-filled desert heat for the past couple hours. Now as we happily settled in wooden chairs within the stone-clad walls of the lodge around 1:30 in the afternoon, the air-conditioned coolness gradually restored our fatigued bodies, while we munched away on our sack lunches.

After an extended rest, we walked, more slowly now, over to our cabin, to check out the accommodations for the next two nights. Curtis and I couldn't help comparing to the El Tovar, though we weren't complaining in the least, considering that the Ranch was the best (and of course the only) place to stay (other than camping on the ground) within nine miles and a five thousand foot elevation gain. And here was a setting like none other on earth.

Entering the rustic cabin, the first sound we heard was the struggling ruckus from an overworked window air-conditioner that was obviously no match for the 100+ degree heat. Nonetheless, it kept the room temperature from being oppressive, if not cool. Like our El Tovar suite, the cabin had two rooms. However, that was where the similarity ended. Instead of the ample king bed in the suite, this cabin sported five creaky bunkbeds, serving ten guests in the cramped quarters. Also, a single toilet and sink would have to do for everyone.

Showers were available across the way in a separate building. But that could wait. As other hikers in our group arrived, they joined us for a nap, some here, and others in the male and female dormitory cabins at the far end of the compound.

Later in the afternoon, after refreshing showers, we gathered around a ring of benches in the shade of a cottonwood tree, near the trail at the edge of the compound, for a ranger talk about condors in the canyon. During the talk, I spotted Marc and Peter just arriving at 4:30 PM. They had passed a slow-moving Karen, our final group member, a little ways back. I left the ring and headed up the trail, finding Karen trudging along with a worn out look on her face. Her spirits lifted as I took the pack off her back and carried it the final quarter mile. Considering her 72 year old age, she had done well, and was relieved as well as contented with her achievement.

When the dinner bell rang at 6:30 PM, we gathered around long tables for a hearty family style meal of beef stew, salad, cornbread, and chocolate cake, washed down with ice tea, beer and wine. Checking my notes after returning home, I noticed that the menus from our stay here nearly 20 years earlier were exactly the same. No need to change a formula that has worked well for so many years.

That evening another ranger talk about canyon critters was given in the amphitheater, located near a grassy area that stirred a memory from my first visit here as a 17 year-old, over 50 years ago. On a one day hike, in and out of the canyon back then, a dip in the ranch swimming pool worked wonders on my overheated young body. Alas, about 10 years later, overuse and water quality issues led to the pool's closure and backfill with soil and vegetation.

"Join me for a walk with my black light to look for scorpions," the ranger encouraged us as her talk about the night creatures came to a close. However, by that time, dead tired, we opted instead for our "inviting" bunks and were in bed by 9 PM. We heard the next day that she had found four of the poisonous arachnids nearby.

Up at 5 AM, Curtis and I were ready for the fresh coffee set out in the quiet morning darkness by the side window of the dining hall. A substantial breakfast of scrambled eggs, bacon, pancakes, peaches, orange juice, milk and coffee brought the rest of our group out at 6:30. All were complaining of sore legs, glad that we didn't have to hike back out that day.

Not wanting to push their luck, Huw and Rachel spent the morning on a leisurely walk along the river trail, while Karen took the same approach on the historic self-guided Ranch tour. But the rest of us headed out the back of camp on the North Kaibab Trail to the Clear Creek Trail, leading in a little over a mile to an overlook high above the Ranch. Still, we were glad to be hiking upward initially, and not downward, since different muscles were used than our calves, which were aching from yesterday's hike down.

The Ranch far below basked in the bright sunlight, as did the muddy red Colorado River, a little further out. From here we could see both the silver and the black suspension bridges in one view, bisecting the river a half mile apart. The black bridge with its solid bottom was used by the mules, so they wouldn't be spooked seeing the river below them.

After lunch, while pondering the prospect of the long, hot hike to the rim the next day, we spotted an intriguing offer posted on the wall. For a fee, our gear could be packed out on a mule. Without delay, most of us were out back stuffing burlap sacks with as much as would fit within the 30 pound limit. That proved to be a huge morale booster as we contemplated hiking without the extra weight.

The wisdom of our decision was confirmed that afternoon by the ranger's talk, which covered tips and precautions for the hike out. The tips included the obvious, such as taking plenty of water, salt and electrolytes, while avoiding the 10 AM-4 PM hottest part of the day. Also, we were advised to eat along the way, dowse the head with water, cover up with long sleeve shirts and pants, wear cotton, wrap a wet bandanna around the neck, and lay over during the heat of the day at Indian Garden. Then the ranger drove her point home, reporting that the temperature was currently over 100°F, and that the record here was 120°F. Hearing that, we took most of the tips to heart.

But members of our group were not the type to sit around for long periods. Conversations at the early dinner sitting that night centered on another way to beat the heat. While enjoying a delicious meal of steak and baked potato, most decided to beat the heat the next morning by departing at 3 AM, to hopefully reach the rim by 10 AM. Not willing to pass up the sumptuous early breakfast at 5 AM, Huw, Rachel and I opted for a later departure, as did Karen, who had pre-arranged a mule ride out of the canyon.

I awoke at 4 AM to an empty cabin, the others having long gone. Sipping coffee in the dark by the dining hall, I was joined by Burkhart from Montreux, Switzerland. He had been here before as a young man, and returned this time so that his wife could share the unique experience. Quickly finishing his coffee, he remarked ambivalently, "I would prefer to stay for breakfast, but my wife wants to get on the trail now." By 4:30, they were off.

Having wolfed down my own breakfast a few minutes later, I waved good-bye to Huw, Rachel and Karen. Free of my pack, I hit the trail with a fast pace at 5:10 AM, just after daybreak. The desert air, though already in the seventies, almost felt cool.

In my haste, I unwittingly made a wrong turn near the river, confused by some construction repairs that altered the path. When the black bridge came into sight, I realized my mistake, which had added a mile to what I already knew would be an arduous hike to the rim. Chiding myself, I crossed the bridge and raced back along the river trail, meeting up with a surprised Huw and Rachel, who were already carefully proceeding, just past the silver bridge. Back on track, I now moved swiftly, waving to Burkhart and his wife a couple miles further along, as they rested under some foliage beside the creek.

Huw and Rachel begin the ascent

The inner canyon revealed a uniqueness all its own. The narrow gorge, fifty feet wide with sheer hundred foot walls rising up from the creek, provided a remarkable contrast to the more expansive canyon landscape familiar to most observers.

Too soon, the precipitous Devil's Corkscrew abruptly returned my senses to the reality that almost a mile in elevation gain rose before me. Two thirds of the way up the Corkscrew, the sun's intense rays broke through and brought the relentless heat that would accompany me the rest of the way.

After a welcome rest and water stop at Indian Garden, the final ascent began. Even without a pack, the oppressive heat and steep incline started to slow my pace. I caught up with and chatted for a moment with Michaele and Aileen from the early risers, while they rested on a rock.

Continuing to trudge along with more frequent stops, I now appreciated a feature that was hardly noticed on the descent two days earlier. Strategically placed, the Three-Mile Resthouse and Mile-and-a-Half Resthouse offered toilets, water and shade at the indicated distances from the rim. Just knowing that they were ahead gave renewed hope to a body that was rapidly wearing down.

At the first one, I passed by Peter and Marc, two more early starters. Proceeding on, I kept telling myself, "one foot in front of the other," wondering if I had enough strength left to make it out. My spirits lifted when I spotted Joe at the second resthouse. From here, we encouraged each other, taking turns leading, as we limply lumbered up the final mile to the top.

Joe nears the South Rim on the final ascent

Totally spent, my rubbery legs seemed like they were on automatic pilot plodding the final hundred yards along the rim, to the long sought after Fountain, where a double dip ice cream cone was the closest to heaven I could ever imagine being at that moment.

After what felt like an eternity sitting immobile, I regained enough energy to walk, like a victor returning from battle, into the El

Tovar. Finding Curtis, who had emerged at the rim fifteen minutes ahead of me, we checked in to our hard-earned "paradise" for the night: The El Tovar Suite. On the third floor, this suite had an even vaster balcony than the Fred Harvey Suite, just below.

A few moments later, padded chairs cushioned our weary bodies, as we eased in with cold beers, to once again take in the matchless panorama. The Canyon rewarded us with a breathtaking thunderstorm, quickly passing over the canyon with a sound and light show that set off the dramatic sandstone cathedrals below.

The scene was a fitting end to an adventure that tested our human limitations against the Canyon's timeless splendor. Though we both relished this moment and the luxurious comfort of the El Tovar, we agreed that we would gladly trade it for another day amidst the grandeur we had found in the canyon depths below.

Celebration dinner at El Tovar Dining room

Part V

Sequoia National Park

Mike, Karen & Curtis explore the Congress Trail

Chapter 11

Sequoia National Park

Home of redwood giants, Bearpaw Meadow and Mineral King

Yosemite and Grand Canyon National Parks are tough acts to follow. But Sequoia National Park offers some hidden gems for those of us willing to explore the out of the way nooks and crannies. Sequoia has its own Crystal Cave, challenging mountain trails, breathtaking panoramic vistas, treacherous winding roads including one leading to a remote spot once proposed as a Disney ski resort, and rustic or luxury camping, depending on which trail you chose.

Without question, the giant sequoia trees are the park's crown jewels. The towering shafts, reaching hundreds of feet in the air and thousands of years in age, span human history much like the mountains link geologic eras. No trip to Sequoia would be complete without a stroll among the red giants along the readily accessible Congress Trail. The trail starts at the world's largest tree by volume, the General Sherman, measuring at 275 feet high, 36 feet in diameter and 103 feet in circumference at the base, and weighing over four million pounds. Other trees along this unique forest path have names like President, Washington, Lincoln, and a grove called Senate.

Our first taste of Sequoia came on Death March 5, as a warm up to our first rafting adventure described in the chapter on rafting. We returned a couple years later to fully focus on this unique area for Death March 7. Gradually learning the fine points of backpacking with each year that passed, I prided myself on this trip from having reduced the weight of my pack from the agonizing 35 pounds carried on Death March 1 to a measly 8 pounds this year. I also learned that sometimes the trade offs in search of lightening the load can be too extreme. For example, the tube tent I took on this Death March, in reality nothing more than a garbage bag, was woefully deficient in most respects out in the back country, as can be imagined.

Driving up from the office on a sunny August Friday afternoon, we reached Lodgepole campground in the evening and took in the ranger talk at the campfire before turning in. Our goal the next day was Silliman Pass and Ranger Lake, an ambitious ten mile hike with a 4,131 foot elevation gain. Having been lulled by the ease of the flat Congress trail, we hadn't anticipated the strenuous nature of this trail. After two steep climbs separated by a welcome and level alpine meadow, Twin Lakes, about half way, provided a pleasant and much needed rest stop for lunch. Then up over the pass and back down to serene Ranger Lake. Hiking time for the group ranged from seven to ten hours. Though dead tired and sore, we found the strength to boil our water, make supper, and hang our food from a high tree limb, since this was, after all, black bear country. The following day we retraced our steps, and though weary, hiked out in better time than the hike in.

Then years later, we returned to a more remote, yet highly enchanting corner of Sequoia known as Bearpaw Meadow, for Death March 17. We had a taste of this memorable spot in the fourteenth year. That was a time when our applications for three different options were all approved. As the years went by, we discovered that more advanced planning was required in order to experience the truly special natural treasures.

The official Death March 14 was the raft trip on the Kern River. But a wilderness permit was also granted for the Whitney Portals trail to Mount Whitney that year, as were accommodations for the Bearpaw Meadow High Sierra Camp. Rather than pass up these difficult to get opportunities, various contingents of Death Marchers participated on one or more of the three outings. Those making that first trek to Bearpaw Meadow knew instantly that this matchless setting must become an official Death March one day.

So it was that on January 2, 1995, Gerry, Steve and George were all up at 7 AM playing phone roulette, hoping that one of them would get through to the reservation desk to snatch a couple nights at the popular camp that sold out within minutes for the upcoming short summer season. Miraculously, we secured the camp's six tent cabins for two nights in July. With twin beds in each cabin, twelve people could be accommodated, plus an additional person could sleep on the floor if desired. As it turned out, twelve made the trek.

The first night we stayed in cabins at Grant Village and warmed up our muscles with a quick walk down the Congress trail. Steve showed his dedication, having never missed a Death March since joining the firm in 1979. He had left town only half moved into his new home, and having just taken his grandmother to the hospital with a broken hip. Fortunately, his wife, Sherry had planned to stay back anyway, and tended to the home base.

Bernie, Don & George on the Bearpaw Meadow Trail

We hit the eleven mile trail the next morning, a gorgeous Sunday where the rain had cleared just in time for a hike, as the Trail Notes recorded, with "spectacular views, sunny with some clouds...Lots of snow in [the] mountains, but very little on the trail... Lots of water in the streams." We marveled at the journey "as the trail wound around the side of the mountain with a broad majestic valley, inspiring us as we go." The rushing water proved challenging. At one point, I slid down a boulder out of control, going head first into the ice cold creek, getting soaked head to toe. The main injury was to my pride. We waded across the creek several times, and the water under one bridge that we crossed had risen three feet by the time Karen and Bernie passed that way a couple hours later. On the plus side, "Wild flowers are in bloom, pink carpets, blue, yellow, etc. with birds and butterflies in abundance."

The camp setting was utterly amazing, set dramatically on the edge of a mountain, looking out across a deep valley to "Snow capped peaks over 13,000 feet and shear granite domes" in the distance. The view was one of the most strikingly beautiful sights we would see on any of the Death Marches before or after. We shared the site with energetic marmots, who accorded us access to their stunning domain for a brief time.

Relaxing at Bearpaw Meadow Camp on the porch

The camp staff were friendly, offering lemonade and brownies upon our arrival, and then filling us with "New York strip steaks, au gratin potatoes, corn, biscuits, salad, apple juice, blueberry and chocolate pie," for dinner. No wonder the Bearpaw Meadow camp was so poplar and sought after!

The pampering continued with a breakfast of "Scrambled eggs, sausage, pancakes, blueberries, orange juice, coffee and granola." Not bad for eleven miles away from civilization. We had a glorious layover day with hiking, reading, card playing and just relaxing in the idyllic back country camp, finished off with a breathtaking sunset and moon rise.

With so many choices for high adventure in the American West, we did not return to Sequoia until eleven years later. Death March 28 brought us to another out of the way part of Sequoia National Park, known as Mineral King. A subalpine glacial valley named for nearby silver mines in the late nineteenth century, the remote area is accessed by a narrow, windy road, over twenty miles long. Walt Disney had planned a huge ski resort here in the 1960's, but fortunately, the valley was annexed into the national park in 1978 instead.

Our home for three nights in August, 2006 was the aptly named Silver City Resort, a quaint array of chalets and cabins surrounding a restaurant and general store. The terrain was similar to other parts of Sequoia with majestic mountain peaks, waterfalls, and green valleys. A unique feature was Soda Spring, a colorful carbonated mineral spring bubbling up, a short hike from Silver City.

We spent two days hiking on trails like East Fork Grove, Paradise Ridge, and Franklin Lakes, past scenic redwood groves, and along mountain and valley trails. Dinners were at the restaurant where the pies were the favorites, especially the razzleberry, a delicious blending of raspberries and blackberries.

The final two Sequoia Death Marches were actually just north of the national park in Giant Sequoia National Monument. We had such a great time at the then new Sequoia High Sierra Camp during Death March 31 in 2009, that we scheduled a return visit five years later.

Crossing a creek in Mineral King

The Sequoia High Sierra Camp was the brain child of Burr and Suzanne Hughes, a Tennessee couple, who turned a dream into reality, when an isolated chunk of land surrounded by the national monument became available for development. An architect whose master's degree had an emphasis on sustainable design, Hughes built an eco-friendly camp using what is known as organic architecture.

Just because the camp is environmentally sensitive did not mean campers needed to rough it. To the contrary, this camp is considered a luxury version of a high sierra camp, and is included in the annals of what is known as glamping, a term that connotes a cross between glamorous and camping. That may have something to do with the eagerness for a return visit.

We started these two Death Marches with a night at the relatively new Wuksachi Lodge, not far from Lodgepole, enjoying a sumptuous bar-b-que dinner in the woods at nearby Wolverton Meadow.

The next day there were two options for reaching the camp. A winding, bumpy road, reminiscent of the drive to Mineral King, could be taken to a trailhead thirty miles away. There, the camp was a mere mile away, along an undemanding trail. The alternative was a challenging twelve mile hike starting directly behind Wuksachi Lodge. As expected, most of our group opted to weather the long drive, so as to have an easy hike to camp. But five of us chose the long hike, which was more in keeping with Death March traditions. Our efforts were rewarded as recounted in the Trail Notes: "Beautiful, sunny day, cool in morning and hot, 90's in afternoon. In forest and meadows, with colorful wildflowers, blue, yellow, red, white. We see a big brown (black color) bear with 2 cubs moving across a meadow (Cahoon) about 200 yards away. She looks at us for a minute and moves on...Long & strenuous, but beautiful mountains & forest views." That was the best bear sighting we could remember from all our Death Marches.

The camp was set on the side of a mountain, making for steep climbs to the cabins from the dramatic, log-timbered pillars of the open air lounge and dining pavilion. The panoramic view over the broad valley toward Kings Canyon was worth it, particularly during a couple outstanding sunsets featuring a blood red sky.

On our first visit, we hiked up 10,365 foot Mitchell Peak. On the second visit, some of us hiked down and around past Lookout Peak and onward all the way to Cedar Grove in the heart of Kings Canyon National Park. The eight mile trek was especially enjoyable, considering that the slope was downhill most of the way. Features of the camp and the gourmet cuisine are described in the next chapter,

Open air dining hall at Sequoia High Sierra Camp

Suzanne & Burr Hughes, gracious hosts and proprietors

Chapter 12

Sequoia's Hidden High Country Gem

A long bumpy road plus a brisk mountain hike are rewarded with dramatic vistas, gourmet meals and a comfy bed

Continuing to call our annual getaway "The Death March" was a stretch compared to the rugged backpacking adventures we shared in years gone by. Yet our group still sought an element of challenge this August, away from the crowds. The Sequoia High Sierra Camp, surrounded by Sequoia and Kings Canyon National Parks, proved just right. Friends and family from our Tustin, California accounting firm huffed and puffed their way up the one mile trail to the camp, at an elevation of 8,282 feet.

The Bed

The camp's 36 spacious canvas tent cabins (www.sequoiahighsierracamp.com; $250 per person per night including meals) were spread across twenty acres of wooded mountainside terrain. The cabins featured concrete floors with colorful rugs, comfortable twin and king-sized beds with warm wool blankets for the cool nights, padded chairs and metal tables. Wood louvered windows opened for daytime air and light, while propane lamps glowed at night. The bathhouse, complete with flush toilets and hot showers, was reached down a solar-lit pathway.

The Meal

The open-air dining hall, ecologically designed by architect-owner Burr Hughes, looked out over a panoramic view of Kings Canyon National Park. Finding gourmet quality cuisine in this remote wilderness setting was a welcome surprise. Chef Brett Laukaitis, from San Francisco, did not disappoint. Hors d' oeuvres served to guests relaxing on the veranda included mushroom caps stuffed with goat cheese and grilled triangles of ham and cheese.

These were washed down with local beers and a worldwide selection of fine wines. Dinners during our two night stay included New York strip steak with pesto sauce and mahi-mahi served with a tomato-based sauce. Flavorful soups and salads came first, while desserts of fruit cobbler and panna cotta completed the meal.

The Find

Owners Burr and Suzanne Hughes, who conceived, built and operate the camp, were delightful hosts. From the first greeting upon arrival, accompanied by ice tea, fresh made oatmeal cookies and watermelon slices, we felt like members of the family, warmly welcomed to their special mountain home. Suzanne assured that our every need was fulfilled, while Burr readily dispensed tips on the variety of hiking trails. A highlight for us was the eight-mile, mostly downhill trek to the bottom of Kings Canyon. A key selling point was the shuttle van Burr provided at the end of the hike that brought us back to camp.

Williams family on trail with baby Brooke

Lesson Learned

By sharing a challenging hiking adventure with people in our lives, we came to know each other in ways that were not readily achieved in any other way. Tramping along a trail together, free of cell phones and TV, we had the gift of time, where the special, unique quality that is within each person, had a chance to shine through and deepen the bonds among us. Having the picturesque, inviting setting of the Sequoia High Sierra Camp, heightened the experience.

Campbell family on trail by Sequoia high Sierra Camp

California coast near San Simeon on Death March 38

Ke'e Beach at start of Kalalau Trail, Kauai on Death March 20

Part VI

Island and Coastal Adventures

Mt Tamalpais DM 33 and dinner on Catalina DM11

Chapter 13

Island and Coastal Adventures

Flowing with the spirit of the alluring Pacific

Over the course of four decades of Death Marches, three took place on islands, and another three along stretches of coastline. The first came on Death March 11, late in August, 1989. Twenty-one of us converged at the Catalina Express Terminal at San Pedro for the 1-1/2 hour boat ride to the tiny village of Two Harbors, located on an isthmus, 18 miles northwest of Avalon on Catalina Island. The village name referred to the harbors that were separated by the half-mile wide isthmus.

Two Harbors was less than a tenth the size of Avalon, with more pleasure boats in the harbor then there were residents, making for a relaxed, laid-back atmosphere. Our group of twenty-one took over the Banning House Lodge, a bed and breakfast, once the summer home of the island's then owner. We knew we were in a different world when we discovered that we shared the area with a free ranging herd of more than a dozen buffalo.

Our objectives for the weekend were two day hikes. The first was a hike up and over the isthmus backbone to the ocean side of the island and then south a total of six miles to Little Bay, "a picturesque little beach with rock outcroppings on each end." Following lunch, a swim and sun bathing on the sandy beach were welcome rewards after the tiring hike. The next day, a hike in the opposite direction to the northwest led to Emerald Bay, where gorgeous views and coves filled with turquoise blue waters captivated us.

On this Death March, six month old Monica Williams made her debut, taking in the hikes, albeit in her father, Steve's backpack.

The other two island adventures were on Death Marches 20 and 23. When number 20 approached, we knew that something special was called for to commemorate this milestone. Much careful planning was required, since our choice, the Kalalau Trail on the Hawaiian island of Kauai necessitated one of a limited number of trail permits that became available a year ahead. The next chapter recounts the unforgettable journey that gave us new found respect for the Hawaiian paradise.

Death March 23 to Channel Islands National Park might be characterized a "cruise," but that would be a misnomer, since the cabins on our "ship" were more akin to steerage than first class. They amounted to a bunk room with tight, curtained-off spaces set against the side of the dive boat's hull. However, this was a Death March, so no one was complaining. In fact, it turned out to be another treasured adventure, as revisited in the following chapter.

Our coastal Death Marches began with Death March 24 to Pigeon Point Lighthouse, near Pescadero, California, a short distance south of San Francisco. This was our first venture with a hostel, this one having taken over a facility formerly used by the United States Coast Guard. From there we explored state parks inland amidst a redwood forest and coastal by an extended family of elephant seals, as detailed in Chapter 16.

Pleased with the efficiency and economy of a hostel stay, as well as the extraordinary seascape setting, we scheduled another one for Death March 33. As if the lighthouse at Pigeon Point was not enchanting enough, this time's hostel was just over San Francisco's Golden Gate Bridge, in the Marin Headlands.

There our group took over a huge old officer's home on a former military base turned into a state park. The eighteen of us were like one large family spread over six bedrooms, and sharing communal breakfasts and box lunch preparation in the kitchen and dining room.

The first full day of hiking took us through Muir Woods National Monument, where once again we enjoyed a stand of majestic coast redwoods. Some of us apparently got caught up in the enjoyment too much, when we discovered that a strategic wrong turn cost us an extra three miles before we reached the inviting Mountain Home Inn, where tasty burgers and bratwurst restored our spirits.

That afternoon, a short hike to the top of Mount Tamalpais highlighted our day with expansive views of San Francisco Bay beckoning in the distance.

The next day the group was ready for a true coastal hike. Point Reyes National Seashore, fifty miles north, filled the bill. We set out on the Palomarin Trail for the four mile trek to gain a view of Alamere Falls.

This hike brought another first for Death Marches. The Young family, with their two boys, succumbed to the ocean's call, racing back to their car to retrieve surfboards for riding the secluded area's inviting waves. The allure soon wore off, however, as the fear of sharks dampened their ardor, after a short foray into the surf.

Alamere Falls proved a worthy destination. From an overlook, we watched as the stream of water formed three successive falls before climaxing with a large cascade over a cliff into the sea.

Our final coastal adventure was the strangest of Death Marches. The widely anticipated Death March 38 drew a record signup of 49 participants. Big Sur was a majestic shoreline that had eluded us until now. We were all set to converge at Big Sur Lodge for two days of hiking and absorbing this unique area on the central California coast.

That is, until a huge, record setting wild fire broke out just weeks before the scheduled commencement of the 38th rendition of the time tested tradition. Our hopes for the fire's containment steadily dwindled, until finally the day before departure, we had to cancel the Death March for the first time in its nearly four decades of annual adventures.

Not to be undone, and with some participants already in route from as far as Chicago, we quickly devised "Plan B" and made the most of "The Death March That Never Was." Chapter 17 recounts all the details.

"This is sacred land. Give it your utmost care, respect and leave knowing you have preserved it for future generations."

Chapter 14

Tramping the Heavenly Kalalau

Note: First published in the Chicago Tribune, January 16, 2000, titled 'Prepare Thee for a Challenge.'

How does a group of backpackers cap off twenty years of hiking adventures? We had trekked in places like Yosemite, the High Sierras and the Grand Canyon, by foot, on horseback, in river rafts and navigating inflatable kayaks. The only requirement: destinations within driving distance of Orange County, California, with hikes that can be accomplished over a long summer weekend. The rationale is quite simple. The group consists of several local accountants and friends that once a year shed their serious, buttoned down image for the world of hiking boots and backpacks.

But this special year, our 20th, seems to call for a unique adventure. I recall a time on the Hawaiian Island of Kauai, five years earlier, when I stood in the rain, at the end of the road, next to picturesque Ke'e Beach. Before me was a signpost that read: Kalalau Trail 11 Miles. I scrambled up the slippery rocks of the first couple hundred yards of the trail and came upon a spectacular ocean vista. Right then I knew that someday I had to return to experience the whole grandeur of this trail. I didn't know if I could persuade anyone else to spend several days in paradise on what is also a hot, muddy path. Besides, it is far beyond "driving" distance from Orange County.

But now as I share my memories of the green-cliffed Kalalau's magical lure, it takes little convincing before the group buys into the dream. However, the advance planning is a greater challenge, starting with the permit to hike and camp on the Kalalau Trail. An application has to be submitted a year ahead, and even then the number of spaces doled out for each day is extremely sparse. Even if you are lucky enough to get picked, your group is limited to a maximum of ten campers. There is no charge, but only after receiving several rejections do we begin to figure out the nuances of the permit request system, the importance of timing, format and sufficient groveling with the all-powerful permit staff. When the precious approval finally comes, the group is ecstatic. The captivating Kalalau is within our grasp.

With permit in hand, we can take a whole year to coordinate schedules, airlines, hotels and condos, and the myriad of other details. Studying guidebooks to assess trail conditions and supply requirements, we learn that this hike is considered as little different in scope from numerous High Sierra treks we'd taken over the years. The guides rate the Kalalau as strenuous, somewhat frightening, and only for experienced hikers. We downplay this difficulty, recalling that such ratings for other trails we'd hiked had proved to be overstated in our case. We estimate that two days should be adequate -- one day in, one day out. Sure it will be hot and humid, but most of our hikes had been undertaken in hot weather, and often at high altitude. The Kalalau starts at sea level and never goes above 800 feet, though the trail reaches both extremes about five times, as it winds in and around the lush green ridges and valleys of the Na Pali coast.

Pack light is our main thought. Tube tent, air mattress, a little food, and lots of water. Oh, and a good book, since there will be the whole afternoon to while away once we get there.

With much anticipation, the momentous weekend finally arrives. Converging on Kauai from various directions, group members rendezvous for a twentieth anniversary dinner at the Princeville Resort, reminiscing on the patio as the orange August sun descends across lovely Hanelei Bay, the gateway to the Na Pali coast and the Kalalau. Tomorrow we find our way ten miles around the bay to road's end, and the beginning of our Hawaiian adventure.

Fighting the temptation to indulge on Mai Tai's around the pool for the next two days, everyone arrives at the trailhead, fresh and ready to go at 8:30 the next morning. Adding to the light hearted, picnic atmosphere, three of the wives and their pre-school age children decide to keep the eight hikers company, joining in for the popular two mile stretch leading to Hanakapiai Beach. There they would wave good-by, wishing us well, as they returned to the comfort of the resort hotels. Confidence at a high level, we instruct them to pick us up at 11 AM the next day at the trailhead. Five hours should give us ample time to retrace our steps from Kalalau, leaving at 6AM.

After a quick group photo beneath the Kalalau trail sign, we are off. Steep, slippery rocks fill the muddy trail from the start. But these warning signs do not color the bright outlook held by all. Nor do the anxious looks on the faces of the mothers after that first two miles. Now they are wondering why on earth they have subjected their small children to this hair-raising introduction to the Hawaiian backcountry.

Lush, jungle vegetation typifies this first section of trail, as it alternately climbs, levels out, and climbs again for a mile. Interspersed are scenes of the gentle surf breaking over the coral reef at palm-lined Ke'e Beach, growing smaller with each lookout point. Pushing through overgrown ferns, guava and broadleaf tropical plants, we reach the top of the first of five fluted ridgelines that accentuate the trail. Far below, sand covered Hanakapiai Beach beckons us. But to get there requires a steep descent, traversing narrow switchbacks, followed by a tricky negotiation of a swift running stream strewn with large boulders. All manage to hop boulder to boulder across the churning waters without falling in. We are rewarded with a break on the deserted shore accompanied by the ocean's pounding surf.

Reaching Hanakapiai has taken us 1-1/4 hours, a slower pace than we are used to. All are complaining of their heavy packs already. But the day is young, the sun well below its peak, and we are still relatively fresh. Before us rises another 800 foot ridge. As we go, we become increasingly wary of the narrow, gravel covered trail, which for long stretches is barely the width of one's foot. Deceptively, the ocean side of the trail is overgrown with low-lying vegetation, giving a false sense of stability. We all learn to our trepidation that stepping just slightly off the trail onto this vegetation can result in a perilous slide toward the sea far below, since the vegetation covers nothing but air. A few careless slips get our hearts pounding as we gingerly make our way forward.

Steve assesses the precarious terrain.

Despite the growing anxiety over the hazardous cliff-like trail, we are exhilarated by the increasingly majestic and haunting beauty of the sheer, green covered mountains, contrasted against the shimmering turquoise and deep blue of the sea far below. As we gaze ahead, the next dramatic ridgeline boldly juts out into the ocean, giving definition to the valley before it. The trail gets tougher on this four-mile stretch and the sun continues to climb, though the overhang of the rainforest offers welcome shade along the way. We pass through the hanging valleys of Hoolulu and Waiahuakua with their numerous streams, before reaching our mid-trail destination of the Hanakoa Valley. While the Hanakapiai Valley had descended gently to the sea, hanging valleys like these end abruptly at a cliff, dropping off straight down to the sea hundreds of feet below.

Jeff and Larry take a break on Kalalau Trail

At our lunch stop by the mosquito-ridden campsite, the steady, rushing sounds of nearby Hanakoa Falls serenade us. The natural beauty of the dense forest of Kukui trees and coffee plants is broken only by the presence of a solitary picnic table and outhouse.

Climbing out of Hanakoa Valley and around the next ridge, we sense a dramatic change in climate. The lush, steamy jungle is replaced with a dry, arid landscape for much of the remaining five miles of trail. Totally exposed to the sun and the steep drop off, we struggle to remain focused as heat and fatigue take their toll. This next mile is especially harrowing, since there is no vegetation to conceal the fact that only a sloping, crumbling thread of a path separates us from a fatal descent. The bleating sounds of nearby wild goats mock our tentative passage through their territory. We pray that the occasional black bumblebee does not appear suddenly, throwing us off balance at such a vulnerable moment.

When the worst is finally over, we pull our eyes off of our faltering footing to gaze out at the breathtaking splendor of the Kalalau Valley spread before us. The green spires reach towards the heavens, accented by delicate clouds at their upper reaches. Confirming that this magical fairyland is, indeed, near at hand, a sign reads in Hawaiian as well as English: "Kalalau – This is sacred land. Give it your utmost care, respect, and leave knowing you have preserved it for future generations."

Spurred on by this renewed inspiration, we cover the final two miles quickly, down the steep, red-earth covered slope and through thick coastal vegetation, including guava and papaya trees. We collapse on Kalalau Beach, an expansive stretch of soft, white sand several hundred yards wide and a half-mile long. After resting for a long while and cooling our blistered feet in the soothing surf, we replenish our water supply from the waterfall at the far end of the beach. The hike has taken us a full eight hours and we are exhausted. Only five of our original eight hikers made it all the way. Not until tomorrow do we learn that one gave up after four miles and the other two camped at Hanakoa Valley before turning back. From the beach, we wave at a passing catamaran tour boat, vowing to sail out of this place, if only it will stop for us. Of course it never does.

As we scout out campsites in the trees behind the beach, an exotic couple passes by, the man wearing a colorful sarong around the waist, while the woman is clad only in a fanny pack. Later, the Moroccan fellow visits our camp, relating to us that his companion prefers to go naked. He has been here a week, nursing a foot infection, so we share antibiotics and he shows us the best caves to camp in. He grimaces in disbelief to hear that we intend to head back tomorrow, without even a day to rest and explore the inner reaches of this special valley.

Knowing that the hike out in the morning will be tough, and regretting now that the wives were told to meet us at the trailhead at 11 AM, we are in bed at 7 PM, too tired even to watch the glorious sunset. Bugs are not much of a problem, but we sleep fitfully amidst the roar of the waves, until we rise at 4 AM.

With the first inkling gray of dawn, camp is broken at 5:45 AM, and the fittest member of the group is sent ahead to retrace our route as quickly as possible. Sadly, we bid farewell to Kalalau and start back. The night's rest and the cool morning air lull us into thinking the return trip may not be so bad. The first two miles go quickly. But then the oppressive sun, heat, humidity, steep slopes, and not least of all our sore, weary bodies, take their toll.

The return hike is more excruciating than the hike in, and becomes a test of will and survival. Water runs short. Needing more liquid than the day before, numerous stops are made, collecting and treating stream water. Each step becomes a major effort as, one by one we "hit the wall," seriously wondering if this ordeal will ever end.

We stare in disbelief upon reaching Hanakapiai beach at the final two-mile mark. What had been an empty stretch of sand early yesterday morning, now bustled with a multitude of swimmers, here for an afternoon of fun at this "secluded" spot.

Somehow, we press on with even slower steps. Gratefully, all eventually return safely to the trailhead, though some as late as 3 PM. All are totally exhausted, covered with dust and mud, and barely able to walk. We have a new found respect to add to our memories of the heavenly Kalalau. All agree that this sojourn in paradise had become more like a death march. Nevertheless, we are hardly off the trail before the inevitable question arises: How will we top this next year?

Our home at sea for Channel Islands Death March 23

Chapter 15

California's Channel Islands

Exploring hidden gems by land and sea

"Juan Rodriquez Cabrillo, discoverer of California, must have seen pretty much the same view when he stood here in 1543," I remarked, peering out over barren San Miguel Island and Cuyler Harbor below. Led by National Park Service volunteer, Andrea Moe, a group of eighteen of us had just hiked up the steep half-mile trail from the beach to this historic, 300 foot high vantage point in the Channel Islands National Park, off the California coast near Santa Barbara. A small, cross-topped monument to Cabrillo commemorates his memory. "Legend has it that he died in these islands from gangrene caused by an injury," Andrea told us.

Having lived in Southern California for over twenty years, I was amazed to learn that this scenic and serene group of islands, the furthest lying less than forty miles away from one of the most populous metropolises in America, is one of the least visited of our National Parks. Indeed, my group of colleagues and friends from our CPA firm in Orange County, California had been taking annual weekend adventures for the past twenty-two years, before we noticed this treasure practically in our back yard.

To be fair, the Channel Islands are not the easiest place to visit. A one to five hour boat ride is required, unless you arrange air service to a dirt strip on Santa Rosa Island. The only overnight facilities available are primitive campgrounds where you must bring all food and provisions with you.

We opted for a somewhat more civilized outing. Truth Aquatics, along with one other concessionaire, runs one day and multi-day boat tours out of Santa Barbara, with sleeping accommodations on board and tasty meals prepared by the crew. Our group converged at the dock after 8 PM on a Thursday evening, and proceeded to settle in on the vessel, Truth, captained by Don Powell.

Margie, one of our firm's bookkeepers, arrived a few minutes later and asked "Where's my cabin?" My colleague, Steve, and I had to fight off a chuckle as I pointed out the "cabin" for her and her two sons, Tyler and Brett, which consisted of cramped three-high bunks in the center of the lower deck. Privacy was provided by a curtain that could be drawn across the narrow space between the three-foot wide single bunks. On the sides of this lower deck were only slightly wider double bunks that couples could use. All in all, the bunks could hold about thirty travelers, though this trip totaled in the mid-twenties.

After loading on our gear, popping Dramamine tablets, and swapping stories of anticipation, we turned in for the night, wondering if we would sleep through the 4 AM departure. It seemed like only moments had passed when the roar of engines broke loudly and suddenly into my peaceful reverie. Sitting up quickly I banged my head on the bunk above, before realizing where I was. The earlier question now answered, I rolled over and, surprisingly enough, went back to sleep lulled by the steady hum of those engines.

The inviting aroma of coffee and bacon filled the air as I awoke at 7 AM. A short time later, while I was emerging up the ladder from a refreshing, but almost scalding shower below the fore deck, Andrea's excited voice came over the loudspeaker. The captain had spotted a pod of six or seven blue whales to the front of the boat. For twenty minutes, she gave a running commentary of their movements, while we all looked on in fascinated awe. "They are feeding," Andrea explained. "See how they come up out of the water sideways. Their mouths are open to catch the food." She noted how lucky we were to see the whales, especially so close. She had been out a number of times with no sightings at all.

Exuberant from this unexpected treat, we moved to the galley for a filling breakfast of eggs, bacon, potatoes, pancakes, toast, bagels, melon, juice and coffee, made to order by the friendly galley staff. Serene San Miguel Island appeared ever closer through the haze, while we ate. As the boat approached the northeastern side, tiny Prince Island, home to countless gulls, pelicans and other sea birds, appeared close by the harbor entrance.

By 9:30 AM, we were heading by motorized skiff, six persons at a time, to make a beach landing on the broad sandy expanse at Cuyler Harbor. It briefly made me wonder what D-day was like, but our crossing was uneventful, and there was not a soul in sight as far as one could see. Everyone hopped from the skiff near the shore and waded through the surf in bare feet, stopping on the beach to don hiking shoes before proceeding up the bluff.

From the Cabrillo Monument, Andrea led us inland on a fairly level, weaving path toward the center of the island. As we walked, she pointed out endemic fauna, including pink island buckwheat and a dormant mini-forest of coreopsis which blankets parts of the island with bright yellow in the spring. Before long, we passed near the Park ranger station and then proceeded over the 831 foot summit of San Miguel Hill, the high point on the island. After 2-1/2 miles, the stark white landscape of our destination, the caliche forest, came into view. Exposed by the work of the strong wind, the small expanse contains the slender trunks of prehistoric trees up to a few feet high that had been covered by sand long ago and then petrified to a chalky white substance, before being exposed once again.

Retracing our steps, we returned to the boat for a lunch of curried chicken salad with turkey and corned beef pita sandwiches. Then Captain Don guided the vessel around the far side of the island for a close up view of the sea lion colony at Bennett Point. The boat floated still in the water about a half mile off shore while we watched the hundreds of seals, sea lions and huge elephant seals on the secluded beach. In the winter months, thousands of the mammals arrive here for the mating season. Even now, the separate harems were evident that the males fiercely guard from rivals.

A little later, excited shouts drew us to the starboard side. Tyler was struggling with his fishing pole deeply bowed at the middle, while he strained to keep control. "I've got a big one," he exclaimed, alternately jerking the pole up and then giving the line some slack. He had been fighting the fish for quite some time and sensed he was close to landing it.

Captain Don appeared with a long hooked pole. Tyler gave one more strong pull on the rod and the large fish sprung out of the water next to the boat. Wasting no time, Don hooked it and pulled the twenty pound halibut into the boat. Still flapping wildly, the magnificent fish was a large oval in shape, three feet long and pure white on one side. The other side was a mixed sandy color, much like the ocean floor where it lived, blending in with the surroundings.

Don quickly finished the fish off with a club, then let Tyler hold it up for pictures. Pulling out a knife, Don had the specimen cleaned, dressed and on the grill barbecuing in minutes. Dinner that evening was especially memorable with a delectable tri-tip steak accompanied by the freshest halibut I had ever tasted. With mashed potatoes, mushrooms, salad and three kinds of pie ala mode to finish off, everyone left dinner stuffed and contented.

Tyler with halibut caught off the side of ship

Sitting in the cool sea air out on the aft deck recounting the day's adventures, we soon started nodding off. The captain had put the boat on a course toward Santa Rosa Island, a couple hours away. By the time it arrived, we were in our bunks fast asleep.

Saturday morning the cooks presented us with another hearty breakfast of French toast, Canadian bacon, eggs, potatoes, melon, juice and coffee. Santa Rosa Island's barren visage rose in front of us. Getting ashore would be easier this day. A wooden pier used by ranchers was large enough for Truth to pull up alongside at Bechers Bay.

Today's venture included a five mile hike following the coastline. Again, Andrea led the way, first past a ranch that is still active, then up a coastal road. Before long she pointed to the hills in the distance. "Look, do you see them?" The hikers all peered in the direction she indicated, clueless to what she meant. With the help of binoculars and some careful coaching, we finally picked out five majestic elk that appeared as specks to the naked eye. When these islands were acquired for a national park, the prior owners were given a concession for a few more years to use the land for game hunting. The elks had been brought here. Hunters paid large sums of money for the chance to come and hunt them. We were glad this "sport" would be coming to an end.

Further along we passed a Torrey Pine forest, one of only two existing stands of the rare species, the other located near San Diego. "No coincidence," Andrea pointed out. In earlier geologic times, the island was a part of the mainland near the other stand of Torrey Pines.

Other evidence of earlier times was also present on this hike. What appeared to be nondescript mounds filled with shells and other debris, were actually middens (trash heaps) for the Chumash Indians who occupied the islands from as far back as 13,000 years ago until the early 1800s. The Chumash were once prevalent up and down the California coast. But the encroachment of modern civilization eliminated many of their vestiges. Consequently, the numerous untouched Channel Islands sites have taken on greater importance for archeologists.

Reaching our destination on a white sandy beach near Skunk Point, we had a few minutes to explore remnant beams of an old shipwreck, one of a number of historic victims that have succumbed to these islands over the years.

Soon our ship's skiff was skimming over the waves to pick us up on the shore We didn't pay much attention to the size of approaching waves as six of us climbed onto the inflated rubber sides of the raft-like skiff. Almost without warning, a huge wave crashed over the skiff, knocking us overboard into the surf. Floundering around dazed by the unexpected plunge in the cold sea, we quickly helped each other scramble back aboard, shivering and fretting over soaked cameras and other gear.

Back on board the Truth, the hot clam chowder tasted especially good after we changed into dry clothes and warmed up again. Hot beef and cheese sandwiches with salad and watermelon rounded out the nourishing lunch.

As the ship pulled out heading in a homeward direction, my colleague, Steve, and I sat contented, feeling we had gotten more than our money's worth on this adventure. But there was one more surprise to come. Captain Don said we would be passing by Santa Cruz Island on our way back, and there would be just enough time for a stop at Painted Cave.

Entrance to Painted Cave on Santa Cruz Island

Santa Cruz is the largest of the Channel Islands at 24 miles long and up to 6 miles wide. Don informed us that Painted Cave is one of the largest sea caves in the world. To prove his point, Don maneuvered the Truth right into the 160 foot high entrance. As if that was not convincing enough, he then proceeded to take us by skiff almost a quarter mile deep into the cave. We were now in total darkness. When Don turned on a flashlight, several seals on a sandy ledge at the end of the cave greeted us. We could also see several of our shipmates who were exploring the cave by kayak. Looking around, the colorful rock formation and lichens attested to the cave's name.

Later, we watched the cave entrance and Santa Cruz Island grow smaller as Truth churned at full throttle toward Santa Barbara. Steve and I agreed that Painted Cave had been the unexpected highlight of a weekend that offered no shortage of delightful discoveries. Nevertheless, we were both glad to be returning to solid ground. Two days at sea were enough for us landlubbers.

Sheila reflecting as we bid farewell to the Channel Islands

Chapter 16

Behemoths of the California Coast

Giants in the forest and by the sea

One does not expect to encounter a 5,000-pound sunbather on a California beach. But one of the largest sea creatures on earth, the male elephant seal, spends the summer basking on a secluded California shore, within miles of one of the largest plant species on earth: the coast redwood. Between colonies of these two behemoths of nature lies another unlikely treasure: a scenic ocean view accommodation for only $20 a night per person.

To experience these wonders near Pescadero, California, just south of the Bay area, was the quest of our group one August. Each year, colleagues and friends of our accounting firm in Orange County, California, take an extended weekend to seek out a unique adventure within driving distance of our home. Though we have often backpacked, camped in tents or remote cabins, this time we had discovered the benefits of the hostelling movement at Pigeon Point Lighthouse Hostel.

Open to travelers of all ages, the hostel was perfect for our group, since our fifteen partakers completely filled one whole building. In other buildings, individual guests were welcome to share space with fellow travelers who arrived for a night's stay in the hospitable quarters.

Pigeon Point Lighthouse is situated dramatically on a cliff overlooking craggy rocks jutting out into the sea about 50 miles south of San Francisco. Erected in 1872 as a mariner's navigational aid, the 115 foot tall national historic landmark got its name from a merchant ship, Carrier Pigeon, that was wrecked against the rocks here almost twenty years earlier. Several more ships met a similar fate before the U. S. Congress finally approved funding and construction at the site.

The lighthouse, now fully automated, still functions today, though the grounds and buildings are used by the American Youth Hostels, in cooperation with the California Department of Parks and Recreation, which leases the facility from the U. S. Coast Guard. In 1980, the four cottages the Coastguardsmen lived in were converted to hostel accommodations.

Arriving late Thursday afternoon after a stop in Santa Cruz for groceries, my friends, Carl Greenwood and Curtis Williams, and I were welcomed by the volunteer on duty. "Some of your party are here already," she pointed out as she led us up the closed driveway to the third cottage, named the Dolphin, just steps from the towering white lighthouse. "When the whole group is together, I'll come back for an orientation."

Once inside, we found our colleague, Patty Woolworth, and her daughter, Madison, who, on behalf of the six women in our group, had already laid claim to the bunkroom with its own private bath. The nine men would have the remaining two rooms that share the other bathroom, situated across the hall. The minimal lavatory amenities presented a challenge, but by the end of the weekend, everyone learned how to get in and out quickly and efficiently.

We distributed the groceries among the two refrigerators, several cabinets and counters in the spacious kitchen. Before long, the rest of our group arrived, including our friend Tom, who drove in from his home near Lodi. While everyone lounged on the three comfortable sofas in the living room, the staff filled us in on the hostel's operating procedures. As is the tradition with hostels, each person is asked to perform a brief clean up task in the morning before departure. Since we had the whole cottage to ourselves for three nights, she simply asked that the group restore the lodgings to their present condition before we left on Sunday.

We all were on our own that evening to relax before the two days of planned hikes. The nearest town in this remote area is Pescadero, a sleepy community with less than a thousand in population, five miles north and two miles inland. Home to only two restaurants, most of the group dined on tacos and enchiladas in a tiny Mexican café, situated in the town's service station.

Carl, Curtis, Tom and I decided to check out Duarte's Tavern, which we had already reserved for the next two night's group dinners. We feasted on the house specialty, Cioppino, served in a hearty tomato broth, brimming with a variety of succulent shellfish. Later, our waitress, Stephanie, could see our disappointment upon hearing that the Tavern's dessert specialty, Ollallieberry Pie, was sold out. "I'll set one aside for your group tomorrow night," she promised.

Afterwards, back at the hostel, the cool night air and the steady, soothing sound of the waves below, helped lull us to sleep. That is, until Tom started snoring. Not until the next morning did we find out that even the girls heard him through the bedroom walls. Before long, Carl was out of bed gently nudging Tom until he was maneuvered into a non-snoring position.

I awoke at 6:00 am to the aroma of fresh coffee wafting through the cottage. Early bird Curtis had started a pot before making an early claim to the bathroom. For breakfast, we set out boxes of cereal, fruits, juices, bread for toast, bagels and milk. Cold meats and other sandwich fixings were also available for folks to make box lunches.

Following a short briefing, the group car-pooled 10 miles south to the entrance of Big Basin Redwood State Park, across the road from Waddell Beach. The plan was to hike in six miles to Berry Creek Falls and then return to the trailhead. The sky was clear and bright as we started out at 9:00 am. The trail first crossed a marshy cultivated valley where we spotted several deer. Then the terrain changed as we moved upward along the side of a densely wooded ridge that followed Waddell Creek all the way to Berry Creek Falls.

The beams of sunlight shining through the trees created striking contrasts of bright greens and browns, interspersed with deep shadows throughout the forest, as we made our way. Before long, redwoods started to appear, sending their massive crimson shafts high above the trail below. At Berry Creek Falls, one mighty redwood stood regally reaching upward from the top of the waterfall, gleaming in the reflected sunshine.

Having gotten to this point by 11:00 am, we realized that if we headed back now, our hike would be over by 1:00 pm. That is when we made a decision that was bound to be remembered for years to come as the infamous "Greenwood Loop." Carl noticed on the map that we could extend our hike a reasonable four miles by branching off on two other trails that looped around back to our current location. Along the way we would see two additional waterfalls and many more redwoods. That was all the incentive we needed.

Up the trail we went. We soon found out there was a lot more up than we anticipated, as the trail got progressively steeper the further we went. Now approaching high noon, another factor became painfully obvious. The sun that had brightened our way so colorfully, was now beating down on us with over 100 degree temperatures. Hiking so near to the usually mild coast, we had not considered the potential impact of the heat spell that had settled in the area. Several in the group ran out of water.

Leading the way, Carl, Curtis and I finally staggered up to Golden Cascade, a picturesque flow of water over a broad yellow sandstone rock face. Wading in, we splashed the cool refreshing water over ourselves and then found a shady spot for lunch. Curtis looked worried. "My two water bottles are empty. I don't know how I can get all the way back this way." Carl and I had little water left, either, though we did not need much to function.

Though we had no purification tablets with us, the only alternative appeared to be filling up from the stream. Risking picking up a bug from the untreated water seemed to be a better choice than dehydration in this heat. Luckily just then, Steve arrived. A veteran hiker, he had extra water bottles with him. "Steve, I am indebted to you for life," Curtis exclaimed gratefully as Steve handed him a full bottle.

With that crisis handled, we started back down the trail, passing Silver Falls on the way. With the prospect of ice cold drinks awaiting us in coolers at the cars, we moved ahead with renewed enthusiasm. Though some of our colleagues needed several more hours to complete the trip, all returned tired but safe and relieved to be done for the day.

Refreshed with showers, naps and just sitting by the ocean behind the lighthouse's fog signal building, the group was ready to share stories of the day's adventures at dinner that night. Duarte's Tavern is a combination small town country bar and regional dining hotspot. Fortunately, we had reserved weeks ago, since the place was packed with hungry diners. The patrons at the equally crowded bar ranged from wizened old cowboys who had likely spent many nights here over the past decades, to "city slickers" like ourselves, trying to escape the pressures of modern life for a night or two.

Dinner at Duarte's Tavern in Pescadero

Stephanie, our delightful waitress from last night stopped by to confirm that our ollalieberry pie was indeed set aside, but our waitress for tonight would be Lieben. Situated in another room of the spacious tavern, two tables were set for us, allowing the young people in our group to have their own. Lieben, a German lady whose name means "love," proved as friendly and fun as Stephanie, trading barbs with us all evening.

Having watched numerous customers revel in the pepper steak last night, several of the group had to try it. They were not disappointed. In fact, all of our appetites, hearty from the hike, were readily satisfied, with the fresh local seafood also a big hit. Not surprising, the group slept well that night, oblivious to any snoring.

Elephant seals on the beach at Ano Nuevo State Reserve

Prior years' experiences had taught us to choose a less demanding hike for the second day. Ano Nuevo State Reserve, eight miles south of Pigeon Point, offered a three-mile trail with a totally different environment. The route crosses the sand dunes along the shore to the elephant seal viewing area. First we stopped in the visitor center, receiving warm greetings from the docents who were just opening up at 8:30 am. A short film depicting the life of the elephant seals would surely have had an R rating for gory violence at a movie theatre. Two male elephant seals fought for domination of the harem of females, banging their trunk-like heads against each other while making bloody gashes with their teeth. Finally one seal conceded and slinked away with a bloodied and battered head.

At the viewing point, a safe distance from the seals' protected beach, we could see several young males lying still in the sun. For a month or two each summer, the seals repeat this molting ritual. All of a sudden, what we thought was a huge boulder started to move. The massive slab turned out to be one of the patriarchs, a 5,000 pounder.

The females were long gone. They would all return in December to give birth to their young and then start the mating game. After molting, the males will leave also, journeying to Alaskan waters to feed. Another docent at the viewing point shared details of the seals' lives, and handed us a piece of the molting hide, which had a rough hairy texture.

On this day, we were all glad to have our hike finished by noon. The group split up, some wanting to relax on the beach, while the women headed for a mall in Santa Cruz. Carl, Curtis, Tom and I drove north toward Half Moon Bay. There in nearby Moss Beach, we spent a leisurely lunch at the Distillery, munching on mussels, artichokes, buffalo wings, cheese bread and beer, next to the shore. The group reconvened at Duarte's Tavern in the evening to share more good food along with the afternoon's adventures.

Sunday morning, all were up early, racing around to clean the cottage, so that we could get on the road for the eight-hour drive home. Diana was impressed with our conscientious efforts and gave us the "all clear," inviting us to return again soon. Bidding farewell, the group departed as we had arrived, in several small parties, all filled with the new wonders we had enjoyed together.

Ready to hike – photo by Paula Novak

Karen crossing Hare Creek in Limekiln State Park

Chapter 17

The Death March that Never Was

38ᵗʰ Annual HMWC Death March Diversions and Plan B

"It's an ugly time to be in Big Sur." So said the voice that answered the phone at Nepenthe, the renowned restaurant dramatically set on the Big Sur coast. I was trying to get a second opinion of the air quality and fire danger near where my Orange County group of 49 was scheduled for a hiking trip in the next couple days.

Representatives from the accommodation we had arranged months ago were alternately stating they were open and welcoming guests, while also noting the fire was just four miles away, most of their guests were now firefighters, and the nearby hiking trails were closed for safety and air quality reasons.

It was beginning to appear that a year of planning and the eager enthusiasm of our ready participants were to be no match for the raging wildfire. With gut wrenching anguish, my partner, Steve, and I finally made the decision to pull the plug, the day before the planned start of the 38ᵗʰ Annual HMWC Death March, an event that had never been canceled in its long history.

With hindsight the decision, though deeply disappointing, proved to be the right one. At the time of the cancellation, the fire covered 35,000 square acres, was only 5% contained, and had closed all the parks where hikes had been planned. The reserved lodge would subsequently close completely as the fire encroached, ultimately reaching more than 91,000 square acres. Fortunately the lodge survived, though the conflagration, known as the Soberanes Fire (named for the creek where it started), would not be completely contained until later in September.

Acknowledging that their inconvenience paled in comparison to those who had already lost their homes and the fireman who had lost his life bravely tackling the inferno, group members contemplated a Plan B. Finding replacement accommodations for so large a gathering in the middle of prime California vacation season was not a realistic option. The logical solution was to "divide and conquer." A benefit of the firm's base in Orange County was the ability to turn in just about any direction and find nearby adventures in the mountains, on the desert, or by the sea.

Gerry had been looking forward to driving the scenic California coast. Word had it that Limekin State Park at the southern end of Big Sur was not affected by the fire. Also, Cambria, popular for pristine Moonstone Beach and nearby Hearst Castle, was only an hour's drive south of Limekin. A quick online search by Gerry's friend, Carl, located what may have been the last handful of available rooms on that part of the coast. So Carl quickly grabbed them, and he, friend Curtis, and Gerry set their sights on Plan B.

Steve, meanwhile, had his extended family group of 20 to redirect, some of whom had come all the way from the East coast and even England. "If it were just me, I would join you going up the coast. But I'd never find enough rooms for my group, so Big Bear is more realistic." Steve had a large cabin in the San Bernardino Mountains above Orange County. That plus a couple rooms at a nearby hotel would work for the family ranging in age from tots to octogenarians.

Jodi and Joe as well as Marc and Peter were already on the road when the cancellation came down. They would need to be contacted, along with two other family groups, two couples and several singles. An urgent email conveyed the sad news to all.

Disappointed, but undaunted, Carl, Curtis and Gerry set out from Orange County early Saturday morning. With the light weekend traffic, they soon arrived in Los Angeles and their first destination: the iconic Union Station, resplendent in the art deco style popular from the era of its construction earlier in the prior century

Right on schedule, the Southwest Chief pulled in on Track 12, bringing Gerry's sister, Karen, from her Arizona home. Gerry had reached her by phone, just as she readied to leave home the previous day for the overnight journey.

After stowing Karen's luggage in Curtis' roomy SUV, the four of us proceeded north on US 101 toward San Luis Obispo. Within minutes, a text message buzzed on Gerry's phone. Jodi and Joe were heading south from Cambria. While touring Hearst Castle, they tasted the smokiness in the air. Concerned that hiking in Limekin, further north, could be unhealthful, their sights were now set on Santa Barbara and a boat trip out to Santa Cruz Island, part of Channel Islands National Park (the sight of Death March 23 in 2001).

Checking the map, I determined that we would be reaching San Luis Obispo from the south about the same time that Joe and Jodi would get there from the north. A couple quick texts and we were on our way to meet up for lunch at Luna Red, a tapas restaurant in downtown San Luis Obispo. Joe and Jodi had a table ready when we arrived for the fortuitous reunion. Feasting on dishes like Cuban press, featuring chorizo, pulled pork and jalapeño, and a meze of peruano bean hummus, quinoa tabbouleh, cucumber tzatziki, and flatbread, we washed it all down with ice cold local favorites, Firestone Double Barrel Ale and Prangster Belgian Gold Ale.

Wishing Jodi and Joe well as they continued toward Santa Barbara, the rest of us were determined to stay the course with our own Plan B, including Limekin. After advancing a few miles further north, now on legendary California Highway 1, my phone rang. It was Marc. He and Peter had checked into the beachfront Moonstone Landing lodging the night before. With the change in plans, they had extended their stay, and invited us to join them later for happy hour on their ocean view balcony, followed by dinner at the highly regarded Robin's, not far from there.

Not long after, another text message buzzed on my phone. This time it was Marley. She and her extended family of eight had found rooms in Morro Bay. They planned to meet us in the morning at Limekin for the hike.

As we wound along the picturesque coast toward Cambria, on California's most famous National Scenic Byway, Steve and his entourage had already completed their two hour drive to the Big Bear cabin, roughly 7,000 feet up the mountain that tops off at almost 9,000 feet in elevation. In good Death March tradition, they wasted no time setting off on the first of several hikes. Known by the Big Bear veterans as the AM/PM hike, the trail found its way over about three miles roundtrip to the local AM/PM Minimart.

By mid-afternoon, Gerry's group was nearing Cambria when a text came in from Paula. A newcomer to the annual tradition, Paula had flown into San Francisco yesterday from her Chicago home. Upon hearing the change of plans upon landing, she quickly regrouped and decided to negotiate the coast by car, to meet up with us. After driving through the smoke and acrid air along the Big Sur coast near the raging wildfire, she no longer needed to question the rationale for the modified arrangements. Instead she embraced "Plan B" and was rewarded with new, unexpected pleasures, like a tour through Hearst Castle, high upon a prominent hilltop in San Simeon. Since her tour lasted later than planned, Paula would meet us at the hotel around 4 pm.

Though Paula was unable to get a room for that Saturday night, Carl had brought along a comfortable airbed that would work well in a suite that Karen agreed to share.

Upon checking in at El Calibri Hotel in Cambria, we were all grateful to have found a place to stay on short notice, but also a little disheartened to not be in view of the ocean. Our disappointment soon lifted when we discovered a wooden, four-foot wide boardwalk proceeding from the back of the hotel a couple hundred yards to Moonstone Beach. From there it branched in both directions for miles along the waterfront. We eagerly followed along to the north for a mile or so, pursued aggressively by hungry squirrels who patrolled for handouts above and below the wood planks.

The steady waves, on their unwavering journey, gleamed with frothy white foam in the bright afternoon sun, then gently washed ashore before us. So engrossed were we that, before we knew it, we had covered four miles out and back along the boardwalk.

Soon after, with Paula now in tow, we were off to Moonstone Landing, and "happy hour" with Marc and Peter. Sharing glasses of wine on their balcony as the sun descended on the horizon, we marveled at the matchless beauty of nature and the shared enjoyment of our long-lasting camaraderie.

Marc and Peter shared tips from their hikes that day to the Limekin and San Simeon sites that we would experience the next day. After a dinner on the patio at Robin's that offered   tasty assortments, such as Roghan Josh, a north Indian lamb curry, and Jidori chicken, we bid farewell to Marc and Peter, since they would head south back to Orange County on the morrow, while we headed north.

Early Sunday morning, we drove the windy, yet enchanting coast road, joined intermittently by the familiar marine layer of clouds that hugged these coastal shores, often in the morning and late afternoon. Within an hour, the entry to Limekin State Park appeared on the left, and we were ready for a hike. Marley had texted that they were running late and would meet us along the trail.

The main trail branched off in three directions, each for about a mile. First came Hare Creek Trail, following the fast flow of the creek through a redwood forest where the sun's rays brightly accented the subtle shades of color. Several times on the round trip, creek crossings were required, alternately on slippery, half-submerged rocks or tenuous tree limbs serving as spans. All of us made the round trip with nary more than a wet foot or two.

Halfway back, we met up with Marley and family, moving briskly along. We stopped long enough for a group selfie, after which our two groups continued, albeit in opposite directions, intending to meet up on the next branch.

Meanwhile, back in the San Bernardino Mountains, Steve's group began the day getting their bearings and the lay of the land at the informative Big Bear Discovery Center, on the north shore of Big Bear Lake. Jointly run by the US Forest Service and the Southern California Mountains Foundation, the Center features natural history and environmental exhibits, as well as providing tips for hiking, camping and recreational activities. From there, Steve's group embarked on a three mile hike to the Cougar Crest Trail Head and along the lake.

Gerry's group at Limekin by that time had started up the waterfall trail, which made up the center fork of the State Park's three-branched trail. Stream crossing encounters continued, some more challenging then those on the Hare Creek Trail. Even so, the effort paid off, when the dual, ribbon-like falls entered our view, stunningly overpowering the senses, as the two strands cascaded down the hundred foot rock face.

After crossing paths with Marley's group one more time, we tackled the final branch to see the park's namesake. In 1887, lime was extracted from a limestone formation here, by constructing four large steel and stone kilns and using redwood timber as fuel. Within three years, the limestone was exhausted and the kilns were abandoned. The fifteen foot high, cylindrical structures are an odd sight at the end of the half mile trail, now sharing the forest with the lofty redwoods.

Savoring our exploration of the picturesque and historical diversity of Limekiln back at the trailhead, we were ready to absorb some more coastal beauty over lunch at the Lucia Lodge, just two miles further up the road. Sunny skies, with rolling clouds here and there, provided a delightful setting on the bluff-side porch of the Lodge, where my order of wild sockeye salmon tacos was the big hit, accompanied by an ice cold local beer.

In one of the ironies of nature, the afternoon brought a phenomenon at Big Bear that would have been heartily welcomed by the current residents of Big Sur. Rain, thunder and hail travelled swiftly and powerfully though the mountain range, producing a refreshingly cooler and moister atmosphere. Though briefly held up, the group there reveled in the experience, which had been a rarity in their Orange County domain.

After checking out the dozens of elephant seals sprawled out on the beach at Piedras Blancas, Gerry's group opted for one more hike, this time along the coast at W. R. Hearst State Park in San Simeon. The stately Hearst Castle loomed from a nearby hilltop in the background. Panoramic views of the shoreline and beach were bathed in the bright afternoon sunshine.

A dinner of fresh sea bass at Moonstone Beach Bar & Grill topped off the day's adventures.

While Gerry's group drove the coast home on Monday, Steve's group hiked a couple miles to the bridge on the lake, and then added a coastal hike to their itinerary Tuesday on the way home, exploring the Upper Newport Bay Nature Preserve. Habitat to several protected bird species and plant communities, the Nature Preserve also incorporated the Ecological Preserve, combining to form one of the largest coastal wetlands in Southern California.

Though the multiple adventures of those past few days were not what had been planned, the spirit of the Death March tradition prevailed during the "38th Annual HMWC Death March That Never Was." Or as Death March first-timer Paula Novak remarked: "Sometimes Plan B isn't such a bad thing."

164

Crater Lake (above), Lassen's Boiling Springs Lake (below)

Part VII

Volcanos

Ediza Lake in Mammoth area on Death March 8

Chapter 18

Volcanos

It should come as no surprise that the focus over four decades for a group of weekend warriors from California would be the iconic natural wonders of the region: Yosemite, Sequoia, Grand Canyon, coastlines, and the scenic rivers that bisect and define them. But an area as vast as California and the American West overflows with an endless array of fascinating and challenging treasures of nature. This chapter highlights another aspect of those gems.

Death March 8 took us to a place better known to Californians for skiing: Mammoth Lakes. Situated directly east of Yosemite National Park, in the Ansel Adams Wilderness, this section of the Sierra Nevada mountain range is rich with alpine lakes and meadows. After camping in Reds Meadows, we started our seven mile hike at Agnew Meadows along the Pacific Crest Trail, climbing from eight thousand to over nine thousand feet elevation. At Shadow Lake, we picked up the John Muir Trail for awhile, finishing off at gorgeous Ediza Lake, set amongst the jagged spires of the Minarets and thirteen thousand foot peaks. There was still plenty of snow there, even in mid-July.

A new challenge on this hike was fording the robust and ice cold San Joaquin River, fed by melting snow and ice as it flowed relentlessly downward. Steve fearlessly waded through the torrent, then strung a rope across to steady the way for the rest of us. Only later while we stood shivering, did we learn that Jeff, who raced far ahead, had found an alternate route, avoiding the crossing altogether.

Another unique feature of this Death March, revealed in the following days, was evidence of the volcanic nature of the region. The highlight was at Devil's Postpile National Monument. Here we marveled at the orderly hexagonal columns of basalt towering over our path. Some four hundred of them stacked together, and reaching sixty feet high, had been formed in the past hundred thousand years, when flowing lava cooled under just the right circumstances, creating the unusual configuration.

Crossing San Joaquin River with rope on Death March 8

Breaking camp on the final morning, we were reminded of one more volatile characteristic of the region. A minor earthquake broke the tranquility, and even toppled a couple of the columns. Such events are common in this area of mountain faults and volcanos, such as nearby Mammoth Mountain, a lava dome last erupting about sixty thousand years ago.

The volcanic nature of northern California would become even more vivid for us thirteen years later when Death March 21 brought us to Lassen Volcanic National Park. Much less familiar and more out of the way than Yosemite and Sequoia, Lassen projects a charm all of its own in the remote northeastern corner of California. The crown jewel is 10,457 foot Lassen Peak, but there are also geysers and other remarkable volcanic features, even if not as dramatic or extensive as those in Yellowstone National Park.

Group back rubs after tough hike on Death March 8

Lassen Peak, an active volcano last erupting in 1915, is part of the Ring of Fire, a far-reaching volcanic and earthquake zone. The Ring stretches from South America, up through North America, including nearby Mammoth Mountain and Mount Shasta, through Oregon, Washington, up over Alaska to Japan, Indonesia, and all the way to Antarctica.

The only accommodation in the National Park is a small, rustic inn, Drakesbad Guest Ranch, popular with families from the Bay area, some of whom return year after year. Accordingly, reservations had to be sought out two years ahead, and even then with a little luck.

Once we got there following a long bumpy ride, a couple from Germany and Switzerland generously catered to our every need, even providing diversions for the young ones. Over the course of three days, there were hikes to places with names like Devil's Kitchen, Boiling Springs Lake, Terminal Geyser, and a drive by Bumpass Hell. Bubbling mud pots, steam vents, and hot springs dotted the park area.

On the Mt Lassen Trail on Death March 21

The heartier members of the group undertook the ascent of Lassen Peak. Though the day beamed bright and beautiful, the five mile hike up the cinder and ash trail proved strenuous, with the altitude and steep incline taking their toll. Sizable snow patches accented the otherwise gray slopes, even in the height of summer. As expected, the sweeping panoramic vistas from the peak yielded a just reward for the effort. The sumptuous home cooking at the Ranch didn't hurt, either.

The richness of the Lassen Death March was memorialized in another milestone for the storied tradition by a feature article in the New York Times. See Chapter 19 for a link to the story in the archives of the New York Times Travel Section.

Our most dramatic volcanic adventure took place on Death March 39, which was spent at Crater Lake National Park in Oregon. Hiking on the rim and boating within the collapsed remains of the once mighty Mount Mazama was another mind-boggling experience. At six miles across and nearly 2,000 feet deep, the lake today projects a quiet power of what once was an immense force that forever transformed the landscape for miles around. Chapter 20 tells the story.

Finally, a part of Death March 40 is planned for Yellowstone National Park, an area created by the country's largest supervolcano. Even the Grand Tetons mountain range, where the 40th will commence in July 2018, consists partly of volcanic material that formed diabase dikes hundreds of millions of years ago.

Anticipating the 40th, Loretta and I reconnoitered the Grand Tetons and Yellowstone at the end of May 2017. We were anxious to assess whether the Moran Suite at Jackson Lake Lodge would be suitable as a gathering spot for our group the following year. So we checked into the Suite for two nights. Actually, 2017 was a milestone birthday year for Loretta, so we had decided to splurge at her favorite national park with a stay at the upscale Jackson Lake Lodge, followed by a few days in Yellowstone, and then finishing up with the even fancier (in a rustic sort of way), Jenny Lake Lodge, named for the lake that would be featured in a Death March hike in 2018.

One lesson learned is that minor adversities should be expected when national park facilities first open after a snowy winter in the mountains, even when a visitor is staying at first-rate accommodations. Even so, the lack of hot water in the Moran Suite that first night quickly paled in comparison to the larger than life view of the majestic snow covered Grand Teton range, spanning across all four broad windows of the multi-room suite. I could hardly tear my eyes away from the magical sight the whole time we were there.

At Jenny Lake Lodge, the water was hot and the cabin and bed were cozy and comfortable. So comfortable that I hardly stirred when a mouse scurried across one rafter than another before disappearing out of sight. Of course I didn't mention it to Loretta though, who was still in the bath room preparing for bed. The following night I was awakened by Loretta's scream when the mouse returned for a repeat performance. The manager sheepishly apologized the next morning, promising a prompt visit by the resident exterminator. I urged him to also ward off the pesky wasp that had been dive bombing us when we emerged from our cushy quarters.

Even that unexpected "wildlife" couldn't deter us from the even more jaw dropping views of the Tetons, which were close up at Jenny Lake, whose shoreline literally nestled at the mountains' base. More of a concern were the trail closures for restoration, both at Jenny Lake and at the Grand Canyon of the Yellowstone, where next year's hikes were planned. Not to worry. The rangers assured us that by the next summer they would be open.

In the meantime, we were not at a loss for a myriad of adventures, such as wolf, moose and bear watching from strategic meadows and valleys, marveling at Old Faithful and multiple geyser basins, and looking out our room window by Yellowstone Lake in the morning, where a mellow buffalo grazed just below. We could hardly wait to share this unique land with our friends and colleagues in the year to come.

Grand Tetons and buffalo-grazing by Yellowstone Lake

Mt Lassen

Chapter 19

Go Climb a Volcano

A tranquil hideaway amidst Northern California's Lassen Volcanic National Park

Note: The story of the 21st Annual HMWC Death March was published in the New York Times on September 3, 2000, under the title: A Steam-Powered Landscape. The story may be found at http://www.nytimes.com/2000/09/03/travel/a-steam-powered-landscape.html?pagewanted=1

Also, see the Trail Notes for further details.

Crater Lake and Phantom Ship

Chapter 20

Crater Lake – A Lake like No Other

A lake with a crater within a caldera

"It's déjà vu all over again," Yogi Berra once said.

Two weeks before thirty-five participants were scheduled to convene at Crater Lake National Park in Oregon for the 39th Annual HMWC Death March, lightning struck the heavy pine forest near the edge of the Park. My first thought was "Here we go again," just as Yogi Berra had put it. Only last year, a massive wildfire required cancellation of plans for Death March 38 at Big Sur, California. That event, which was a year in the making, necessitated a last minute reconfiguration to Plan B, including a reduced version, partly centered around the southern Big Sur coast line below the fire, and partly up in the Big Bear Mountain region, east of Los Angeles.

As this year's fire proceeded deep into the National Park over the following week, the West Rim Drive was forced to close, as well as several trails. Subsequently, a Stage 1 Evacuation Alert was announced. Fortunately, thanks to some rain, a drop in the record temperatures, the path of the fire moving into a less vegetated area, and heroic work by the firemen, the fire slowed to a halt, and the restrictions were lifted, merely days before our arrival.

After countless hours setting up group lodging, meals, boat rides, and convincing people to sign up, another cancellation would have been devastating. Though selling the wonders of Crater Lake should have been easy, the following exchange demonstrated the challenge, even without the threat of a fire.

"What's so great about Crater Lake?" a friend asked as I tried to recruit him for the upcoming Death March. "After all, it's just another lake." I scratched my head thinking "He does not know what he is missing."

Over the years, when I shared about the destination for the annual event, I would at times get similar replies, such as "I stopped once to look at the South Rim of the Grand Canyon," or "We've driven through Yosemite Valley," or even "Zion is pretty tame compared to the other nearby canyons."

I may have initially felt that way, also, when as a youth I first saw Zion National Park from my parents' car window. No more! Not after hiking the Zion Narrows knee deep in the middle of the Virgin River, or peering out from the Angels Landing Trail with thousand foot drops on both sides, during Death March 26. Tame is not the word I would use to describe life changing experiences like that, which are common on our annual Death March events.

But reaching a point where mind-blowing transformation becomes a possibility requires getting out of the car and onto the trail. But if that is the case, you might ask why it took nearly forty years for the HMWC Death March to venture to Crater Lake National Park. I would posit that the answer lies more in the distance from our Orange County, California base, rather than from a lack of enthusiasm. After all, the American West holds countless jaw-dropping scenic wonders, many closer to home, making the competition for the prized destination each year intense.

The diverse modes of transport to Crater Lake illustrated how distance has impacted our departure tradition when commencing a Death March. In the earlier years, participants would converge on a starting point in Orange County, California, and form a car caravan driving to the Death March location. As the number of participants and the distances grew, the favored options for travel expanded as well.

This year, Steve's extended family followed the traditional caravan approach, taking two full vans on the journey north. With a nostalgic nod to the past, they spent the first night, pre-Death March, at Morrison's Rogue River Lodge, near Grants Pass, Oregon, where the kayaking Death March 19 was based, nearly two decades earlier. The accommodations and fine cuisine were just as they remembered, especially the renowned, freshly baked orange dinner rolls.

Williams family at Crater Lake Lodge

Marley with her family of seven and first-timer, Tristan, HMWC computer specialist, also drove separately, stopping along the way.

Gerry, Carl and Curtis flew up from Los Angeles to Medford, Oregon, then drove the final 75 miles, as did Robert, another first-timer and HMWC Tax CPA, who was met in Medford by his father from Portland.

While Paula, a second-timer, winged her way in from Chicago, the furthest to travel were Scott and J.T., who hailed from North Carolina. They ventured first to Alaska on their own before dropping down to join us at Crater Lake.

Karen took the Southwest Chief train from Arizona, and then caught another, the Coast Starlight, in Los Angeles. She enjoyed the scenic and relaxing ride all the way to Kamath Falls, then caught a trolley for the final 40 miles to the Park.

Marc and friend Ray were joined by Marc's son, Jeff, and his family, whose home is in Portland, Oregon.

The others made their way to Oregon in variations of the above approaches, with the whole group meeting up for a welcome dinner at Annie Creek Restaurant in the National Park's Mazama Village. That is, all but Paula from Chicago. Thanks to both an Uber and a taxi not showing up, she missed her plane, and would not arrive until a day later.

Crater Lake did not disappoint anyone, even the most veteran members of the group. The National Park catered to all, who ranged from 4 to 75 years of age, and varied in stamina from couch potatoes to marathoners.

Wanting to promote togetherness, the first hike, characterized in the brochure as "easy," weaved along for a mile on a flat trail through an evergreen forest to the delightful Plaikni Falls. Flowing over a volcanic and glacially carved rock formation, the falls cascaded through a glade accented by colorful wild flowers. The idyllic setting proved an ideal backdrop for family photos, bathed in sunlight forming rays through the trees.

HMWC group at Plaikni Falls

The heartier group members followed the Plaikni Falls hike with a more challenging five mile roundtrip ascent of Mount Scott, at 8,934 feet elevation the highest point in the Park. From the peak, broad panoramas of the Lake and nearby area extended dramatically in all directions, accented with smoky haze from the fire in low lying valleys.

Others opted for more easily accessible walks, like the Castle Crest Wildflower Trail, a blissfully serene half-mile stroll along and across a gurgling stream that meandered through a meadow of multi-colored blooms.

On top of Mount Scott

These three hikes already highlighted sought after features common to many parts of the American West. But the qualities uniquely associated with Crater Lake were yet to unfold. These would only be revealed out on the Lake itself.

We were scheduled to take a shuttle boat the next day to Wizard Island, the cinder cone protruding from Crater Lake. Once there, we planned a hike to the ancient summit. Ironically, though the island is just off the western shore of the lake, the shuttle departs from the far northern shore, requiring an eleven mile drive and a steep one mile hike to the dock, followed by a half hour boat ride to finally reach the island.

The night before I was asking a clerk at the Lodge front desk about driving time to the dock, when another clerk overhead the conversation. "There was a report that the boat had mechanical problems, so the shuttle won't be running tomorrow," she said. "Check with the boat operator. They are going to try to take the shuttle passengers on the two hour lake tour boat instead. But they won't be stopping at Wizard Island."

The cancellation portended to be a major disappointment. Glad at least to find out ahead of time, I quickly relayed the bad news to the group. Though the change in plans was regarded as a temporary setback, we were to realize later that the lake cruise would turn out to be the highlight of the trip for fully grasping the timeless grandeur of this geologic wonder.

The lake boat tour is where the captivating diversity of the crater came to the fore. After a few awkward moments at the dock where the operators did their best to accommodate as many anxious guests as possible into the available seats, the motorized craft embarked across the smooth sapphire waters.

Here we were in the middle of what remained of the mighty Mount Mazama, once a 12,000 foot high mountain. Formed over hundreds of thousands of years of lava flows and eruptions, the mountain finally succumbed to an enormous blast more than 7,500 years ago. The traumatic event caused a massive collapse, resulting in the caldera that now surrounded us. About a mile's worth of the mountain's previous height was blown off, leaving a crater that eventually filled with rain and snow melt to a lake depth of nearly 2,000 feet. The purity of the water source along with the great depth produced the deep cerulean blue color that characterizes the lake today.

We were privileged to have Audrey, a National Park Ranger, share the many facets of the lake with us. Early on, she pointed out the layers of hardened lava on the wall of the caldera, as the boat pulled close to the shoreline. The seam-like deposits were evidence that we were observing the remains of a stratovolcano, built up over several hundred millennia.

Further along, a jagged vertical wall, reaching from the shore up a thousand feet to the rim, came into view. The Devil's Backbone, resembling vertebra-like protrusions, was a dike of once molten lava that filled in cracks and then stood out when the softer pumice eroded away. Pumice was created during an eruption when rapid cooling caused gaseous bubbles to form within the lava, giving the stone a lighter weight and texture.

Speaking of pumice, a spectacular formation of the porous orange colored stone that still stands below the East Rim is known as Pumice Castle. Revealed when the great collapse occurred, Pumice Castle was left over from an earlier eruption and hangs dramatically on the side of the cliff wall like a European fortress of old.

The most haunting formation appeared through the slight haze at the southern end of the lake. The Phantom Ship rose up like the legendary ghost ship from the Wagnerian opera, The Flying Dutchman. At 170 feet high, 500 feet long and 200 feet wide, the leftovers of an early volcanic fissure would dwarf modern tall ships only half its size. Nevertheless, the eerie Phantom Ship appears to sail along on an endless journey, fascinating all who behold its mesmerizing presence.

As our boat circled the mystery ship, the lake's larger island loomed in the distance like a wizard's hat, for which it was named. We got a little wistful as Wizard Island grew closer, lamenting the bad luck that prevented us from hiking up the cinder cone that protrudes 755 feet above the lake's surface. The cone at the top, known as Witch's Cauldron, is about as wide as the Phantom Ship is long. Audrey told us that certain individuals were known to take sleds there in wintertime to slide down the hundred foot slope inside the cone's interior.

As we drew near, the barrenness of the island became apparent. Other than sporting a trail to the summit, Wizard Island appeared rather bleak. After the abundant manifestations of volcanic phenomena observed while traversing the far reaches of the lake, our curiosity for this island was amply satisfied by taking in the various angles of its visage while our launch circled the shoreline. Audrey explained that Wizard Island was the result of numerous smaller eruptions that occurred over the course of hundreds of years following the major collapse of Mount Mazama.

Not all the mysteries of Crater Lake have been solved. While pausing by the dramatic Palisades on the north end, Audrey informed us that some water seeps out of the lake, but no one knows for sure where it goes. The broad Palisades cliff, originating from a volcanic flow, rests atop glacial till and other permeable rock extending below the surface of the water. That explained how the water got out. We learned from Audrey that water has a unique identifying marker much like a fingerprint. Tests of all the nearby lakes and rivers uncovered no evidence of Crater Lake water. Apparently, the water sinks into a deep aquifer. There is enough snow melt and rain to maintain the depth at a steady level. Trickling waterfalls could still be seen even now in August, replenishing the lake from remains of the winter snow pack.

Though the boat ride was relaxing as well as powerfully enlightening, reality struck when the tour finished. The only way back to the car was by the steep mile long trail to the rim. It didn't seem all that bad going down. But by the time we reached the top, we appreciated in a much more physical way the massive force that was released so long ago to generate the lofty caldera wall.

Dinner that evening in the dining room of Crater Lake Lodge afforded a fitting conclusion for our storied tradition. Built in 1915, the Lodge is a classic national park property perched strategically on the rim overlooking the lake. Resisting the trend of other national park lodges to expand by adding numerous surrounding cabin units, Crater Lake retains the rustic charm of a quaint hunting lodge with strong stone interior walls and rich wood paneling and ceilings. The 71 sought-after rooms have been updated with modern amenities.

Marley & Eric Jue and family at Crater Lake Lodge dinner

Not configured to handle a group our size, the dining room seated us in five groups staggered at fifteen minute intervals. That worked just fine with our ongoing happy hour celebration in the Great Hall, while watching one final orange-hued sunset over the lake.

"What's so great about Crater Lake?" Be prepared for a lengthy passionate response, if asking anyone from our group, as we reluctantly bid farewell to a magical sojourn at this unique wonder of nature.

Epilogue

Almost another decade has passed since I reflected back after thirty years of Death Marches in Chapter 2. A number of adventures, some new, some familiar, have been added to the list.

We returned to the Canadian Rockies of Banff National Park, this time to Skoki Lodge, and we completed a farewell trek to Phantom Ranch at the bottom of the Grand Canyon. Though most of our recent events were based out of lodges or cabins, we relived the experience of camping under the stars, on top of sandbars while rafting along the Colorado River.

While some of the hikes rivaled the challenges of those in earlier years, some proved more accessible, thereby attracting a new class of Death Marcher's to the storied ritual.

Over time, the Death March had lost the ominous nature that the name implied. Though the moniker originated partly from a bit of gallows humor, the tradition's current style and direction reflected an ongoing maturation.

I am now retired from the active accounting practice. But the Partners I wrote about nearly ten years ago, are still together, and have carried the firm to even greater heights than I could ever have imagined, leaving me most gratified as well as humbled in their presence. I am filled with pride and appreciation for what we and they have built together and separately. As I have told them before, the most prized accomplishment in my career with the firm has been to have the wisdom and good luck to have hired such talented and trusted colleagues, long before the potential of their special gifts and stalwart characters were fully realized.

A favorite lithograph by artist Douglas Andrews of Sedona, Arizona, hangs above my desk. The view is from the brink of the Grand Canyon, looking down at the Colorado River winding through the multi-layered labyrinth, thousands of feet below. Above the artists signature is the title, "Decisive Moment of Life." Those words resonate with me over and over, as I consider my life with the firm and on the trail - as I go from ledgers to ledges.

From Ledgers to Ledges

Appendix A

Summary of Death Marches

Number	Location	Dates	Participants
1	Mt. Whitney View, Shepherds Pass, Trail Crest, Whitney Portals	*7/19-22/1979*	*5*
2	Kearsarge Pass, Onion Valley, Southern Sierra Nevadas, California	6/25-27/1980	5
3	Southern Sierra Nevadas - Onion Valley, Kearsarge Pass, Glenn Pass, Baxter Pass, Oak Creek Trail head	7/29-8/1/1981	3
4	Grand Canyon - Trans-canyon from North Rim To South Rim	9/16-9/19/1982	4
5	King's River - King's Canyon & Sequoia National Parks	8/12-8/15/1983	8
6	Yosemite National Park - Tuolumne	9/6-9/9/1984	9

	Meadows to Yosemite Valley via Sunrise High Sierra Campground		
7	Sequoia National Park	8/23-8/26/1985	7
8	Mammoth Lakes, Devil's Postpile National Monument	7/17-7/20/1986	7
9	Havasupai Canyon, Grand Canyon National Park	9/5-/98/1987	19
10	Yosemite National Park - Glen Aulin & May Lake High Sierra Camps	8/18-8/21/1988	21
11	Santa Catalina Island, Two Harbors	8/25-8/27/1989	21
12	Yosemite National Park -Merced Lake High Sierra Camp	6/ 28-7/1/1990	14
13	Virginia Lakes, California - Horse Packing Trip	8/22-8/25/1991	15
14	Whitewater Rafting, Lower Kern River, Lake Isabella, California	7/26-7/28/1992	12
14 Take 2	Mount Whitney	8/5-8/8/1992	4
15	Tuolumne River Rafting and Yosemite National Park	7/17-7/21/1993	21
16	Yosemite National Park - Vogelsang High Sierra Camp	7/8-7/11/1994	8
17	Sequoia National Park	7/8-7/11/1995	12

	- Bear Paw Meadow High Sierra Camp		
18	Grand Canyon – Phantom Ranch	8/23-27/1996	13
19	Rogue River/North Umpqua River Kayaking Trip, Oregon	7/31-8/3/1997	23
20	Kalalau Trail, Kauai, Hawaii	8/15-8/19/1998	8
21	Lassen Volcanic National Park, Drakesbad guest Ranch, California	7/30-8/1/1999	16
22	Yosemite National Park -May Lake High Sierra Camp	8/26-/29/2000	12
23	Channel Islands National Park	9/6-9/8/20001	12
24	Pigeon Point Lighthouse Hostel, California	8/8-8/11/2002	15
25	Yosemite National Park-High Sierra Camps – 7 day guided hike	8/3-8/9/2003	6
26	Zion National Park	8/14-8/17/2004	14
27	Grand Canyon – Colorado River Rafting	8/6-8/11/2005	15
28	Mineral King, Sequoia National Park	8/10-8/13/2006	16
29	Hetch Hetchy Valley, Yosemite National Park	7/28-7/31/2007	28

30	Shadow Lake Lodge, Banff National Park, Canada, and Sperry Chalet, Glacier National Park, Montana	7/29-8/2, 2008	21
31	Sequoia High Sierra Camp, Sequoia National Park	7/30-8/2/2009	14
32	Grand Canyon – Colorado River Rafting	8/1-8/8/2010	16
33	Marin Headlands - Golden Gate National Recreation Area	8/12-8/15/2011	18
34	Wawona, Yosemite National Park	7/28-7/31/2012	29
35	Skoki Lodge, Banff National Park, Canada	8/3-8/6/2013	9
36	Sequoia High Sierra Camp, Sequoia National Park	7/31-8/3/2014	24
37	Grand Canyon – Phantom Ranch	7/10-7/14/2015	19
38	Big Sur and Big Bear, California	7/31-8/1/2016	40
39	Crater Lake National Park	8/31-8/16/2017	35
40	Grand Teton and Yellowstone National Parks	7/29-8/3/2018	Est. 40-50

Appendix B

Trail Notes

First Annual Death March

Location: Mt. Whitney - Symmes Creek Trailhead, Shepherds Pass, Trail Crest, Whitney Portals

Dates: July 19-22, 1979

Participants: George DiGaetano, Gerry Herter, Kirby, Ernie Ortiz, Russell Ortiz

Trail Notes:

Day 1 - Thursday, July 19, 1979

Left home at 4 AM. Arrive at Lone Pine at 9 AM. Have breakfast at the Sportsman's Cafe. (This starts a long tradition of meals at the Sportsman's Cafe before and after various marches). Drive north to

Symmes Creek Trailhead.

Hit trail at 11:30 AM (elevation 6,000 feet). Gerry has forty pounds of pack and canteen. Attire is T-shirts, shorts and boots. Rain starts to fall just as the hike begins.

Kirby leads the way, followed closely by Ernie and Russell. Gerry struggles far behind them, while George brings up the rear. (George must have 60 pounds in his pack. This starts a tradition of George having every conceivable backpacking item along in his pack. It also causes George to suffer terribly on most death marches, and to be good naturedly noted to bear a striking resemblance to a pack mule).

Follow Symmes Creek for a while, then up and catch Shepherd Creek late in the day. Clear, fast rushing, ice cold water. Stop for lunch at 4 PM. Thunder heard at stop. A little rain on the way, but not much. Overcast, so temperature was nice and no sunburn.

View got progressively more spectacular. Snow in crevices, high in mountains. Sheer, craggy mountains. We hike 7.5 miles and gain 5,200 feet in altitude to Anvil Camp (11,000 feet). Hike is very strenuous and steep - TORTURE. Make camp finally at 8 PM. Cool in evening. Long jeans and sweater for last part of hike.

Supper - dehydrated turkey tetrazzini cooked on GAZ stove. Worked great and freeze dried meal very tasty. Trail mix and candy bars along the way.

Day 2 - Friday, July 20, 1979

Breakfast - Granola & blueberries (another tradition in the making) and coffee. Chilly in the morning. Bathed in a stream.

Kirby an excellent hiker. Ernie and Russell pretty good. George and Gerry not in very good shape. We suffered the most. Camp amidst pine trees near tree line. Near the pass. Good night sleep - 9:30 PM to 6:00 AM.

Broke camp at 8:30 AM. Headed over Shepherd's Pass - grueling climb to 12,000 feet. Packs are killing us. Crossed snow glacier. Overcast - in the clouds at the top. Raining steadily half the day. Everything soaked. Melted snow at top with stove for hot chocolate. Beautiful scenery between the clouds. Crossed an alpine meadow with streams passing through. Then met up with the John Muir Trail and headed to Wallace Creek, where we made camp at 4:30 PM.

Set up tents and climbed into sleeping bags rest, warm up and dry off. Later fixed supper: beef stew, tang, applesauce, cheese and crackers. Gerry built a fire and we dried our clothes and got warm. Almost burned the boots while drying them near the fire. Going to be cold tonight. Stream next to camp for drinking water and washing. Camp amidst pine trees.

Day 3 - Saturday, July 21, 1979

Breakfast - granola and blueberries

Broke camp at 6:30 AM and headed to Crabtree Ranger Station - 5 miles up and down. Ranger said Mt. Whitney had storms. Suggested wait until tomorrow. Some in party (Kirby) couldn't. So decided to hike over Trail Crest (13,700 feet) and on out to Whitney Portals trailhead. Hike from Crabtree to Trail Crest extremely steep and grueling. Met high winds and hail. Lunch half way up - trail mix and beef jerky. Chilly weather.

Gerry falls behind. At Trail Crest, others are far ahead, out of sight. Hiked the final ten miles down to Whitney Portals trail head, the final few miles in darkness, groping for the trail. Arrive at trailhead at 9 PM. Others are nowhere to be found. Half hour later, others arrive with car. They had driven over to our starting point to pick up the car we left there. Exhausted, but anxious to get out of there, we drive home, arriving about 3 AM.

Beautiful mountain scenery and lakes near Mt. Whitney set off an

otherwise treacherous and soon to be entitled "Death March."
Contrary to this title, everyone did survive, and vowed to never go
backpacking again!

Second Annual Death March

Location: South Sierra Nevadas - Onion Valley, Kearsarge Pass

Dates: June 25-27, 1980

Participants: George DiGaetano, Gerry Herter, Ernie Ortiz, Russell Ortiz, Steve Williams

Trail Notes:

Day 1 - Wednesday, June 25, 1980

Left from the office at 6:25 PM. Stopped for pizza in San Bernardino. Arrived at Lone Pine Campground about midnite and set up camp.

Day 2 - Thursday, June 26, 1980

Got up at 6 AM and went to Sportsman's Cafe for breakfast. Stopped at sporting goods store for fishing rod for Ernie. Drove to Onion Valley (9,150 feet elevation).

Hit the trail at 9:45 AM. Lots of snow. Had to cross two snowbanks, about 1/2 mile across each. Gerry reached Kearsarge Pass (11,823 feet) at 2:30 PM, followed shortly thereafter by Steve. Ernie, Russell and George set up camp about 1,000 feet and 1/2 mile below. Gerry & Steve camped on pass next to snow. No room for tent. Night cold and windy. Full moon.

Day 3 - Friday, June 27, 1980

Get up at 6 AM. Snow frozen. Break some off and melt for coffee. Last night melted snow to make supper. Gerry and Steve hike down to rest of group. Ernie collapsed through snow and almost fell down steep snow bank. George and Russell had their fill of snow. So we hike back out, after breakfast. Down at 1:30 PM.

All the lakes were frozen, so no fishing. We learned another lesson the hard way this year. Don't back pack into the Sierras in June. There is still too much snow and ice, making conditions treacherous and cold.

Third Annual Death March

Location: Southern Sierra Nevadas - Onion Valley, Kearsarge Pass, Glenn Pass, Baxter Pass, Oak Creek Trail head

Dates: July 29 - August 1, 1981

Participants: George DiGaetano, Gerry Herter, Steve Williams

Trail Notes:

Day 1 - Wednesday, July 29, 1981

Steve and Gerry depart from office at 5:10 PM. Stop at Outpost Cafe near 395 and 15E Junction, for supper. Arrive at Oak Creek Campground at 10:10 PM. Meet up with George, who arrived earlier. Sleep out under the stars.

Day 2 - Thursday, July 30, 1981

Rise at 6 AM. Have breakfast - cantaloupe, pancakes, orange juice, and coffee. Drop George's car at Oak Creek Trailhead. Drive to Onion Valley and leave car at trail head.

Start hiking at 8:10 AM. Pass Little Pothole Lake, Gilbert Lake, Matlock Lake, Heart Lake and finally Big Pothole Lake. Arrive at Kearsarge Pass (11,823 feet) at 11:40 AM (5 miles). Hike was strenuous and grueling. Chipmunks at the top appear well fed. Lakes are deep green in center and light green around shallow edges. Very little snow. Only in high crevices. One fairly strong stream running out the valley. About 10 hikers at top when we arrived. Checked by rangers for passes at trailhead and near top of pass. Temperature in low 70's on trail. Feet a little hot. Perspired a lot. Breezy at pass. Wore t-shirt on trail and put on windbreaker at pass. Slight headache - probably the altitude. Not much appetite at pass. Couple handfuls of trail mix, beef stick, and cup of orangeade. George arrives at pass at 12:40. Sunny and clear.

Leave pass at 1:35. Hike down steep grade for 3 and 1/2 miles, past Kearsarge Lakes and Bullfrog Lake, to Charlotte Lake, arriving at 3:40. We set up camp next to the lake. Rest awhile. Have headache and nausea from altitude. Supper - dehydrated chicken chop suey. We string up our food in the trees since bears have been sighted in the area. To bed at 8:30 PM.

Day 3 - Friday, July 31, 1981

Up at 5:50 AM. Breakfast - granola & blueberries. Chilly in morning - 45-50 degrees. Moisture on side of tent. Break camp at 8:10. Head up over Glen Pass (2 miles - 11,900 feet). Beautiful view of a dozen lakes from pass. Hike down to Rae Lakes (2 miles). Steep downhill grade. Hard on feet. See marmots along trail. Continue on to Baxter Lakes. We miss the trail junction and go three miles out of our way. Back on the trail. We don't make it to Baxter Lakes by nightfall. Camp about a mile short in the woods. It is a very dry year. A lot of the brush grass is brown in some areas. Lakes appear to have a lot of fish, i.e. brook trout, and fishing is good. We are really dead by the time we make camp. My big toes are black and blue and blistered from the rough terrain we hiked over. We pitch tents (8PM) and hit the sack. Cup-a-soup for dinner. No lunch, no appetite. A couple of hard candy pieces.

Day 4 - Saturday, August 1, 1981

Up at 5:30 AM. We are low on water. So we strike camp quickly (6:15) and hike a mile to a creek. Fill up on water and then on a short distance to Baxter Lake, where we stop and have breakfast. Granola & blueberries, tang and coffee. Leave at 8:55 AM. Then up over Baxter Pass (12,400 feet). Very steep, all over rocks. Very barren area, all rocks and sheer mountain sides. Bowl shaped like an old volcanic crater. Snow bank in one area, but not on path. Spot a herd of 12 bighorn mountain sheep climbing side of mountain. Arrive at pass at 10:10. Majestic view. Town of Independence can be seen in the valley 15 miles away. Sheer mountain faces, with snow in crevices.

Start down at 10:40. Very steep, rapid descent, again over all rock for first couple miles. Finally back to tree line which provides intermittent shade, as we get lower and the sun gets hotter nearing the desert below. Baxter Creek flows down through the valley and is quite strong. We cross it twice on the descent, requiring agility to step over stones and fragile logs without toppling into the water. Fill our canteens each time. Water has been sparse today, so we fill up where ever possible. We don't treat this water with iodine, since it is flowing so fast and seems fresh and pure. Earlier in trip, purified our water with iodine, because of expected presence of a protozoa organism. May be related to the dry year and large number of hikers. They recommended treating all water, even fast flowing, since organism can be present.

The hike down remains fairly steep the whole distance - 7 miles. And is very hard on the feet, because of rocks and jarring on the steep descent. As we near the bottom, the forest vegetation (fir trees, etc.) gives way to desert scrub. With extremely sore feet and fatigued muscles, we finally reach the trailhead where George's car is parked, at 4:10 PM.

This trip we learned the importance of having good trail maps and of following them closely, since trails in the back country are not always marked well. Also, surprisingly enough, we discovered that downhill hiking can be tougher than uphill, especially on the feet, and where the trail is rocky and rough.

Fourth Annual Death March

Location: Grand Canyon - Trans-canyon from North Rim to South Rim

Dates: September 16-19, 1982

Participants: George DiGaetano, Gerry Herter, Steve Williams, Kay Ferbrache drove car around from North to South Rim

Trail Notes:

Day 1 - Thursday, September 16, 1982

Departed from office at 1:50 PM. Raining all the way. Arrived at Las Vegas at 6 PM. Had dinner at Holiday Casino buffet - $3.47. Departed Vegas at 7:15 PM and drove through, arriving at the North Rim at 11:30 PM. Total of 550 miles. Drive into camp ground. Sign says it's full, but we find place. No ranger around at this hour. George sets up tent. Gerry & Steve sleep under the stars. The next day we find out it is illegal to camp as we did. We avoid fine by sweet talking the female ranger.

Day 2 - Friday, September 17, 1982

Arise at 6 AM. Break camp. Breakfast at Grand Canyon Lodge - North Rim. Get passes in lodge, drive to trailhead and start down trail at 8:55 AM. Weather cloudy mostly and cool - pleasant. In a continuing effort to lighten the load, Gerry takes a flimsy day pack this year. Expecting warm weather, less heavy clothing is taken. Also, since there purportedly is a snack bar at the bottom, less food is taken. Except for Steve and George who feel that canned ravioli and such would taste good, and decide the extra weight won't be so bad. Steep descent. Pass by Roaring Springs - water gushing out of side of cliff forms Bright Angel Creek. Arrive at Cottonwood Campground at noon and have lunch. George's feet are suffering. Cool off feet in creek and then depart. Stop at Ribbon Falls. Beautiful, unique, feather of water drops 30 feet to cone-like pedestal and flows down all sides like ribbons. Continue through canyon, which gets very narrow. Starts to rain near end. Arrive at Phantom Ranch at 5 PM. Lemonade at snack bar. Ahh! Campground is next to ranch. Set up tents, cook dinner and go to bed at 8 PM. All are very tired. Hike was 14.2 miles

Day 3 - Saturday, September 18, 1982

Up at 7 AM. Have breakfast and wash up. Gerry heads up trail to Phantom overlook and Clear Creek. George rests feet and Steve swims. Buy sandwich at ranch for hike. Spectacular views of river, South Rim, and temple (Zoroaster) along Clear Creek Trail. After at camp, swim in Bright Angel Creek. Rinse out clothes. Relax, dinner at 5 PM. Campfire talk with ranger at 6:30 PM.

Day 4 - Sunday, September 19, 1982

Up at 3:40 AM. (Yes, that is 3:40 AM). On the trail at 4:30 AM. Daylight about 5:30 AM. Hike in dark along the river. Cool, but humid and sweaty. Steve and Gerry arrive at Indian Gardens at 6:45 AM. Have breakfast. George arrives at 7:30, just as Steve and Gerry are leaving. See you at the top, George! Sure, he says, as though only a certified miracle will bring that result.

Rest of climb becomes steep and hot. Pass several mule trains and many day hikers now. Arrive at top at 10 AM., with Steve just behind. George miraculously makes it to the top at 1PM, once again disproving all laws of physics, and looking more and more like a member of one of the pack trains we passed along the trail.

Kay is waiting for us with the car at the Bright Angel Lodge. We take showers in camper area and put on fresh clothes, much to Kay's relief. Have lunch and start home at 3 PM. Arrive home about 12:30 AM., despite a tangle Kay has with a picky Arizona highway patrolman over her driving speed.

Truly a memorable way to experience the grandeur of the Canyon, as one hikes through hundreds of millions of years of history colorfully layered in the rock formations of the canyon walls and temples. I don't think Steve and George will carry cans of food again, either. The garbage cans at the bottom are cleverly secured so that none of your garbage can be left in them. It all has to be carried out on your back.

Fifth Annual Death March

Location: King's River - King's Canyon & Sequoia National Parks Raft Trip

Dates: August 12-15, 1983

Participants: Gerry Herter, Loretta Herter, Jeff Hipshman, Jackie (Jeff's girl friend), Sue Johnson, Ted Johnson, Steve Williams, Sherry Williams

Trail Notes:

Day 1

In a major departure from the first four death marches, this was not to be a march, but a "death cruise," rafting along the treacherous, icy cold waters of the King's River. We were without George this year, the only death march he was to miss out of ten; something about impending fatherhood. Since this was not a traditional march, no trail notes were prepared at the time. Therefore, sketchy memories from six years later must be conjured up.

Departed with three vehicles, Steve's silver Honda hatchback, Loretta's brand new Toyota Camry on its maiden break-in run, and the Johnson's camper. The first night's destination was the campground we had reserved at Sequoia National Park. We arrived early, set up tents, and then took some short hikes among the magnificent redwoods (thereby qualifying the trip officially, though stretching the point a tad, as a death march). Dinner at the nearby cafeteria, possibly a ranger talk, then to bed. Bears in the area, so all food must be secured in bins permanently affixed at the campsite.

Day 2

We break camp after breakfast to make the two hour drive to the river, so as to arrive for lunch before disembarking. The Johnson's are anxious to get there and depart earlier than the rest. Twenty minutes later they return to pick up the ice chest they had left behind. Roads in and out of Sequoia are windy and mountainous, making it a long haul to the King's River Expeditions' base camp.

Once there, we are welcomed with a hearty lunch, and about forty other adventurous souls. With full stomachs, we are given a briefing, life jackets, and some are fitted for wet suits. Loretta is practically launched into space attempting to don hers. With one fellow holding each side as she steps into the tight, stretchable rubber leg, they lift upward as she steps down, sending her heavenward.

Next they pile us into pre-World War I buses for a harrowing ride along a cliff on the side of the river canyon, along what must have been a pioneer's trail, about half a lane wide and impassable. Half an hour later, pale and wan, we arrive at the starting point. I think they took us that way so the river wouldn't seem so treacherous by the time we got there.

About six rubber rafts are lined up on the bank. Each holds six rafters plus a guide. We split up with the Williams, Johnsons and Hipshmans taking one raft, and the Herters joining two couples who are a little older. Gerry is a little disappointed being with this group, but Loretta is relieved, especially later after hearing of the escapades in the other raft. It seems their guide was a bit of a maverick and not averse to trying adventurous maneuvers.

We spent the morning rafting down the river. The rapids were fun and exciting. The water was COLD!!! Jerry, not having much padding on his bones, felt it more than Steve. What does that tell you? At one point, there was a dead tree sticking up in the river with a rope hanging down from a limb. The guide asked for a volunteer to grab the rope and hold tight. Surprisingly, someone did. As the raft rushed by, the crazy one grabbed the rope and was swung way into the air, out of the raft and into the waiting river with a huge splash. Since the current was moving swiftly, the fellow was swept along like the raft, and easily caught up and was shiveringly hauled back in. He said it was a ball. Gerry at the time figured the icy water had affected the guy's brain, but the next day when the opportunity arose again, Gerry was the crazy one from his boat.

After crossing several challenging rapids, holding on for dear life, and getting thoroughly drenched (from the river as well as from a light rain that fell intermittently), we floated back to the base camp late in the afternoon. Most were exhilarated, some were grateful just to have survived. Now there was time to relax and clean up before dinner. Next to the camp was a swimming hole, at a slow spot in the river. A tree hanging out over the water had a rope hanging from it. We took turns swinging out on the rope, dropping into the river at the farthest point. Refreshing now that the afternoon had turned hot.

Dinner was superb, with big, juicy steak kabobs, along with all the fixings and drinks you wanted. Afterward the leaders and raft guides started a campfire, entertaining us with songs and skits. We all slept well that night, in our tents. There were showers and toilet facilities, softening the remote roughness of the terrain.

Day 3

This morning, after another hearty meal, we again load on to the death wagons for a repeat of yesterday's heart-stopping ride, only today the drive is twice as far. We board the rafts like experts and proceed down the river covering new territory in the morning, and finishing the afternoon over the same course as yesterday. At noon we stop on the riverbank for a lunch of sandwiches and fresh fruit. The sky is sunny and warm. Everyone is more adventurous today, having gained confidence from our experiences the day before. The front seats in the raft are now the prized ones, providing the most excitement as heavy rapids are crossed.

The final rapids were passed about a half mile from camp, leaving calm waters for the finish. The guide in Steve's boat felt his guests needed one more thrill, so he dumped the raft several hundred yards from the end, requiring the rafters to swim the remaining distance. The guys enjoyed it, though the gals were not overly thrilled. But everyone made it safely, and considered the trip a big success. Ted broke all land speed records with his van on the drive home, negotiating the mountain curves with uncanny idiocy.

One sad note to the trip. One of the couples joining us on the rafts had brought their dog along. He was a bulldog, so ugly he was lovable, by the name of Charming Choppers. They prized the dog, which had a long pedigreed lineage. We noted during the first evening that he seemed to have difficulty breathing, but assumed it was just the funny configuration of his snout. During the second day, he was left in camp while we rafted. It was a hot day. Upon returning from rafting, we heard a blood curdling scream. The owner had found the dog dead on the ground, apparently unable to take the heat. We wondered why they had brought him along, but also shared in their sorrow.

Sixth Annual Death March

Location: Yosemite National Park - Tuolumne Meadows to Yosemite Valley

Dates: September 6-9, 1984

Participants: Julie Bond, George Digaetano, Gerry Herter, Jeff Hipshman, Gina Ray, Susie Ray, Steve Williams, Scott Williams, Jeanie ?

Trail Notes:

Day 1 - Thursday, September 6, 1984

Departed from office at 6:45 AM. Susie and Julie give the guys a sendoff. They will meet us at Yosemite along with Gina and Jeanie, this evening. Stop for breakfast at McDonald's near Magic Mountain at 8:30. Stop for lunch at 1 PM at A & W in Oakhurst. Arrived at Yosemite Valley at 2:45 PM. Got wilderness permit and set up camp in Upper Pines Campground. Dinner at the Loft Restaurant in the

Village - expensive. Girls arrived at 8 PM.

Day 2 - Friday, September 7, 1984

Up at 5:45 AM and broke camp. Breakfast at Curry Village cafeteria. We drive to Tuolumne Meadows and arrive at Cathedral Lakes Trailhead at 9:30. Susie will drive car back to our camp in the Valley where she and Jeanie will stay while we are on the trail. She will later wish that she had been with us on the trail. We head across the green, stream covered, alpine meadows, going past the angelic Cathedral Rock and over Cathedral Pass. We reach our destination, Sunrise High Sierra Camp, at 2:30 PM, a distance of 7.5 miles.

Our first precursory exposure to a High Sierra Camp, Sunrise contains tent cabins, dining hall, solar heated showers, wash tub, flush toilets, and water. They charge $46.50 per night to stay there. We camp next to this wilderness enclave and take advantage of the showers and toilets, except for Julie who gets kicked out for not being a paying guest (neither were we). The camp is situated on the side of a mountain with a beautiful panorama of Long Meadow, with meandering streams and mountains on the far side. Dinner varies from turkey tetrazzini to cup of soup to cup of noodles. In bed at 8 PM. No one sleeps well. Cabin campers have campfire next to us and sing until the wee hours.

Day 3 - Saturday, September 8, 1984

Up at 5:45. Breakfast of granola & blueberries, breakfast bars, tea and hot chocolate. On the trail at 7:00. Slight climb, then all downhill for 14 miles. Beautiful views of domes and peaks of Little Yosemite Valley. Hike around backside of Half Dome. At junction to Half Dome trail at 9:30. Tempted to hike two miles to summit, but wisely decide not to. Feet are not in good shape at this point. Continue on to Nevada Falls at 11:00 and then to Vernal Falls at 12:30. Trail is very steep and all rocks. Very hard on legs and feet. Falls are flowing fairly strong. Impressive.

Jeff and Gerry reach trailhead in Yosemite Valley at 1:30, followed by Gina and Julie at 3:00, Steve and Scott at 4:00, and George at 4:30. Scott, at five years old, becomes the youngest participant to complete a Death March.

The only casualty of the trip is Susie, who didn't even hike! While staying in the Valley, she gets thrown by a horse. The result is a crushed vertebrae. She spends two nights in the park hospital. Husband Roger drives up and brings her home. Quite a disappointment for the marchers who were expecting her to have a steak dinner prepared for them upon the completion of the hike. We camp in the Valley. In bed at 10 PM and up at 6 AM of Day 4. Head home at 7AM.

Except for Susie's mishap, an enjoyable trip, with endless high sierra scenery. The hike is considered extremely strenuous and exhausting by Julie and Gina, who never again want to hear of another Death March.

Seventh Annual Death March

Location: Sequoia National Park

Dates: August 23-26, 1985

Participants: Merv Anderson, George DiGaetano, Gerry Herter, Jeff Hipshman, Karen Spivey, Scott Williams Steve Williams

Trail Notes:

Day 1 - Friday, August 23, 1985

Departed at 12:45 PM from office and George's house. Gerry's pack weighs in at 8 pounds, a world record. After seven years, many sore backs and aching bones, he has gradually trimmed down his pack and contents from the 35 pounds taken on the first death march. Key elements making this possible are use of a daypack, tube tent (glorified garbage bag), new light-weight sleeping bag and little else.

Arrived at Sequoia at 7:15 PM. Supper at the deli. Camped at Lodgepole. Took in the ranger talk at the campfire. To bed at 10 PM.

Day 2 - Saturday, August 24, 1985

Up at 6 AM. Breakfast at the bakery. Hit the trail at 8:35. Start climbing immediately. Then trail levels off for a couple miles. Then steep climb into Twin Lakes. Jeff and Gerry arrive at noon with Merv close behind. Rest for two hours. No sign of others. Head up over Silliman Pass at 2:30 and reach Ranger Lake at 3:30 (2 mile per hour pace). Climb over the pass is steep. Very tired. Others arrive at 6:30. Karen is very sore. Supper and boil lots of water. To bed at 8:30 after hanging food in tree, to keep it safe from the bears. Beautiful weather. Clear, hot and not too cold at night.

Day 3 - Sunday, August 25, 1985

Up at 6:00. Start out at 8:30. Karen's pack is too heavy, so some gear is switched to others. Make it to pass at 9:30. Leave there at 10:15 and decide to hike all the way out. Jeff and Gerry back to trailhead at Lodgepole at 1:40, followed by the rest at about 3:40. Showers, cold drinks and pizza. Ahhhh. Park ranger campfire show that night. Camp in campground.

Day 4 - Monday, August 26, 1985

Up at 6:00. Depart at 7:30 or so. Breakfast in Visalia. Home at 2:30. Hike was tougher than expected, all agree. Many sore legs and feet. But all make it, vowing as they do every year, never to do this again. They obviously have very short memories.

Eighth Annual Death March

Location: Mammoth Lakes, Devil's Postpile National Monument

Dates: July 17-20, 1986

Participants: George DiGaetano, Gerry Herter, Jeff Hipshman, Julia Peck, Karen Spivey, Scott Williams, Steve Williams

Trail Notes:

Day 1 - Thursday, July 17, 1986

Departed from office (Santa Ana) at 12:15 PM. Drove to Riverside for lunch stop. Into Mammoth Lakes about 7PM. Pick up wilderness permit from ranger station night drop. Supper at Grumpy's (Julia's nickname). Then drive 15 miles to Red's Meadows campground and make camp. Jeff and George put up tent, but rest are too tired and sleep in car or under the stars.

Day 2 - Friday, July 18, 1986

Up at 6 AM. Break camp. Didn't sleep very good. Some guy next to us barfed loudly all night. Breakfast at Mulehouse Cafe at Red's

Meadows. Good food. Then to trailhead at Agnew Meadows. And we're off at 8:55 AM. Easy trail for a couple miles (flat). Then a real steep stretch for a mile. We stop for lunch and get ambushed by mosquitoes, so we move to a better place. Hike by Shadow Lake and then a gentle climb.

The highlight of the day is fording the San Joaquin River. It is too deep, fast and wide to walk across rocks or logs. So Steve wades across (knee deep) and strings a rope that the girls can hold onto while crossing. Take socks off, but need shoes because of rocks. So all have wet shoes. Jeff had gone way ahead and we discover later there was another way to go without crossing the river. Oh well. Another mile and we arrive at Ediza Lake and hunt around for a campsite. All are tired, but the hike was not bad, 7 miles. Altitude 9300 feet - has everyone winded. We rest awhile and fix supper. Then Steve and Scott fish with no luck. In bed at 6:45 PM. It's getting cold, so the sleeping bags are the only warm place. Beautiful setting. The lake amidst the Minarets, with lots of snow in the crevices. Big snowbank next to our tents.

Day 3 - Saturday, July 19, 1986

Up at 6 AM. Cold! Breakfast of oatmeal, hot chocolate, blueberries and granola. Change of original plans. Ranger and hikers indicate that there is a lot of snow over the pass to Iceberg Lake. Risky. So we decide to hike back to Shadow Lake and take alternate loop that goes to Rosalie Lake, Gladys Lake, Trinity Lakes and out to Devil's Postpile. Start out with 22 switchbacks and 650 foot climb. Many streams to cross on logs, rocks, and sometimes have to wade through. Sun is hot and trail is dusty. George hikes out the original trail to pick up car and meet us at Devil's Postpile. Hike is tiring, but is a good distance and difficulty for a death march. Everyone makes it out in pretty good shape at about 4 PM. We shower at Red's Meadows, hot water only, from a spring. Set up camp at Devil's Postpile Campground and go to ranger campfire show. In bed at 9:45.

Day 4 - Sunday, July 20, 1986.

Up at 6 AM. Brisk morning half mile hike to the Postpile. Deer along the path. Impressive, volcanic formations of hexagonal columns towering over the path. Break camp at 8:30 AM and head home. Breakfast at Bishop. Learn of minor earthquake at 9 AM that toppled a couple columns of the Postpile. Just missed it.

Ninth Annual Death March

Location: Havasupai Canyon, Grand Canyon National Park

Dates: September 5-8, 1987

Participants: George DiGaetano, Keith Falconer, Gerry Herter, Jeff Hipshman, Mary Hipshman-to-be, Marley & Eric Jue, Julia, Joe, and Jennifer Peck, Lois, Jeff, and Jenny Richardson, Karen Spivey, Karen Williams, Steve, Sherry, and Scott Williams, Vivian Young

Trail Notes:

Day 1 - Saturday, September 5, 1987

Departed from Newport Freeway and Chapman Avenue, Orange, at 5:10 AM with four cars. Breakfast at Carls Jr. in Barstow at 7. Depart Barstow at 7:50. George and Lois' cars make wrong turn. Go up 15 instead of 40. Steve and Karen cars arrive at Kingman, Arizona at 11:10 and gas up. Lunch at Burger King. George and Lois' cars arrive via crossover route at 11:50. Depart Kingman at 12:10. Arrived at Haualapai Hilltop at 2:05 PM. Met up with Karen Williams and Vivian Young who drove up from Phoenix. Hilltop was loaded with cars. At trailhead was a mule pack train waiting to depart. Majestic, expansive view of the Grand Canyon. Steep drop off. Sparse facilities here: two chemical toilets.

We start down trail at 2:45. Steep descent with switchbacks for first mile or so. Beautiful scenery as we go. After this, trail is almost flat for the rest of the way. Group spreads out quickly. Large distance between Karen S. in front and George & Kay in back. Trail goes into a narrow canyon with initially 50 foot walls and 100 foot width, that grows to walls several hundred feet high, red limestone and sandstone eroded by wind and water. Runs along a stream bed. We had light rain just before arriving at trail head, but it stops. So temperature is pleasant starting out. Later, sun comes out and it gets in the 80's.

Arrive at Supai at 5:45. Small Indian village, self contained, store, cafe, school, clinic, and a dozen or two homes. Arrive at lodge which has modern motel rooms. Check in 8 rooms. Rest of group arrives piecemeal with George bringing up the rear at 6:45. All are tired but in reasonably good shape. Dinner at the cafe on Indian fry bread, beans, tacos, stew, burritos, and etc. Relax and cool off for a while by motel and then to bed early - 8:30-9:00, after watching the moon rise.

Day 2 - Sunday, September 6, 1987

Up at 7:30 and hearty breakfast at the cafe. Pleasantly cool in the morning. Then two mile hike to Havasu Falls. Passed Navajo Falls on the way. Easy trail. Beautiful falls cascading over travertine overhang. Terraces of limestone form pools below. Turquoise blue water. Clear. Falls is forceful. Water is cool and refreshing. Swim out to terraces and sit on them with feet in water. Big rope hanging from tree. We swing out on it and drop into the water. The ultimate swimming hole. Later hike another mile to Mooney Falls. Treacherous climb down the cliff face to reach the base of the falls. Chains fastened to the rocks and spikes are needed to hold onto as the descent is made. Also a couple of tunnels. Falls is even higher and more spectacular than Havasu. Also has terraces. We swim to the base of the falls, where the intensity of the pounding water is like a hurricane, with the mist blasting us in the face. We can only take the power of it for a few moments, and then swim back. The sun is hot now and we hike back, passing through the campground as we go. Outhouses and running water in the campground. Cold drinks in the cafe and then relax and play games on the tables outside the lodge. Dinner at the cafe. Crowded tonight. More games and to bed at 9:00-9:30.

Day 3 - Monday, September 7, 1987

The main group is up early and departs at 5:40 AM at daybreak. Hoping to hike out before the heat of the day. George and Kay follow at 5:50. Steve and family leave at 6:15. Joe, Jennifer, Karen Spivey, Karen Williams, Vivian Young and Gerry ride out on horses leaving at 8:00, along with pack of several others. Riding provides a unique perspective. We feel like cowboys. Indian guide who owns horses goes along and tells us what to do. Horses are tame and obedient. Very pleasant ride. Starts cool. Gets hot later when out of the canyon shade. Hikers move fast and get most of the way before hot sun comes out. Hiking time out is about the same as the time in, three and a half hours. Riders meet up with George and Kay about a mile from top. Kay is hot and tired. Gerry lets her have his horse and he hikes the rest of the way. Hikers out about 9:15. Horses out about 10:45.

Hot, tired, but fulfilled. Everyone made it. Drive two hours to Kingman Holiday Inn. We have lunch and then relax by the pool or cooling off in the rooms. 35 miles to dinner at the Colorado Belle Casino in Laughlin, Nevada. And a little gambling.

Day 4 - Sunday, September 8, 1987

Breakfast at Bob's Big Boy at 8 AM. Then leave for home at 9. All had a great time. This trip began a turn in direction for death marches. For the first time, the nights were spent not in a tent, but in a comfortable bed in a motel. Though we did have to hike 8 miles to get to it.

Tenth Annual Death March

Location: Yosemite National Park – Glen Aulin & May Lake High Sierra Camps

Dates: August 18-21, 1988

Participants: George DiGaetano, Kevin Falconer, Gerry & Loretta Herter, Jeff Hipshman, Marley & Eric Jue, Mark Lewinter, Julia & Joe Peck, Julia's friend Chris, Karen Williams, Scott Williams, Steve & Sherry Williams, Laurie Williams, Vivian Young, Dave & Mary Beth Zaczyk, Dave's parents

Trail Notes:

Day 1 - Thursday, August 18, 1988

Steve and group depart from park & ride at intersection of 91 and 5 near Buena Park, at 5:20 AM. Marley & Eric were to go with them,

but they did not show up. Steve called their home and Eric
answered. Marley was gone, on the way to the rendezvous without
Eric. The group left without them. It turned out Marley was going to
the starting point to let them know that they weren't ready yet.

Gerry departed at 8:30, as did Dave, and Marley shortly thereafter.
Drive was smooth and pleasant. About seven hours including a half
hour lunch stop. Early group arrived at noon and hiked Vernal and
Nevada Falls in the PM. Rooms were at Yosemite Lodge. Others
arrived at 4:30-5:00. Karen Williams & Vivian arrived driving up
from San Francisco. Dinner in the Valley. Ranger show and to bed
about 9:30.

Day 2 - Friday, August 19, 1988

Breakfast at 7:30-8:00. Depart at 9:00. Drive to Tuolumne Meadows.
Drop off three cars at May Lake trail head. Take four cars to Glen
Aulin trail head. Depart from trail head at 11:25. Beautiful scenery
through the meadows with Granite peaks and outcroppings along the
way. The meadows are partly brown due to dry weather. After an
hour or so the trail goes along the river. Stop for lunch on shore. Pass
several waterfalls and two bridges, arriving at Glen Aulin High
Sierra Camp, some at 2:00, the rest at 2:30 or so. About six miles.
Beautiful setting next to a cascading waterfall. About 10 cabins,
with four beds each. Showers, flush toilets, store with lemonade,
candy and tee shirts. Hot supper at 6. Outstanding: cream of celery
soup, salad, Austrian-Hungarian goulash, pasta, stir-fried vegetables,
and apple crisp - a gourmet feast. College students worked the camp.
Sunset and moonlight by the waterfall. In bed at 9:00.

Day 3 - Saturday, August 20, 1988

Up at 6:00. Cool, but not too cold last night. Warm wool blankets.
Comfortable beds. Wood stoves in cabins. Coffee & cocoa at 7:00.
Breakfast at 7:30. Hot cereal, bacon, eggs scrambled with
vegetables, potatoes, apple juice and coffee. Delicious. Break camp
at 8:45, on the way to May Lake, eight and a half miles away. Trail

is good most of the way, much up and down. Cool most of the morning. Part of the way through forest, part over granite mountains. Spectacular views and vistas of the Sierras and lakes.

Jeff, Mark, Scott and Kevin make a wrong turn and end up at Tenaya Lake, an extra four miles out of the way. Box lunches are consumed along the way: chicken sandwich, apple, raisins, trail mix, cookies and apple juice. After a couple grueling climbs up switchbacks, we arrive at beautiful May Lake about 2 PM. Lemonade awaits us. Towering white granite Mount Hoffman rises from the far side of the clear lake. We relax by the lake, playing Scrabble while Mark rows the kids around the lake in a boat, and George soaks his feet in the water. Karen W. and Vivian straggle into camp about 4:00. Vivian has severe back trouble and was lucky to make it. She says a couple pain pills will put her back in good spirits.

About 4:30 a thunderstorm rumbles in, bringing sheets of rain and hail. We watch the spectacle safe and dry in the dining hall, except for Marley, who had hiked out to the trail head and got caught in the downpour on the way back. She had heard that bears had broken into some cars parked there, and she was worried because of food left in the car. All was OK. The chill from the storm was incentive enough to light up the wood stoves in the cabins for warmth.

Dinner at 6:30 was steak, rice, corn, salad, mushroom soup, homemade bread, and chocolate surprise cake. Delicious! After dinner some hike to a nearby bluff to catch a glimpse of sunset and Half Dome in the distance. In bed at about 8:30. A pretty dull group - except the two Karens & Vivian who have a wild time until Larry, the camp manager, finally bangs on their tent cabin and tells them to shut up.

Day 4 - Sunday, August 21, 1988

Up at 6:00. Light the stove. Up to the bluff for a beautiful, peaceful sunrise over the Sierras. Disappointed that no bears appeared last night despite numerous assurances that they were around. So remains intact a death march record. No time in the ten years of marches has a bear been encountered on the trail. Hearty breakfast at 7:30 like yesterday. We break camp at 8:30 and hike the 1.2 miles to the trail head by 9:00. Drivers are shuttled to the starting trailhead to pick up cars, and we're ready to depart in our different ways by 10:00.

A most successful trip. All made it and had an enjoyable time. After ten long, suffering years, we finally found the ideal way to make a backpacking trip. The High Sierra Camps will be hard to beat.

Eleventh Annual Death March

Location: Santa Catalina Island, Two Harbors

Dates: August 25-27, 1989

Participants: Mike, Glynna & Jeremy Ampe, Christine Couts, George, Kay, Tommy & Gene DiGaetano, Gerry & Loretta Herter, Jeff Hipshman, Mark Lewinter, Julia & Joe Peck, Steve, Sherry, Scott & Laurie Williams & Monica (6 months old), Kevin & Sherry Falconer.

Trail Notes:

Day 1 - Friday, August 25, 1989

The group met at the Catalina Express Terminal, Berth 95, San Pedro, under the Vincent Thomas Bridge, at 11:15 AM. Chris' friend, Bruce, was the first casualty and had to cancel at the last minute, because of a suspected appendicitis. Boat departed at noon. Boat holds about 50 people. The ride was smooth. Somewhat overcast, but calm. Flying fish spotted along the way. Drinks available on the boat. (Unbeknownst to everyone but me, Loretta spills her ginger ale all over her shorts).

Arrive at quaint Two Harbors at 1:30 PM. Harbor is filled with pleasure boats (about 200). About 150 people live permanently in Two Harbors. All facilities are run by Doug Bombard Enterprises. We disembark and are taken by shuttle the 1/2 mile up a hill and out of the little bustle of the harbor to Banning House Lodge, originally the summer home of the former owners of the island. Situated with a panoramic view of Isthmus Bay, where we came in, and also Catalina Harbor on the opposite side of the isthmus. A rustic lodge with ten nicely decorated and furnished rooms. A lodge room has hunting trophies, buffalo head, complete mountain goat, peacock, turkey, fox and several others, along with a massive fireplace and views of both harbors. Also a dining room for breakfast.

After checking in, everyone is on their own. Ice cream at the snack bar and various walks around the harbors. The first two buffalo are spotted high on the hillside and encountered by Mike and the boys. Jeff and Mark hike all the way to Emerald Bay, about 8 miles. Dinner at 6 at Doug's Harbor Reef Restaurant, the only one in town. A fairly large place, service is efficient and the food very good. This is the social center of town, and later on a band plays oldies 'til the wee hours. At dark, we are given a slide show on the beach, by Misty, a naturalist, who tells us all about the island, its features and history. Then to bed early. About 10 PM.

Day 2 - Saturday, August 26, 1989

Up at 7 AM. Continental breakfast provided by the lodge: croissants, muffins, oranges, cantaloupe, coffee, tea and orange juice. Our box lunches arrive about 9:20 AM. We depart for our day hike at 9:25 AM. Our route is up the old Banning House Road to the main road and on to Little Harbor. The first mile or so is very steep. Little Gene DiGaetano has had enough after a few steps, so Kay decides to stay back with him. Behind the lodge, about 15 buffalo have wandered in and graze. We get some good close-up views and pictures as we start out. As we go, the island is very arid and dry and dusty. Lots of prickly pear cactus and brush. The sky is overcast and keeps the temperature cool for the difficult part of the hike. Views are spectacular as we climb higher. Several little coves full of boats can be seen looking toward Emerald Bay. The ocean unfolds on the other side. After several intermediate hills, we reach the top and start a very steep descent. After 3 miles, we meet up with the main road at the Buffalo Corral. Now the hike is fairly level and pleasant the remaining 3 miles to Little Harbor. Steve and Sherry carry 6 month old Monica on their back the whole way.

Little Harbor is a picturesque little beach with rock outcroppings on each end. The sun comes out and we lay out our beach towels and have lunch. Then a swim in the clear, cool waters. Beach is sandy with some stones. We arrive at noon. About 1:00 PM, Kay and Gene come plodding over the sand, having caught the bus here. We all relax and sunbathe while the boys explore and come back with a lizard.

At 3 PM, a special bus picks us up for the return trip to Two Harbors. Julia, Joe, Jeff and the boys decide to hike back. We see more buffalo along the way. Arriving back at 3:30 PM, we clean up and recuperate at the lodge. At 6, seven of us return to Doug's Harbor Reef for dinner, while the kids take the parents to the snack bar for hot dogs and burgers. The band plays oldies again tonight, while the families play some spirited games in the lodge room. To bed at 10, except Jeff and Mark who watch band and listen to tall stories by boat people 'til 11:30.

Day 3 - Sunday, August 27, 1989

Continental breakfast at 8 AM. The Ampe's need to catch a 9:45 AM boat back to the mainland, so we have a quick breakfast and farewell. Today is left flexible. Joe, Julia, Chris, Jeff, Mark, George and family take the boat to Avalon for the day, departing at 10:15. Steve and family hike to Emerald Bay, 6 miles each way, departing at 10:15. Gerry and Loretta head out the road toward Emerald Bay, departing at 10:45. The hike yields ongoing spectacular views, as cove after cove are revealed, each with turquoise blue water and numerous boats. The road is level and about 200 feet above the water. One contains a Boy Scout camp, complete with canoes, tent cabins and archery range. Along the way, two deer are spotted. Emerald Bay is a broad expanse of turquoise blue water. Steve and family climb down to the beach and stay for 1/2 hour before the return hike. George and Kay return from Avalon at 3 and take to the beach at Two Harbors, joined by Gerry and Loretta. The rest return from Avalon at 5:15. Julia, Joe and Chris took in the shops and bring back a crazy duck. Jeff and Mark rented bikes for 2 hours and check out all areas of Avalon.

All have a bite to eat at the snack bar, change clothes, and board the boat for the return trip to the mainland, leaving at 6:45. Mark has talked his way onto the bridge for the crossing. Ship arrives and we are on our way home by 8:30 PM. All have had a terrific time and plan to return to Two Harbors.

Twelfth Annual Death March

Location: Yosemite National Park -Merced Lake High Sierra Camp

Dates: June 28 -July 1, 1990

Participants: Christine Couts, George & Tom DiGaetano, Kevin Falconer, Gerry Herter, Jeff Hipshman, Paul & Justin Nash, Julia & Joe Peck, Steve & Scott Williams, Dave & Frank Zaczyk.

Trail Notes:

Day 1 -Thursday, June 28, 1990

The group met and departed at 6:15 AM from the Park & Ride lot at the intersection of 1-5 and 1-91. Steve drove his van with Jeff, Gerry, Paul and the boys. Joe drove in with Julia, Chris, Dave and Frank, and George drove. Traffic through LA is not bad. Breakfast at 7:15, at McDonalds at Magic Mountain. Disney Trivial Pursuit along the way, men vs. boys. Lunch at Oakhurst at 11:45.

Arrive at Yosemite Lodge at 2 PM and check-in, 3 cabins -5 to a cabin. Explore the valley via the shuttle, hitting each ice cream stand along the way. Temperature 83, at night 51. Dinner at Four Seasons after 20 minute wait, that was actually an hour. Steve, Paul, George and boys get pizza. Ranger show, 8:30 -talk and film on Sequoia trees. All have neon orange hats this year. We are the talk of the valley; can be spotted for miles. They consider kicking us out of the park as an eyesore. To bed at 10 PM.

Day 2 -Friday, June 29, 1990

Up at 6 AM. Breakfast at cafeteria at 6:30. pick up box lunches (2 sandwiches, apple, egg, cookies). Catch tram for Happy Isles at 7:30. On trail at 7:55 AM. Mist trail is steep and strenuous. Views of Vernal Falls and Nevada Falls are spectacular. Group starts to spread apart quickly. After 3 miles of steep climb, trail levels off for awhile. Per Julia, this is the first time she has sweat in her life, running down her face. Sunny and hot. Lunch after 3-1/2 hours. After 9 miles, another steep section, and after 13.1 miles, Merced Lake comes into view. Jeff and Gerry arrive at High Sierra Camp at 1:45 PM, followed by Dave and Frank at 1:50. Steve and boys pull in at 2:45. Paul and Justin Nash come in at 3:15. Julia arrives at 3:45, with Joe and Chris close behind. Finally, George and Tommy show up at 5:15 PM, in keeping with tradition.
Camp is large with 23 cabins and a capacity about 50. All tent cabins with beds, tables, shelves, but no stoves. There are two shower tents, johns, mess tent & building. Pleasant setting amongst stand of tall evergreen trees. Merced is large lake with river flowing in with small waterfall at far end. We cool off feet in stream, have lemonade at mess tent and buy T-shirts. Relax on benches by campfire, waiting for hikers to arrive. Kevin and Scott go fishing.
Dinner at 6:30. Chicken, zucchini, fettuccini, soup, salad, spice cake, coffee and hot chocolate. After dinner, sit by campfire awhile and eat popcorn. Report comes in that a bear is around. Everyone races over to the area of the sighting. No bear is seen, but on the way back, Julia slips and severely sprains her ankle and leg. She is in much pain. A gal from the camp comes and looks at it. We carry her back to camp and put her in bed. Ice is put on the leg and she takes some

pain killers. We all go to bed by 10-10:30.

Day 3 -Saturday, June 30, 1990

Up at 7. Breakfast at 7:30. Cream of wheat, broccoli and cheese omelet, bacon, muffin, grapefruit, coffee and cocoa. Julia is carried to breakfast and to the ladies room. After breakfast, we put her in the stream to soak her leg. Frank fishes in Merced Lake -catches four trout. Dave reads. Joe stays with Julia. The rest hike three miles to Washburn Lake where the boys fish. We have our box lunches - sandwich, peach, cashews, M & M's and apple juice. Jeff, Gerry and Chris return to camp at 1PM.

The park ranger examined Julia and decided she should be taken out by helicopter. Her ankle and leg are swollen and stiff. Five minute chopper ride to the Valley. Julia is embarrassed and disappointed. Because of other emergencies, Julia has to wait until 4 PM to get lifted out. We stay with her. Ranger Bob puts an inflatable plastic splint on her leg. A stretcher is improvised from a canvas and eight of us move Julia to a big wide rock formation where the helicopter will land.

The fishermen return just before the helicopter arrives. Everyone caught at least one fish and they brought them back to have cooked for breakfast. The chopper finally arrives and Julia is placed on a real stretcher and loaded into the rear of the chopper. The chopper tries to lift off, but is too heavy. It lands again and one of the crew hops out and waits for the chopper to come back and pick him up.

We all shower and then have dinner: steak, corn, beans, rice and cherry cobbler. A pleasant campfire and popcorn. To bed by 10.

Day 4 -Sunday, July 1, 1990

Up at 6:00. Coffee at 7:00. Breakfast at 7:30. On the trail at 8:20. Traveling out, primarily downhill, is faster than going in. Dave and Gerry set a blistering pace of 3.2 miles per hour and finish in four hours at 12:20 PM. Gerry, determined to keep up with upstart Dave, trips while jogging down the Mist Trail and sprains hand & shoulder and bangs knee, ripping jeans, but otherwise is ok. Jeff is out at 12:50 (4-1/2 hrs.) followed in 5 minutes by Frank. Steve and boys come out at 1:30. Paul and Justin are here at 3:30, followed by Chris and Joe at 4.

We give up waiting for George, who was last to leave camp this morning. Dave and Frank will wait for him, only because they need a ride home. We all pig out on cokes, root beer floats and icees at Happy Isles Trailhead. A tall, athletic blond girl, who was with her parents at Merced Lake, arrives at the trailhead about 2:30. She proceeds to Curry Village to get a beer. Half hour later she returns to wait for her parents and gives us a big can of Fosters Beer to share. We take the shuttle back to the lodge and clean up. Julia is waiting and has a cast from knee to toe. Don't know if anything is broken yet. She'll need to see her doctor when she gets home. She stayed in the lodge last night. But they didn't hesitate to boot her out this morning when she didn't have any money.

We depart Yosemite about 5 PM for the long ride home, arriving very late.

Thirteenth Annual Death March

Location: Virginia Lakes, California - Horse Packing Trip

Dates: August 22 - August 25, 1991

Participants: Mike & Jeremy Ampe, Mark Carter, Christine Couts, George & Tom DiGaetano, Lyndi Dykstra, Kevin Falconer, Gerry Herter, Jeff Hipshman, Julia & Joe Peck, Karen Williams, Steve & Scott Williams.

Trail Notes:

Day 1 - Thursday, August 22, 1991

Departed at 8:15 AM from 91 & Imperial Highway. Steve drove van with Scott, Kevin, Mike, Jeremy, George and Tom. Gerry drove Mark, Jeff and Karen. Julia drove Joe, Chris and Lyndi. Made Lone Pine at 12:00 noon. Two cars stop for lunch at Sportsman's's Lodge. It has been remodeled since our last visit five years ago. We sit where kitchen used to be. Wise cracking waitress keeps us on our

toes. Julia has the chicken breast. The van has more boys than men
(4-3), so they vote to hold out until Carl's Jr. in Bishop, an hour
further. Rest of group gets there about 2 PM.

Arrive at Lee Vining, Lake View Lodge at 3 PM. Settle in and then
check out the town. Drive to Mono Lake for guided sunset hike.
Fascinating geology of the lake — highly saline and alkaline with
tufa formations and volcano cones. Naturalist stressed concern over
Los Angeles taking water from the lake, causing the water level to
decrease and salinity to increase, endangering birds and brine
shrimp. Lee Vining is a small town with very few restaurants. We
wait one-half hour to get table at 8:30 PM. Boys skip nature hike and
watch movie in room. To bed at 10:15 PM.

Day 2 - Friday, August 23, 1991

Up at 6 AM. On the road at 6:55. Arrive at Virginia Lakes Pack
Outfit at 7:30. We unload our gear and have breakfast of eggs &
bacon. We break into two groups. The boys and dads plus Jeff leave
first at 8:30, followed at 9:00 by the rest. The horses are very
cooperative. Two cowboys go with each group and two more lead
four mules with our gear. Scenery in mountains is spectacular. Trail
goes up over a pass. Reminds us of Baxter Pass years ago. Weather
is beautiful and riding allows us to take in all the views. Coming
down from the pass is treacherous. Steep and over rocks, making it
exciting. Julia is scared to death. We stop for lunch on the trail. First
group gets to camp about 12:30 and has lunch. Other group arrives at
2. All are stiff and sore. Pass several alpine lakes on the way. Tents
are all assembled. Two to a tent, we settle in. Boys go fishing. Steve
catches one. We hike and rest 'til five. Then have wine, crackers &
cheese by the fire. Supper at 6:30 - chicken fajitas. Getting cold! To
bed by 8:30 PM.

Day 3 - Saturday, August 24, 1991

Up at 6:30. Coffee ready. Good and hot. Hot chocolate, also. Cold
this morning! A gigantic sausage, pepper & onion omelet is made in

a 16" Dutch oven. It takes two hours to cook. We all watch it while keeping warm by the fire. It was delicious!

Breakfast is finally over at 10:30. We all head out at 11 for day hike. Steve's group heads down main trail along creek, to fish in pools. No keepers were landed. Julia, Joe & Chris go part way down same trail. Gerry, Karen, Jeff and Mark head uphill for two hours and finally reach picturesque Shepherd's Lake. The view and panorama and Shepherd's Crest are spectacular. Deer are seen along the way and a mountain lion is spotted among the rocks. We alter our route, needless to say, with Mark leading the retreat. Back to camp at 4. Steve and group about 5.

Karen gets attacked and stung by renegade bee in her tent. Julia gives her Crest toothpaste to treat it. Lyndi is reading on edge of camp and deer comes and sniffs her toe. Must be quite an aroma. Everyone is pooped out and rests awhile. Wine and crackers at 5. The cowboys and cook are agreeable characters and socialize with us. Dinner of Lasagna and crispas. Very tasty! Bad jokes around the campfire and then to bed at 9:00.

Day 4 - Sunday, August 25, 1991

Up at 6:15. Breakfast of French toast and sausage. Pack up and wait for horses which have been kept in a meadow a couple miles away. We leave at 10:15. Beautiful, sunny, breezy day. Views are again spectacular. Ride out is quicker. Horses are anxious to get home. We stop for lunch by a creek and then out to Virginia Lakes at 2:00. Pack mules arrive at 2:30 and we're on the road home at 3:15.

Fourteenth Annual Death March

Location: Whitewater Rafting, Lower Kern River, Lake Isabella, CA

Dates: July 26-28, 1992

Participants: Mike & Jeremy Ampe, Mel Drury, George Di Gaetano, Gerry Herter, Ken & Cindy Little, Karen Williams, Steve & Scott Williams, Kevin Falconer, and Mike (George's wife's brother-in-law).

Trail Notes:

Day 1 - Sunday, July 26, 1992

Departed at 4:10 PM from Yorba Park Medical Group parking lot, at Chapman and Newport Freeway in Orange. Gerry's Lexus, Mike's MBZ, and Ken's Jeep V6. Two and a half hour drive to Bakersfield. Arrive at the Ramada Inn at 6:40 PM. Special rib dinner, but we wait almost all night to get it. Busy with teenage wedding in the next room. After dinner, watch Olympic swimming in Barcelona, then to bed at 10-10:30.

Day 2 - Monday, July 27, 1992

Up at 6:00. International House of Pancakes has the same pace as last night's restaurant, so we don't get on the road until 8:25 AM. Make Lake Isabella main dam meeting place at 9:30 AM, and meet up with the other rafters. (Note: These trail notes went through many soakings in the river over the next two days, leaving them next to unintelligible).

Guides meet us at 10:00 - Whitewater Voyages. Leave cars at fenced in parking lot and then bus to river for instructions and into the water at 11:00. Five rafts with five people in each plus guide. Steve, Mike and boys in one raft. Gerry, Karen, Mel and Little's in another. George, Mike and others in a third.

Weather is great. Sunny and hot, and pleasant breeze. Drive into Lake Isabella is a scenic canyon. 50 miles from Bakersfield. River is swift and narrow. After first rapids, we encounter a downed tree in the river. Guides get all in one raft and maneuver around tree and place rope around it and pull it out. We go over several exciting Class IV rapids. On White Maiden Falls, George goes in the river as his raft goes over the falls. He flounders in the river bobbing up and down in front of and under the raft for 100 feet down the rapids. It looks like he is doomed to smash against a massive rock. Somehow he misses it. His guide, who is a pretty, tanned young girl, pulls him out.

We stop on a beach for lunch of sandwiches, vegetables, fruit, cookies and lemonade. Then down the river and several more rapids. At about 4, we pull out and are bused to the camp along the river. We make camp, play volleyball, swim in river, and snack on chips and sodas and beer. Supper is steak, chicken, fettuccini, corn, Caesar salad, and brownies. Excellent. We talk around the campfire with the personable guides and watch the stars. To bed about 10:00.

Day 3 - Tuesday, July 28, 1992

Up at 6:30 AM. Coffee is on and guides are busy fixing breakfast. Guides are well organized and work together as a team, cooking meals as well as running the river. They are safety conscious, and you always feel that they know what they are doing. On each rapid, the guides station themselves and their rafts at various strategic vantage points, to be able to view and react to any situation where help may be needed.

Breakfast is hearty with scrambled eggs filled with onions, peppers, cheese, along with hash brown potatoes, bacon, cinnamon coffee cake and fruit. We break camp and continue our adventure down the river at 9:30 AM. The camping spot had been delightful. The river was running fast there. We could jump in with our life vests and float down about fifty yards very quickly and then swim out. Portable outhouses were also available.

Today we covered the last few rapids from yesterday and then experienced numerous more through out the day. When the river was calm, we hopped off the raft and drifted along for awhile, cooling off from the heat of the day. At one point we encountered a Class V rapid. Since this was too treacherous for our group, we portaged about 100 hundred yards around it, carrying the rafts up and over a rock face and dropping them back in down stream.

Lunch again was along the river. One of the rafts is turned upside down to function as the serving table. The boys get into the cookies first, which seem to disappear quickly. The final hours are passed with rapids of colorful names like Deadman's Curve and the Staircase. At various places, rafts attack each other deluging everyone with paddle spray. We reach our destination at 5:00 PM, and pull the rafts out of the river. Made of rubber-like material, they seem quite heavy. Plenty of beer and soda for all, as we take the final bus ride back to the starting point. We all buy t-shirts and order photos. Everyone has had a great time and declares this one of our best death marches.

Fourteenth Annual Death March - Take Two

Location: Mount Whitney

Dates: August 5-8, 1992

Participants: Tom Ahling, Gerry Herter, Dick Willner, Dave Zaczyk

Trail Notes:

Day 1 - Wednesday August 5, 1992

Not willing to settle for one death march this year, four hearty souls set out to conquer Mount Whitney. You will recall that Mount Whitney was the goal that eluded us on the original death march in 1979. Over recent years, with the popularity of various nearby destinations, obtaining reservations or permits to these places has been extremely difficult. This year, in hopes of getting approval for one of our desired locations, we put in requests for three: rafting, Mount Whitney, and Bearpaw Meadows. Were we surprised when all three came through. Not wanting to lose any of the opportunities, we decided to open all three to whoever could go.

Not knowing how the hike would go, we took two cars, since some had to be back by Friday night, while others could take an extra day if needed. We all met at Dick's in Claremont. Gerry and Dick drove, departing from there at 1:30 PM. The trip to Lone Pine was smooth, arriving at the Mount Whitney Ranger Station at about 5:00 PM, with views of the peak coming into view just as we approached the town. We pick up our permit at the night box, and then head to the Sportsman's Cafe, to once again uphold the old tradition. The drive to Whitney Portals is 13 miles and takes us to 8300 feet elevation. A campsite is found at the trail head. After setting up, we have pie and coffee at the little shop there, and muse about how the hike will go and when we'll get to the top. Into bed about 9PM. Dick sleeps in car. He admits to a snoring problem. The other three crowd into

Tom's dome tent. Sleeping is not very good at this altitude.

Day 2 - Thursday, August 6, 1992

We oversleep as no one hears Gerry's watch alarm. During the night, it rains two different times, not a good omen. Dave gets up and covers our packs outside. Up at 5:45 AM. Dave fixes breakfast while we break camp. We're on the trail by 7:30 AM. Gerry & Dave are in the lead. Ten minutes into the hike, Dave discovers he forgot his sunglasses. He goes back. Gerry continues on alone for about an hour. Then Dave and Tom catch up. Dick is taking a much slower pace and is not seen for several hours. The day is beautiful, sunny with patchy clouds, and no trace of the rain from the night before. The air is so dry, the ground has completely dried out already.

The first objective is Outpost Camp, 3-1/2 miles, which we reach at 9:00 AM. This is a flat, vegetated area with a stream running through. After a brief stop we continue. The trail steepens as we go upward. Dave moves out ahead. By the time we make Trail Camp, 2-1/2 miles further, Tom is not feeling good, the effects of the altitude coupled with the strenuous ascent. Dave arrived at 10:30, followed by Tom and Gerry at 11:00. Tom is debating whether to go back down. Trail Camp is at 12,000 feet. Dave and Gerry are still feeling good and decide to forge ahead. Camp is set up at Trail Camp, and packs are left there, with only water and snacks to carry to the top. We also take sweatshirts and wind breakers, as the temperature is cooler.

Dave and Gerry head out at 11:45. The climb now is steeper and increasingly difficult in the thin air. Down below, Dick arrives at Trail Camp at about 12:15, in good shape, but deciding to wait until tomorrow for the climb to the top. He and Tom set up camp, as Dick tries to convince Tom to hike to the top with him tomorrow.

The further they go, the more worn out Dave and Gerry get. The switch backs (100 of them) go on and on. All the while the view is getting more and more spectacular. When the sign for Trail Crest finally comes into view, we get a burst of adrenalin, as we feel the worst is over. Trail Crest is at 13,873 feet above sea level, and marks the closest point we got to the summit back in 1979. It looks much more inviting now with the sun shining, then it did with the storm clouds back then.

We rest a bit, before completing the final 2-1/2 miles. We quickly realize that these will be the toughest miles of the climb. Not that they are treacherous, although the view is awe inspiring. But the altitude, combined with tired muscles has all but sapped what energy we have left. After each few steps, we have to stop and rest. How can we go on? The top is so close, yet so far. Several times Dave suggests that we're close enough, hinting we may as well head down. Each time Gerry replies, just a few steps at a time, and before you know it we'll be there. Amazingly enough, we do finally make it, and collapse on the boulders for a fifteen minute nap. You feel like you can see forever on this vantage point at the top of the country. The view is truly spectacular. At top is a little hut, infamous a year or two ago as the place where a couple of hikers were struck by lightning in a storm.

Dave is not feeling good, so Gerry signs the log for both. We arrived at the peak at 4 PM. We are lucky, the weather has held up and we have sun, with a few scattered clouds. But storms can rise quickly late in the day, so we head down at 4:20. The going down hill is much, much better. It is hard on toes and knees, but a real break for the cardiovascular system. About a mile from camp, we are met by Dick who was worried about us. We had estimated we would be back by 4 or 5. We hike into camp, where Tom has the chili prepared ready for dinner. Dave's wife, Mary, had made the chili and froze it for us. We kept it cool in the lake during the day. It was delicious, a real treat at 12,000 feet. We socialize with some of the numerous campers, watch a beautiful sunset and moonrise over the mountains, and then to bed at 9:00 or so.

Day 3 - Friday, August 7, 1992

Up at 6. We sleep hardly at all last night. The altitude gave us headaches, and we toss and turn. Dick was able to sleep some. He is feeling good, and is ready now to tackle the summit. He does not succeed in getting Tom to do it with him, nor Dave or Gerry to do it again. We're anxious to get back down to a lower altitude, hoping that will cure our headaches.

Dick departs at 6:45 on a beautiful sunny day with no clouds at all. The rest break camp and start the descent at 7:20. The downward hike goes very fast, and we all feel progressively better as we descend. Tom is especially feeling good as he takes off beating us down by ten minutes, arriving at the Portals trailhead at 10:45. We get a much needed shower at the little shop, lunch in Lone Pine, and then head home.

Day 4 - Saturday, August 8, 1992

Dick was expecting to hike to the summit and then return to Trial Camp for the night on Friday. Saturday, he would hike out and return home. We left a tent and stove for him to use. There were a lot of people on the trail and in camp, so we did not feel he would be alone.

Fifteenth Annual Death March

Location: Tuolumne River Rafting and Yosemite National Park

Dates: July 17 - July 21, 1993

Participants: Tom Ahling, Mark Carter, Bill Decker & son, George DiGaetano, Kevin Falconer, Gerry Herter, Jerry, Jeffrey, Jimmy & John Higashi & two friends, Patrick Meehan, Jennifer Peck & friend Melanie, Karen Williams, Steve & Scott Williams and Dave Zaczyk.

Trail Notes:

Day 1 - Saturday, July 17, 1993

Jerry Higashi, Bill Decker, sons and friends departed Friday night about 8PM, driving to Fresno, and then begging for $300 rooms at 1AM, having discovered that a Jehovah's Witness convention had swallowed up all available accommodations.

Steve, Scott and Kevin converge at Gerry Herter's house for a 7:25 AM departure, along with Dave, George, Karen and Patrick. As Dave packs Steve's bunch into his truck, his backpack turns out to be conspicuously missing. So off they go with a detour to Fullerton in search of the missing backpack. Gerry heads up the main route - 1-5 - with plans of meeting up with Dave in Bakersfield. Thanks to a wreck along the way, Gerry is delayed and Dave reaches the California Street truck stop rendezvous first.

On to Oakhurst for a McDonald's lunch at 12:40, then into Yosemite, arriving at Curry Village at 2:30 PM. Check into cabins, then check out the shops for snacks and supplies for tomorrow's hike. The Higashi group arrives this morning and tackles the hike to Yosemite Falls. A lot of sore muscles by the time we meet up with them in late afternoon. Dinner at the cafeteria, reading to the fading daylight at the amphitheater, ranger show at 8:30 PM - Yosemite Meadows - and to bed before 10.

Day 2 - Sunday, July 19, 1993

Up at 6:30 AM. Breakfast at cafeteria at 7:00. Tram to Happy Isles trail head at 7:30. Dave, Gerry and Patrick are on the trail to Half Dome at 7:50. Karen and George follow along, headed to Vernal and Nevada Falls. Steve and the boys head to Yosemite Falls trail. Jerry Higashi and group, still sore from yesterday hikes, decide to take it a little easier. We order them 8 box lunches.
Dave, Gerry & Patrick make it to Vernal Falls at 9, Nevada Falls at 10, and Half Dome Summit at 11:30 (11:40 for Gerry). Climb is strenuous and steep. Last mile is stairs up the rock and then cables up sheer side of rock face for last 500 feet elevation gain. Cables are 3-4' apart in width with a wood 2x4 every 10'.

Big pile of gloves at base of cables. Use these to get grip on cables to not hurt hands when they slip. Cable stretch is very steep and hands and feet slip as you go from one 2x4 to the next. Rest at each 2x4. When people come down, you have to stay at one side so they can pass.

Once on top, views are spectacular in all directions. Yosemite Valley is spread out below with beautiful green meadows. We lay on our stomachs and peer over the edge down the 4,000' cliff face. There are about 15 people on the summit including Austrians and Germans. We start back down at 12:30 and reach the Happy Isles trail head at 3:40 PM. Wonderful experience, but very strenuous - 14 miles and 4,800' elevation gain. Beautiful clear, blue sky and hot weather.

We hit showers and have pizza for dinner. Boys do pool after their hike. We discover that Jennifer and Melanie arrived about 8 AM this morning, having driven all night after a wedding. They spent most of the day sleeping.

About 10 PM, Mark and Tom arrive having driven up today. We set them up in tent cabins for the night.

Day 3 - Monday, July 20, 1993

Up at 6:15. Pack up, have breakfast at the cafeteria at 7, and shoot for a 7:30 departure. Our cars are lined up in the parking lot as we await the Higashi group in final loading mode. A police ranger drives up, so our car caravan takes off, meandering through the rambling parking area as we try to elude the officer intent on giving us a ticket. We finally succeed and are anxious to make tracks when Jerry rushes up exasperated. "We're missing a kid," he yells. With their active group of eight, that is not hard to do. Miraculously, the missing one appears, and we're off at 8 AM, with an hour to cover the hour and a half drive to meet the rafting outfitters at 9, near Groveland.

With Dave in the lead, driving like his life depended on it, we sail along, pulling into the meeting point at 9 sharp. From then on, when we needed to make time, we knew Dave was our man.
The outfitters provide us with large plastic bags for our gear, and then canvas duffel bags to cover them. These bags contain

everything we'll need for a night on the river: tent, sleeping bag, clothes, etc. We hop into a rickety old bus and proceed down a perilous, one lane (at best), dirt road, slowly descending in forty five minutes down the five hundred foot canyon side to the Tuolumne River.

Three paddle rafts and three oar rafts await us. The head guide briefs us on safety and procedure, we don life jackets and helmets, grab paddles, and head to the six man rafts. Patrick and Jimmy volunteer to paddle with an oar raft. Each oar raft has a guide with oars and carries all our supplies for the trip. The Tuolumne is a remote river, and so we'll be out of touch with the outside world for the next two days. The rest of the group is six to a raft plus a guide.

No sooner do we start out then we are faced with the Class IV Rock Garden rapids. Jerry is not fully aware of the power of the rapids, and does not secure his feet like the rest of us. Out he flies on the first steep rapid. He almost takes Mark with him. Fortunately, or unfortunately, George manages to grab Jerry's foot as he goes over, and holds on to it. That succeeds in keeping Jerry near the raft, but also makes it impossible for him to get upright, so he trails along a ways, before yelling to George to let go. We finally pull him back in and he checks out his foot holds closely for future rapids. The water is COLD!!! We had debated wearing wetsuits, but the air is hot, so we opted not to, except for Jimmy and a couple others with spring suits.

We continue one thrilling rapid after another, pulling onto a beach about 1:30 for lunch. Guides go to town fixing lunch of meats, cheeses, fresh cut vegetables, fruits, cookies and lemonade

After lunch we are ready to tackle Class V Clavey Falls. This is a surprise. The brochure only mentioned Class IV on this trip. All are excited and scared. Now we know why we have helmets. The guides are very professional about this. They stop just before Clavey Falls and have us walk down to the rapids. From this vantage point, they brief us on how to run the rapid, what to expect, how to react to unforeseen events like getting thrown out of the raft, etc. Also, those who prefer not to run the rapid are allowed to walk past it. Karen and George wisely decide not to risk it. The rest return to the rafts reviewing in their minds the detailed instructions. The important thing is to keep focused and respond immediately to all instructions from the guide as we paddle through the wild, foamy torrent. Several rafts on the previous trip had tipped over. On we go. Amazingly enough, the guides had prepared us well. All three rafts go through like pros, without a casualty. Now we all feel invincible. The rest of the trip pales in comparison to this milestone of successfully negotiating a Class V rapid.

In late afternoon, we pull into a beautiful, secluded beach and set up camp. While we put up tents and sleeping gear, the guides open happy hour with soda, beers, wine, cheeses and crackers. All are thirsty and tired, but exhilarated. Nap time, football on the beach, swimming. Later a delicious dinner of grilled chicken, steak, broccoli, pasta salad, garlic bread, salad and brownies. Lots of sharing of stories, of the river, of our lives far away in the civilized (?) world. To bed early. Sleeping under the stars, with thousands of stars we rarely see back home, and the constant roar of the river at our feet.

Day 4 - Tuesday, July 21, 1993

Guides are up at 6, putting on the coffee and starting breakfast. A port-a-potty is set up back in the woods. A paddle set in a strategic place serves as the door. The user takes the paddle with him. So if the paddle is gone, you know the john is occupied and don't unexpectedly surprise someone.
Hearty breakfast of eggs filled with peppers, onions, mushrooms. Also, bacon, sausage, blueberry muffins, fruit and juice.

We break camp and pack up all our gear for the day of rafting to the end of the wilderness. While waiting for the river to rise, we hike to an old, abandoned mine shaft across the river. Built a hundred years ago by Chinese laborers during the gold rush, the shaft goes a hundred feet into the mountainside. We use head lanterns and step on the rail tracks leading into the shaft. Cool, damp and spooky.

Upon returning to the river, we discover Jerry Higashi sprawled out on the sand. He made an unusual motion tying his shoe and threw his back out. He is in considerable pain and his sons try to put it back in with only partial success. Since we have no contact with the outside world, the only way out is down the river. One of the oar rafts is rigged up so Jerry can lay down as we raft out. We proceed cautiously down the river. After a while, Jerry is feeling a little better, and rides sitting up on the cushioned back of the raft. It is fitting. He looks like an ancient monarch perched on his throne, as his subjects row him down the river.

The river is very late in coming up. The Hetch Hetchy Reservoir is the source upstream, and so we are dependent on it releasing enough water to make a good trip. We finally depart about noon and have a lot of river to cover. Several more Class IV rapids are run providing an exciting and enjoyable day. All along the narrow river canyon, the canyon walls reach immediately upward at a steep slope about five hundred feet. The golden hills the state is known for are dotted with green bushes and trees.

Late in the afternoon, the last of the rapids is run, and we paddle the final mile to a bridge where we take out. As we hike up from the river to the bridge, Jimmy, Melanie and Patrick get the urge and jump from the sixty foot bridge into the river. All are impressed and think they are crazy. Fortunately no one gets hurt. Beer and soda all around as we hop on the old white bus again. Spent and satisfied, we are too tired to worry about the harrowing drive to the top.

We reach our cars about 6:30 PM. Knowing we have to be at the Wawona Hotel to get dinner no later than 8:30, we put Dave in the lead again and are on our way at 7, trying once again to cover 2 hours' worth of some of the most scenic and winding mountain roads around, in an hour and a half. Obviously, Dave got us there for a meal of celebration. Showers later all around and to bed about

10:30. The Higashi group headed home directly from Groveland arriving back in early morning.

Day 5 - Wednesday - July 21, 1993

After a good night's sleep, we are up at 7 and on the road by quarter to eight. Breakfast is at our favored McDonalds in Oakhurst. On to Bakersfield for lunch at the In-N-Out at the Panama Street exit, and then home, reaching Gerry's about 2:30. Everyone seemed to have a great time and started dreaming of our next adventure.

Sixteenth Annual Death March

Location: Yosemite National Park -Vogelsang High Sierra Camp

Dates: July 8 - July 11, 1994

Participants: George and Tom Di Gaetano, Kevin Falconer, Gerry Herter, Karen Williams, Steve & Scott Williams and Dave Zaczyk.

Trail Notes:

Day 1 - Friday, July 8, 1994

Departed form Herter's at 8:21 AM, except for Steve who drove to Fresno on Wednesday, flew to Kansas City, and flew back Friday night to drive the rest of the way early Saturday morning. (Steve had an important medical consulting seminar in K.C.). Gerry and George drove. Pit stop at Bakersfield (California Street) at 10:55-11:15. Lunch at Fresno at 12:50-1:20. To Yosemite Valley at 3:30 and Tuolumne Meadows at 4:40 PM. Stop at Tuolumne Meadows Lodge High Sierra Camp - tent cabins, 4 beds per cabin. Dinner at camp at 6:30 - chicken, burgers, taco salad. To bed at 9:30 PM.

Day 2 - Saturday, July 9, 1994

Awoken at 5 AM by the sound of bears rummaging through stuff. Look out window but see none. Find out at six that it was Tom starting a fire in their tent stove. George, Tom, Scott and Kevin in one tent. Gerry, Karen and Dave in other. Hearty breakfast at 7. Eggs, French toast, ham, bacon, etc. Pack up and wait for Steve. He arrives at 8:45 having left Fresno 3 hours earlier. Gets quick breakfast. Head to Dog Lake Parking and pick up trail head. 6.8 miles to Vogelsang.

Depart at 9:40 AM. Scott and Kevin will camp out, so they have heavy packs. Everyone else will stay in tent cabins. Hike is beautiful, level at first, then a steep climb, then long, gentle incline across spacious meadow valley. One more steep climb the final mile into camp. Dave arrives at 12:40, with Steve and Gerry 10 minutes later. Scott and Kevin arrive at campground at 1 and set up camp. George comes in at 2:30 and Karen at 3.

Camp is beautiful setting at 10,181 feet altitude, surrounded by 11-12,000 foot mountains, with a stream flowing through it and several lakes nearby. Right near the tree line, so camp is among trees, with rocky slopes going up to the peaks. Friendly marmots frequent the camp. About a dozen tent cabins, each with 4 comfortable beds with warm blankets, comforters and a stove with wood.

We eat our box lunches in dining room/store and buy T-shirts. The rest lunch on the trail. The hike was a workout and the altitude took its toll. But all in all, a great hike with much scenic beauty. We rest most of the afternoon, reading john Grisham's latest novels (Client & Chamber).

Dinner at 6:30. Filet Mignon, zucchini, mashed potatoes, corn chowder, salad, bread, and apple crisp, coffee, tea and hot chocolate. Card games and reading. To bed at 8:30-9.

Day 3 - Sunday, July 10, 1994

Dave and Gerry don't sleep much. Altitude, overexertion, etc. Others do OK. Tom was sick last night after getting chill in stream, and missed supper. But he recovered later to win three rounds Spinner 10. Coffee at 7, breakfast at 7:30: cream of wheat, spinach & mushroom omelet, bacon, strawberry muffins.

Steve, George and boys go fishing and catch a few. Dave stays near camp and reads. Karen and Gerry head to Vogelsang Lake. Karen goes over pass. Gerry climbs to summit of Vogelsang Peak at 11,516 feet. No trail, so cross country up scary cliffs. Spectacular views of all parts of Yosemite, from Tuolumne Meadows, to Half Dome, with Merced Lake and many others in between. Hike takes four hours -9 to 1. Then lunch in dining room. Others wade in stream and sun. Mosquitoes a little pesky here this time of year.

About 40 people for dinner last night, although several cabins available. Tonight only 14 at dinner. Karen and Gerry to bed by 9, the rest a little later.

Day 4 - Monday, July 11, 1994

Karen and Gerry up at 5 AM and make fire. They pack up and head down the trail at 5:40 AM. Peaceful, downhill hike as the sun rises. No wildlife spotted until a single deer in the final half mile. Out at the trail head at 8:30. Then to Tuolumne Lodge for breakfast, cleanup and on the road home at 9:50. Three miles down the road, get caught for 20 minutes for road construction. Take the eastern route down the backside of the Sierras. Stop in Olancha at Ranch House Cafe for lunch and arrive home at 5 PM.

The rest stay in camp for breakfast at 7:30. They break camp at 8:25 after George and Tom have a head start leaving at 8. Dave bets Tom that Dave will catch up with him before the end of the hike. So they both race down the trail. Dave finally catches him within a mile of the entrance and is out by 10:30, including a lot of running. Steve and boys are out by 11. They shower and hit the road with a stop in Oakhurst for lunch.

George, Dave and Tom almost make it home down the eastern route, when George's car loses power, not long after the air-conditioning goes out. They end up needing a tow off of the freeway. They get a jump and limp along to Dave's house. On the way home from there, the car goes out again and George needs another tow, getting home very late. I t turns out to be a bad alternator. Fortunately, everyone gets home safe and the breakdown didn't occur in the middle of nowhere.

Seventeenth Annual Death March

Location: Sequoia National Park -Bear Paw Meadow High Sierra Camp

Dates: July 8 - July 11, 1995

Participants: Carl Greenwood, George and Tom Di Gaetano, Gerry Herter, Bernie Jeltema, Don Silber, Karen Williams, Steve & Scott Williams, Simon, Steve and Bryan .

Trail Notes:

Day 1 - Saturday, July 8, 1995

Carl picked up Gerry and Karen at 7:15 AM, then Bernie at 7:30. Met up with George & Tommie at the Sheraton Anaheim. Then on up the I-5, stopping in Visalia at In-N-Out Burger for lunch at 11:46. On to Sequoia at 12:30, arriving in Giant Forest Village at 2:00 PM. Checked in the 6 rustic cabins, then did the Congress Trail in 45 minutes. Dinner at the Lodge Dining Room at 5:45. Steve and his group arrived at 6:30. Steve overcame endless adversities of selling

his old home and moving into his new one. Only half moved before leaving. The main move left up to Sherry and the girls, today. Also, last night, Steve's grandmother fell and broke her hip, with surgery this morning. Steve and group dine at cafeteria, then to ranger show. Bears make an appearance at dinner. Showers and to bed at 9 PM
.

Day 2 - Sunday, July 9, 1995

Up at 5:30. Clean up and breakfast at 6:30, plus pick up box lunches. Drive to trailhead and start out at 7:55 AM on 11.3 mile hike, from 6,500' to 7,800'. Some rain this morning at 5:30 and 6:00. Fortunately, it stopped before hike. Temperature pleasant. Shorts and T-shirts. Hike provides spectacular views, sunny with some clouds. Hike together for awhile, then Carl and Gerry go ahead with Steve's group next, George and Tom, Bernie and Karen.

Lots of snow in mountains, but very little on the trail, one little spot. Lots of water in the streams. Cross several little ones, then the first big one, Panther Creek. While scouting out the beat place to cross, Gerry starts sliding down a boulder, loses control and goes face first into the rushing creek. He is soaked head to foot with ice water. Luckily, only a few minor cuts and scratches, but his canteen pops out and disappears. He picks himself up and continues to the other side. Carl, wisely, just walks through the water, getting only his feet wet. The others follow later, taking off their shoes and socks and crossing in tennis shoes.

Continue on and have to wade through Merhten Creek and one other before getting to Buck's Creek and the bridge. Water is rushing under the bridge. By the time Karen and Bernie pass here a couple hours later, water is going over the top, about three feet higher. Wild flowers are in bloom, pink carpets, blue, yellow, etc. with birds and butterflies in abundance. The final mile is steep and tiring, but passes quickly. Then on to Bearpaw Meadows Camp. Carl and Gerry arrive at 1 PM, Steve's group at 1:30, Simon and Steve at 2, George and Tommy at 3:30, and Karen and Bernie at 4. All make it safely.

Carolyn and Paul are running the camp and are very friendly. Cool lemonade, brownies, coffee cake and wine refresh us. The view of the Great Western Divide from the porch of the dining room is beautiful and dramatic. Snow capped peaks over 13,000 feet and shear granite domes. Cloud formations change every few minutes. We all get warm, refreshing showers. The marmots are in residence. As each group arrives, they rest on the porch with refreshments and then hit the showers. Then some nap, play backgammon, chess, read novels and take in the natural beauty. Everyone marvels at how beautiful and scenic the hike has been, as the trail wound around the side of the mountain with a broad majestic valley, inspiring us as we go. The rushing waters of the creeks provided added adventure and challenge.

Dinner at 5:30: New York strip steaks, au gratin potatoes, corn, biscuits, salad, apple juice, blueberry and chocolate pie. Relax on the porch and watch the view of the mountains and snow as sun descends, shadows grow, and moon rises. Some play cards. To bed at 9:00.

Day 3 - Monday, July 10, 1995

Carl is up at 5:30. Others up at 6. Coffee ready. Breakfast at 7. Deer in camp. Scrambled eggs, sausage, pancakes, blueberries, orange juice, coffee and granola. Carl, Bernie & Gerry hike to Hamilton Lakes and beyond. More spectacular side of the mountain trail and scenery. Four mile hike to lake. Carl and Gerry go two miles further up toward Kahweh Gap, about 9,000 feet. Lunch at lake and head back. Trout in lake (golden). Carl steps in deep crossing stream and gets shorts and camera wet. Leave for Hamilton Lakes at 8. There at 10. Lunch at 11:30. Return at noon. Back at 2. Shower, nap and read.

Karen and George stay in camp and relax, read, while Tommy chops wood. Steve's group hikes over the hill trail for a couple miles. Then read and play cards. Dinner at 5:30. Joanie and Mike are our hosts today. Card games, watch the sunset and moon rise. To bed at 8:30-9:00.

Day 4 - Tuesday, July 11, 1995

Up at 5:30. Coffee and pack. Breakfast at 7:00. Egg soufflé, sausages, biscuits, hash browns, peaches and orange juice. George and Tommy on trail at 7:15, Karen, Gerry, Carl at 7:25, others at 7:45? Pleasant hike out, cool at first, creeks a little lower. Scott and Bryan out at 11:15. Steve and Simon out at 11:30. Jerry and Carl out at 11:40. Karen at 11:45. Steve and Don at 11:50. George and Tommy at 12:20. Bernie at 12:30.

All agreed this was one of the prettiest and most enjoyable death marches!

Eighteenth Annual Death March

Location: Grand Canyon –Phantom Ranch

Dates: August 23-27, 1996

Participants: Sheila Ashrafi, Carl Greenwood, George, Kay, Tommy and Gene DiGaetano, Gerry and Loretta Herter, Marley Jue, Don Silber, Karen Williams, Steve and Scott Williams and Glen.

Trail Notes:

Day 1 - Friday, August 23, 1996

Steve's group departed at 6:00 AM from San Juan Capistrano. The rest met at Chapman Medical Center and departed at 7:45. Lunch in Needles at 11:30. Scattered rain along the way. Steve arrived at the Grand Canyon at 3:30 followed by the rest at 4:30. Check-in at the El Tovar Hotel. Loretta will stay there the whole four nights and serve as the base camp. Later on, Kay and Gene decide the El Tovar looks pretty good and decide to stay the four nights also. Part of group has dinner at the El Tovar Dining Room and the rest at the cafeteria. To bed at 10.

Canyon is awe inspiring as always. Overcast so not too hot. Cools off in the evening. Nice breeze. El Tovar employees are helpful in straightening out our reservations.

Day 2 - Saturday, August 24, 1996

Up at 5:00 AM. Ready for 6 A M Breakfast at ice cream fountain: coffee, fruit, juice and muffins. Catch shuttle ($3) at Bright Angel Lodge at 6:30 to ride over to Kaibab Trail Head. Because of heat, trail is closed at 7, so need to start down by then. After a group photo, we are on the trail at 7:05. Beautiful, sunny day. Views of canyon are increasingly spectacular with changing hues of red, purple, brown, yellow and green. Scott takes off in the lead followed by Carl and Gerry, Steve, Don , Glen and Karen, George and Tommy, with Marley and Sheila bringing up the rear. This is Sheila's first hiking experience, so she's a little worried.

We start out with a cool breeze that warms up before long. Since we are early, there are small stretches of shade as we go from one side of the trail to the other. We descend from 6,800' to 2,600.' Scott is first to arrive at Phantom Ranch at about 9:45, followed by Carl and Gerry at 10, Steve's group at 10:15, Karen at 10:30, George and Tommy at 10:45, and finally Marley and Sheila at 11:30. Sheila looks pretty pooped out, as do all when they arrive.

We have a cabin with bunk beds for 10, a john and air conditioning! The three ladies are in the female dorm. Stream behind cabin flows cool and fast. We soak our feet for a while. Office/store/dining room is air conditioned as well, with four long tables for 12. Drinks, snacks, souvenirs and supplies are available. We check in, have cold drinks and relax. Read, nap and play cards. Dinner at 6:30 - stew, salad, cornbread, chocolate cake, ice tea and coffee - great.
Ranch is located a short distance from the Colorado River, up a side canyon. An oasis with trees and plants. Friendly rangers and staff. Deer and chipmunks at rim. Lizards and squirrels below.

Day 3 - Sunday, August 25, 1996

Up at 6. Breakfast at 6:30: scrambled eggs, bacon, peaches, pancakes, orange juice and coffee - great. Relax and chat for a while. Then all but George and Sheila hike up the Clear Creek Trail to Phantom Point for view of ranch 1,000 feet below, and a little further to a spectacular viewpoint overlooking the Colorado River both up and down stream. Kaibab Trail across the way. We marvel at its steep rugged appearance and that we had covered it yesterday.

Lunch in the shade of a ledge, while absorbing the grandeur of the inner canyon, river and rim above. Beautiful, sunny day, in the 80's in the morning, over 100 at noon. Return to camp and cool off in dining room with cold drinks, read, play cards and nap. Afternoon by the creek (Bright Angel) just behind the cabin. Don trunks and swim in cool, refreshing water, a couple feet deep with little trout nipping at the toes. More reading and naps. Showers. Carl finds a scorpion in the men's shower. A little guy, he looks pretty soggy by the time I get there.
Ranger talk at 4. Knowledgeable local native answers questions about canyon. Several months ago, a controlled flood out of Glen Canyon Dam was done to flush out the river and re-establish the natural sand bars and inlets the fish use for spawning. It appears to have worked. They will watch for five years and then decide if needed again. The Phantom Ranch pool, used by Gerry in 1962, was closed in 1970, because of overuse and pollution by increasing number of hikers (over 1,000 a day before controls were put in place). Stew dinner again at 6:30.

Day 4 - Monday, August 26, 1996

Up at 4:30 AM! Breakfast at 5. On the trail at 5:25 AM. It is just barely light out. The temperature is pleasant and the sky is clear. Scott takes the lead again, followed by Carl, Gerry and Steve, Don and Glen, Karen, George and Tommy , Sheila and Marley. We head to the river and then up the Bright Angel Trail. The hike to Indian

Gardens is pleasant. Mostly in the shade. Trail is increasingly more populated the further we go. We are lucky with the weather. Not so hot and lots of shade since we left early. Carl, Gerry and Steve arrive at Indian Gardens about 7:30.

Views are increasingly spectacular as we climb. Somewhat level stretches intermixed with steep switchbacks. Scott is first one out at the top at about 9:20 - 3 hours and 50 minutes! A record. Carl, Gerry and Steve top out at 10:40 - 5-1/4 hours - a record for us. Don and Glen arrive at about 11:00, Karen at 12:15, Tommy, Sheila and Marley about 2:15, and George at 2:30. Not bad for the whole group. Family of deer, parents and two fawns, spotted along the way. All head to the ice cream fountain (humans, that is) for root beer floats at the top. Then showers and lunch. Kay, Gene and Loretta are waiting for our arrival. They have had a pleasant two days on top, Kay and Gene sightseeing, Loretta working on a book.

All are exhilarated by the trip and the accomplishment. Tired but satisfied. Dinner at the El Tovar and Bright Angel. Enjoyed meeting folks of many nationalities at Phantom Ranch as well as at the rim, especially English, German and French. Also, many friendly skunks on the rim by the El Tovar. We are entertained that last night as a curious skunk wanders into the lobby, sending worried guests in all directions before being shooed out by the staff.

Nineteenth Annual Death March

Location: Rogue River/North Umpqua River Kayaking Trip

Dates: July 31-August 3, 1997

Participants: Curtis Campbell, Jeff (Curtis' friend), Gerry and Loretta Herter, Jeff, Mary & Ryan Hipshman, Bernie & Sally Jeltema, Don & June Silber, Steve & Roz Silber, Karen Williams, Steve, Sherry, Scott, Laurie, Monica and Megan Williams, Patty and Madison Woolworth and niece.

Trail Notes:

Day 1 - Thursday, July 31, 1997

Participants left at different dates and times, and by various means. Bernie & Sally left Saturday and went via Idaho. Steve Williams's group left Monday and drove by Monterey and Sacramento. Gerry, Loretta and Karen left Tuesday night and drove through San Francisco. The Silber's left Wednesday and drove by Ukiah. The

Hipshman's left Wednesday night, flying to Medford, as did Curtis and Jeff on Thursday. Patty and family flew to Redding and drove from there.

All arrived at Morrison's Rogue River Lodge on Thursday afternoon. Morrison's is a rustic lodge with cabins in a beautiful wooded setting right on the Rogue River, outside of Merlin, Oregon. Folks relax and play cards, watching jet boats and rafters pass by on the river. George DiGaetano, a veteran Death Marcher, missed this year due to his wife's high school reunion. The lodge is quaint and comfortable, and the folks are friendly. Dinner at 7:30 is a gourmet feast of Salmon, roast pork, onion soup, salad, heavenly orange glazed rolls, and blackberry cobbler alamode. Delicious! We all go to bed early, by 9 or 10, to rest up for the adventure tomorrow.

Day 2-Friday, August 1, 1997

Rafters are up for breakfast at 7:45 AM . Non-rafters get to sleep in 'til 9. Hearty breakfast of eggs, pancakes, bacon, sausage, potatoes, coffee, fruit, juice and muffins. There are 9 kayakers (Gerry, Jeff, Steve, Bernie, Curtis, Jeff, Dan, Scott and Steve) and 7 rafters (Patty, Madison, niece, Sally, Karen, Laurie and Monica) today for the Rogue River. This is a Class 2 section, so all can learn how to use the kayaks.

We depart the lodge at 8:30, picked up by the Orange Torpedo Trips in a van. We stop at their office in Merlin and get outfitted for life jackets. Then a short drive to the Rogue River put in. The kayaks are the one-man, orange, inflatable types. The rafters are on two rafts, each with a guide, plus 2 guides in kayaks. After instructions, we start out on a calm section of the river. When we hit our first Class 2 rapids, Bernie has the distinction of being the first to pop out of his kayak and into the river. (In fairness to Bernie, at the end of the day, the guide said his paddling in the afternoon was the best). As we go, we learn and practice the fair art of the feather stroke, hitting the waves head on, and if that is not possible, then leaning into the wave to avoid being tossed out.

We go through a number of tame rapids (Class 2) and long stretches of calm before stopping for a lunch of burgers, chicken and fixings, at Indian Mary Park. Then more easy rapids, good for beginning kayakers to hone their skills on. Scenery is beautiful with green forested banks and rock outcroppings, especially as we go through Hellgate Canyon and past Morrison's. Sherry, Mary, June, Ryan and Megan are on the beach as we paddle by and wave from afar. We finish rafting about four o'clock, and the guide pronounces us all ready to tackle colder, swifter, Class 3 North Umpqua River tomorrow. After a long discussion as to whether some would rather go in a paddle raft than a kayak, all nine finally agree to kayak, with three of the girls - Karen, Laurie and Monica - going on an oared raft.

Back at Morrison's at 4:30 with time to hike, nap and happy hour until dinner. Another gourmet delight - beef tenderloin, cucumber soup, salad and Swiss walnut torte. Excellent! The movie for tonight is "The River Wild," partly filmed on the Rogue. All are in bed early to rest up for tomorrow.

Day 3 - Saturday, August 2, 1997

The rafters are up early to catch the van at 6:15. Bernie decides to stay back today and turns in his gear. Box breakfasts are provided, with Egg McMuffin, juice, muffin and orange. At the office, we are fitted for wetsuits and wind breakers. Than a two hour ride north past Roseburg, and to the North Umpqua put-in. Before launching, the guide tells us that yesterday, they were easy going and fun, but today they will be serious, because the river is more treacherous. We are all real happy to hear that!

We start out in the cold, swift river, and, after a Class 2 warm-up, we hit our first Class 3 at Right Creek, where 12 of 13 rafters go flying into the water. Jeff Hipshman is the only one to get through it in his kayak. His prestige is short lived though, as he goes in the river on the next Class 3. After this inauspicious start, all are dreading what the day will be like. As it turns out. Right Creek was the toughest rapid of the trip and practically a Class 4. Still, the guides said they had never had so many rafters go in the river at one time. We all do much better on the remaining four Class 3 rapids. Most go in the water a second and some a third time. But no one gets hurt. The Class 4 rapid looks too tough, so the guides have us portage around it.

The Umpqua is quite scenic and remote. We hardly see any other rafters, unlike the Rogue where we encountered a lot of rafters. We see deer on the way and numerous birds, like osprey, herons and hawks. By lunch time at one o'clock, we are all pretty tired. Kayaking is hard work. Fortunately, the rapids after lunch are not too bad or long. We finish up at 3:30, tired, but pleased that we made it through.

Back to Merlin (two hour ride) and Morrison's. Our final dinner is halibut and pork tenderloin with blueberry cheesecake. We all share rafting stories on this final night. All had a great time.

Day 4 - Sunday, August 3, 1997

All head their separate ways, some home today, others to vacation more.

Twentieth Annual Death March

Location: Kalalau Trail, Kauai, Hawaii

Dates: August 15-August 19, 1998

Participants: George & Tommy DiGaetano, Carl Greenwood, Gerry Herter, Jeff Hipshman, Steve & Scott Williams, and Larry Swartz. Also along: Kay & Gene DiGaetano, Mary & Ryan Hipshman, Sherry, Laurie & Monica Williams, Diane & Aaron Swartz.

Trail Notes:

Day 1 - Saturday, August 15, 1998

Hipshman's. Swartz's and Williams' leave together, as well as Gerry Herter on a different airline, departing LAX at 8:30-9:00 AM, arriving in Honolulu about noon and Kauai about 1:30, where all rent cars. All but Gerry head to the picturesque Princeville Resort on the side of the bluff overlooking Hanalei Bay. Gerry proceeds to the Hanalei Colony Resort, on the far side of the bay, on the beach in sleepy Haena. Beautiful, sunny day, with green covered formations rising from the ocean. Check in, buy groceries & supplies, relax, explore and take in the beauty of the area. Gorgeous sunset over the bay. About 9 PM it pours rain for about an hour.

Day 2 – Sunday, August 16, 1998

Carl and the DiGaetano's come in today. Carl staying with Gerry, and George & family at south end of the island. Those arriving Saturday enjoy Sunday swimming, snorkeling, sunning and resting up for the hike. Carl arrives at 4:30 PM.

The 20th Annual Death March Celebration Dinner is scheduled for 7 PM at Café Hanalei in the Princeville Resort. Carl, Gerry, George & family arrive a few minutes early and proceed to Steve's room to check out. Beautiful plush furnishings and an ocean view on the 10th floor with adjoining rooms. George is staying at a client's condo in Kapaa, about 20 miles from Princeville.

Café Hanalei is on a patio overlooking Hanalei Bay, and we take in a gorgeous Hawaiian sunset. Dinner is excellent, though pricey, a far cry from the Sportsman's Cafe in Lone Pine, California, from Death Marches of old. There are 17 of us in all at dinner. We pass out the trail permits, last year's trail notes, as well as the special premium quality 20th Death March commemorative shirts, designed and produced by Steve's sister. We reminisce over the past 20 years. Steve remarks that he was not much older than his son, Scott, when he did his first Death March (24 vs. 20). We make arrangements for car pooling to the trail head tomorrow, then bid our goodnights early, so all can get a good rest.

Day 3 – Monday, August 17, 1998

Up at 6 AM. Breakfast and load up accompanied by an inspiring soft hued sunrise over the bay. Steve picks up Carl & Gerry, whose condo is just 2-1/2 miles from the trailhead, at 8:00 AM. We meet the others at Ke'e Beach by the trailhead at 8:15 AM. After the traditional group picture, we are on the trail at 8:33 AM. Sherry & Monica, Mary & Ryan, and Diane & Aaron join the hikers for the first 2 mile stretch to Hanakapiai Beach. The morning is pleasant, already some swimmers at Ke'e Beach and other hikers. The trail starts out steeply uphill, with rocks & slippery mud. After a few hundred yards, it levels off a bit and provides the first ocean vista and view of Ke'e Beach below. More uphill through jungle-like foliage for the first mile. Then Hanakapiai Beach comes into view far below and we start the descent. A beautiful white sand beach, but to get there requires negotiating across a river strewn with large boulders. A little tricky, but all make it and take in the scenic beach with its pounding surf. Some adventurous types swim, though it is not recommended. 1-1/4 hours to here.

Here the wives and children turn back, and the 8 hikers proceed (Gerry, Carl, Jeff, Larry, Steve, Scott, George & Tommy). All complain about their heavy packs, though as usual George's is the heaviest. Scott heads out in front, followed by Gerry, Carl & Steve, then Jeff & Larry, with George & Tommy picking up the rear. Carl doesn't seem to have his old energy and starts to fall behind.

The hike consists of crossing over five valleys and corresponding mountain outreaches that extend to the sea. The views of the steep, dramatic green-covered sheer mountains become increasingly majestic and hauntingly beautiful. As the angle of the sun changes, new hues and shadows are revealed. They contrast with the shimmering turquoise and deep blue of the sea far below. The height of the trail ranges from 0' to 800.'

After six miles, we reach the Hanaloa Valley with the rushing sound of a waterfall nearby. Also a picnic table and outhouse. Steve and I break for lunch. I have a half a sandwich and a Pepsi. Along here, Jeff and Larry catch up with us. They left Carl at about the four mile mark. He was turning back. Carl has just recovered from a stubborn respiratory virus that has hampered him for a couple months.

Apparently his lungs are not back to 100% and he doesn't have his normal stamina.

The four of us proceed. As the scenery becomes more magnificent, the trail gets dicier and in spots scary. Generally, the trail is good, but narrow and overgrown in places. Where the vegetation is lush, if you step a little off the trail into the vegetation next to it on the ocean side, your foot would slide down the side, as there was nothing below the vegetation. We all did this a few times, which was unnerving. Steve in the most extreme incident slid down all the way to his shoulders, holding on to a plant trunk at the last minute. I ran over and grabbed his arm, but he managed to gain control and pull himself up. I also had a scare when we found a few big rocks to sit on at an overlook to rest a minute. As I sat, the weight of my pack tipped my balance and I started to fall back. As I gave a yelp, Steve reached out and pulled me back into balance.

While the first half of the trail was lush jungle, with all sorts of leafy vegetation, guava, nuts, and in spots extremely muddy, with numerous streams and a few little waterfalls, the second half became arid and dry. While still having some vegetation, there were arid sections like a desert or the Grand Canyon, While traversing one such section of reddish gravel covered mountainside, the trail got extremely narrow with a drop-off seemingly almost straight down for 800' to the sea. While it was reasonably negotiable as long as you concentrated and watched your footing, we all found it a little scary, nonetheless.

Glad to be past that section and one more cliffhanger like it, we glimpsed our first view of the expansively spectacular Kalalau Valley. Here at about 9 miles a sign welcomed us to this sacred land, requesting our respect and reverence for this special place. We started our descent down a steep red gravel covered slope, with the inviting Kalalau Beach below. Along the way through the day, clouds and sun alternated, with a few minimal showers that refreshed us from the oppressively hot sun and muggy air. The peaceful stillness of the Na Pali coast was often broken by the din of sightseeing helicopters flying over this most popular spot.

We reach the beach at 4:30 PM, exhausted after 7 hours and 50 minutes on the trail. We all collapse on the sand. Scott is there waiting for us having arrived 1-1/2 hours before. The sand is soft and comforting. We remove our boots and cool our feet in the pounding surf. Kalalau is a huge beach, several hundred yards deep and a half mile long. Only a handful of people are in sight. A couple kayakers are down the beach.

At the far end is a waterfall. After resting a long while, we walk down the beach and fill the water bottles and treat them with tablets. Then back down the beach to a camping area just behind the beach. We set up camp, Steve & Scott with a tube tent, Gerry with a tube tent, and Jeff & Larry with a tarp given to them by Carl when he turned back. Jeff had lost his tent along the way and hadn't noticed it. There are caves in back of the camp, taken by others.

An exotic looking character from Morocco whose name is Tariq stops by our camp to talk and warns us of the hard rains here and that there are more caves nearby he will show to us. We look but decide to stay put. Tariq shares a tent nearby with a somewhat heavyset woman we notice wearing only a fanny pack. He says she likes to go naked. He wears a brightly colored sarong-like towel around his waist. He has been here a week and expects to be here a few more days while an infection on his foot heals. We give him some Neosporin for it. Tariq has been in the states about ten years and had an import business which he sold.

We blow up our air mattresses which takes forever, munch on trail mix, power bars, and the like, and are in bed before dark at 7 PM, too tired to watch the sunset. Bugs are not much bother, but we use repellent anyway.

Day 4 - Tuesday, August 18

Up at 4 AM. Steve & Jeff had told the wives to pick us up at the trailhead at 11 AM. We now realize that is unrealistic, even leaving real early. We hesitate to start out in the dark. At 5:45 AM, camp is broken, the first gray of dawn brings a little light from the blackness, so Scott is sent ahead to meet the wives and let them know we will be late. The rest of us leave a few minutes later about 5:50 AM. The quiet solitude of Kalalau surrounds us as we hike along the ocean front while the day slowly begins. By the time we start to climb, daylight brightens our way and we cover the first two miles in an hour.

We are refreshed and ready to move out quickly, despite sore shoulders and blistered feet that we bandages up before starting out. Unfortunately, our pace slows down quickly as heat, humidity, steep slope climbing and hike wearied bodies take their toll. We worry about Carl, George & Tommy who we haven't seen since early yesterday. We hope George did not try to traverse the difficult portion of the trail late in the day.

The hike out gets increasingly excruciating, hot, tiring dry and slow. We watch as far below on the ocean, the kayakers we saw in camp pass by on their way back, looking like they are making much better time than we are. Again the valleys and mountains of Na Pali share their natural beauty with us, though our enjoyment is tempered by the weariness in our eyes. Up and back we pass a group of black, brown and white goats who complain and scurry away as we approach. Also, a large white heron is spotted in the valley below.

After a long time, we reach Hanaloa Valley and take a break. Water supplies are replenished and treated in a nearby stream. Steve lost a water bottle while crossing a stream. One stream was tricky with rushing water and wet slippery rocks, so we removed our shoes to get across.

After Hanaloa, Jeff & Larry moved out ahead, with Steve & Gerry behind. Climbing up each of the 5 mountains was bone & muscle wrenching, intensified by the blazing sun. After each climb, there was a level portion going around the mountain, which enabled the muscles to recuperate. Then a downward stretch, while not as strenuous, was hard on the knees & toes.

Steve & Gerry reach Hanakapiai Beach about 12:15 PM and see Jeff & Larry crossing the river rocks. After Steve & Gerry cross, Gerry moves on ahead while Steve rests awhile and talks to other hikers.

The final two miles are not as easy as I remembered yesterday, and the sun & heat are worse than ever. One mile from the trailhead, Gerry meets George. George & Tommy made it 6 miles to Hanaloa Valley and camped there. George is hiking out.

After as a tortuous hike, we finally make it back to the trailhead. Scott was amazing, getting out at 11:00 AM, 5-1/4 hours. Jeff & Larry are out about 2 PM, Gerry 2:30 PM, George 2:45 PM, and Steve 3:15 PM. All are safe and sound, but physically and mentally exhausted. The wives and kids are all there waiting for us and worrying. Carl has been at the trailhead since 11:00 AM. He brought a cooler of drinks and a book. While hiking out yesterday, Carl got caught in heavy showers and got soaked. It rained hard for four hours. Those who hiked in, missed all the heavy rain.

Our legs and feet are caked with red mud and wet. Our shirts are soaked in sweat. We are each greeted with cheers as we reach the trailhead. All are glad to have made this once in a lifetime adventure, and all are very tired and sore. After a long rest at the trailhead with cold drinks and beach showers, we say our farewells, with Steve, Jeff, Larry & families heading south to Poipu Beach and the Hyatt Regency for a few days, George back to Kapaa for the rest of the week, and Gerry & Carl to return to California tomorrow.

End note: Flying out of Honolulu on Wednesday, Carl's flight is cancelled so his return home is delayed.

Twenty-first Annual Death March

Location: Lassen Volcanic National Park

Dates: July 30-August 1, 1999

Participants: Gerry Herter, Steve, Sherry, Monica, Megan and Esther Williams, Jeff, Mary and Ryan Williams, George, Kay, Tommy and Gene DiGaetano, Larry, Diane and Aaron Swartz.

Trail Notes:

Day 1 – Friday, July 30, 1999

All participants left home a day or two earlier and spent the night before as follows: Gerry flew to Reno; Steve drove to Chico; Jeff and Larry flew to Redding; George drove to Red Bluff.

All drove in to Drakesbad Guest Ranch in the southern part of Lassen Volcanic National Park. Steve arrived at 11, Gerry at 11:15, George at noon, and Jeff & Larry at 1:30. Drive from Reno takes 2-3/4 hours. Sunny drive through meadows & low mountains, through

Susanville & Chester. 17 miles from Chester, the last 3 miles are rough dirt & rock.

Drakesbad registration in dining hall. Ed & Billie Fiebiger are the hosts. Separate lodge building with 6 rooms on 2nd floor & lounge on first with fireplace & soft chairs & couch. Pictures, books, nature exhibits & t-shirts & goodies for sale.

Lunch at ranch consisting of buffet of salads & sandwiches & cookies. Our group is at one long table.

After lunch we hike to Devil's Kitchen – 3.2 miles round trip. Across green meadow, up into the forest. Devil's Kitchen consists of several large steam vents, bubbling mud pots and boiling stream. Very unusual & awe inspiring. Lassen is along a line of volcanos.

After hike, we swim in pool – fed by hot springs. It is warm like a bathtub. Refreshing. Then showers by the pool.

Dinner at 6. Kitchen crew has one of the kids ring the dinner bell. We are all at the same table. Dinner consists of Mahi Mahi with pineapple salsa, mixed vegetables, arroz (pasta that looks like rice), salad, & vanilla ice cream with caramel sauce. Wine & other drinks & coffee.

After dinner – horseshoes, ping pong, marshmallows & s'mores around the campfire by the lodge, scary stories for the kids, "farfel" & other dice games in the lodge. To bed at 10.

Day 2 – Saturday, July 31

Up at 6:30 am. Breakfast at 7:30. Coffee is ready earlier outside of dining room. Breakfast of buffet fruits, toast, bagels, muffins, cereal, yogurt, oatmeal, juice & then hot entrée of quiche with heated cheese & coffee.

After breakfast, pick up sack lunches & prepare for hike. Kids are going to take a 45 minute horseback ride with moms, then hike to Boiling Springs Lake & terminal Geyser.

Rooms in Lodge are Spartan with double bed, some with a second single bed, chair, dresser, hanger rack, shelves, two windows, light wood finished walls, bathroom with sink & commode.

Gerry, Jeff, Larry, Steve, Monica, Tommy & George depart at 9:00 in George's van for Lassen Peak. On the way, we spot a short cut, which after an hour plus on a dirt road, we discover we can't find our way. We turn back & go the normal way, finally arriving at the trailhead at 11:55. We start up the steep, stark trail consisting of cinders & ash. Elevation 8,500. Soon Larry & Jeff pull out ahead, followed by Tommy & Gerry, Steve & Monica, with George pulling up the rear.

Beautiful sunny day with bright blue sky. Gray mountain with large patches of snow & intermittent trees that gradually disappear. Lots of people on the trail. Walk for a while with family from Ulm, Germany. Spectacular vistas all around as Mt. Lassen rises above all other nearby mountains. Tough, strenuous hike, steep & high altitude makes it tough.

Jeff & Larry make summit at 1:15, Gerry & Tommy at 1:25, Steve & Monica at 1:35. Windy at top. We rest & have our lunch. Views are awesome, with Mt. Shasta in the distance.

We head down, Jeff & Larry at 2:00, rest at 2:15, race down getting out at 3 pm. On the way back we stop in Chester for A & W Root Beer floats & arrive back at camp at 5.

Head for the showers & then dinner at 6. Prime rib, artichokes, mashed potatoes, salad & strawberry cheesecake for dessert. Horseshoes & sitting by the campfire in the evening. To bed at 10 pm.

Day 3 – Sunday, August 1.

Up at 6 am. Gerry, Jeff& Larry take an early morning hike to
Boiling Springs Lake (.9 mi). We make a wrong turn & go an extra
mile. The lake is spectacular. Steam rising intensely from milky
surface about 300 yards across. Along edge, mud pots are bubbling
in places. The path circles the lake. On the far side, strong sound of
the hot spring bubbling as it enters the lake. At various spots,
bubbles percolate in the lake. Getting close to a mud pot, Gerry's hat
gets splattered with an exceptionally large burst. We step back a
little. Areas of red & beige barren spots where former or intermittent
vents or mud pots or springs have been. The water temperature per
the sign is only 125° F.

We get back to the ranch just in time for breakfast at 7:30. French
toast and sausage with some blueberries & blackberries along with
the usual buffet items.

After breakfast, we say our farewells, pay our bills and depart. A
card on our breakfast table thanks us for our stay, welcomes us back
next year, and wishes us a safe journey home. Ed & Billie, our hosts
have shown us a pleasant, enjoyable time. Ed is from Garmisch-
Partenkirchen, Germany & Billie from Bern, Switzerland. In the US
40 years, they spend the winters at Lake Tahoe working there – ski
instructors.

Jeff & Larry head back to Redding to catch a flight to San Francisco
for a stay at the St. Francis. Steve & Sherry are heading to Mammoth
for a few days. George & Kay are heading to Reno/Tahoe for a few
days. Gerry heads to Reno for a flight home.

All had a great time, making this a hard Death March to top next
year.

Twenty-second Annual Death March

Location: May Lake High Sierra Camp -Yosemite National Park

Dates: August 26-August 29, 2000

Participants: Gerry Herter, Steve and Monica Williams, Jeff and Ryan Williams, George, Tommy and Gene DiGaetano, Carl Greenwood, Curtis Williams, Patty and Madison Woolworth.

Trail Notes:

Day 1 – Saturday, August 26, 2000

Gerry, Carl, Curtis, Steve & Monica, George & boys depart at 6:30 AM. Patty & Madison departed on Friday and overnighted in Fresno. Jeff & Ryan departed at 4:40 AM on Sunday.

Picked up coffee & bagels at Starbucks and headed out. One stop for gas in Fresno, then lunch at Burger King in Oakhurst. Beautiful, sunny day; 80's at Yosemite.

Arrived at Yosemite Valley at 12:30 PM. Checked into motel units at Curry Village. Cancelled two tent cabins and ten wilderness permits. Two double beds in room, so Curtis volunteers to sleep on cot with air mattress.

Over to Ahwahnee Hotel for a beer and to scope it out. $279 per night. Short hike to Happy Isles, 2 miles roundtrip. Patty arrived early and toured Valley.

Get keys at 4 PM, then back to Ahwahnee for a drink. Then to Mountain Room at Yosemite Lodge for steak dinner. Patty does buffet. Steve & George do pizza. Steve does ranger talk on Curry history. To bed at 9:45 PM.

Day 2 – Sunday, August 27

Up at 5:45 AM. Showers, then over to Coffee Corner at 6:30 AM for coffee and box lunches. Breakfast buffet at 7: AM. Cashier asks who was president in year we were born. Clever way to tell if we qualified for senior citizen discount.

We all gather after breakfast and are ready to leave at 8:30 AM. Caravan an hour to Tuolumne Meadows and May Lake trailhead. Group photo, then hit the trail at 9:50 AM. Easy uphill slope for 1.2 miles to May Lake. Beautiful sunny day again. A few clouds in the sky. Temperature in the 60's at departure. Soon in 70's. Carl leads way with Tommy. George, Gene & Patty in rear. Arrive at camp at 11:20 AM. Peaceful and quiet.

Steve, Gerry, Carl, Curtis, Monica, Madison and Tommy drop packs at 11:45 AM., take water and box lunches and head out for Mount Hoffman. Patty, George and Gene relax at camp. May Lake is beautiful and serene. Mount Hoffman rises steeply from its far shore.

Trail leads around left shore of lake, then starts climbing steeply. We are soon huffing with the high altitude. Was 4,000' in the Valley,

8,500' at trailhead, 9,000' at May Lake, and 10,850 at the summit of Mount Hoffman.

Trail is not well maintained, so is rocky, and goes off in several sub-trails. It gets increasingly tiring. Near the top, there is all rock and large boulders that have to be climbed over. At a couple spots, it gets downright scary, but we manage to pull ourselves up by finding handholds or footholds. Reach the summit at 12:45 PM. Spectacular views in all directions: Clouds Rest, back of Half Dome, top of Valley, and mountains in distance. Antenna and solar panels and small locked container (3x3x6).
.

Relax and have lunch on summit: turkey sandwich, orange, egg, cookies, apple juice, coke. Two other couples up there.

We're apprehensive about getting down scary parts. Turns out not to be so hard or scary. We go facing down on all fours at times. Hike down is much faster, easier on the lungs, but slippery (sand), so nerve wracking trying to avoid slipping.

Back at camp at 2 PM. Get cabins – 4 beds to a cabin, put on sheets, unpack and rest. Then showers. Steve with Gerry's group in a cabin. Jeff with George's group, and Ryan with the girls.

Read by the lake in relaxing afternoon sun. Youngsters, Jeff & George play cards in dining hall. Jeff & Ryan had arrived by time we returned from hike. Carl & Curtis bring out bottle of wine before dinner.

Dinner at 6:30 PM. Turkey, mashed potatoes, zucchini, soda bread, tomato soup, salad, apple cobbler and coffee. Very good. Carl fixes campfire. Getting chilly. We are impressed with group of hikers: one guy 79, one 78 still hiking after many years. To bed by 9:30 PM.

Day 3 – Monday, August 28

Up at 5:45 AM. Can't sleep anymore. Dress, then coffee at 7:00 AM. Beautiful sunny morning. Lake is like glass. Mirrors Mount Hoffman. Breakfast at 7:30: Omelet with cheese, pepper and tomato, potatoes, biscuits, cream of wheat & cold cereals, cantaloupe and coffee.

After breakfast all but George and Gene hike back to trailhead, hop in cars and drive a couple miles to Porcupine Creek trailhead.at 8:45 AM. We hike first three miles to Indian Rock arch. A little up and down, some in woods. Getting warm but not bad. Indian Rock is a white outcropping that sticks out above the forest. A dramatic view of Half Dome is had from the top and especially through the arch. We climb up to the arch. Precarious footing. Tommy gets way up on arch in a scary spot. Get some good pictures. A trio from England and Germany is on the arch when we get there.

At this point, Patty, Tom, Jeff and a reluctant Ryan turn back. The rest head on, inspired toward North Dome, two miles further. More up and down but not extreme. After hiking across the exposed white rock of the dome, we reach the top, and are rewarded with a spectacular view of Yosemite Valley. Half Dome is right in front of us, like you could almost touch it. Across the way, Glacier Point, El Capitan and Yosemite Valley below. We lunch over this awesome sight. All see this as a highlight.

Head back about 12:30 PM. Pleasant hike, hot in the exposed areas, but cooler in the woods. Back to trailhead at 2:30 PM. We decide to drive a few miles (15?) further to Tuolumne Meadows and the general store for ice cream, cold sodas and beer. Buy wine and chips for tonight. Thunder & lightening. It starts raining. We drive back and hike in rain back to May Lake. Of course, we left ponchos at camp, so get wet. Back at 3:45 PM. George & Gene hiked a little around the lake. Showers, then chips, salsa and wine in the tent while it rains.

Dinner at 6:30 PM. Chicken with tomato, penne pasta, broccoli, minestrone soup, salad, biscuits, peach cobbler and coffee. Good.

Go up on ridge after and watch sunset. Campfire Tommy builds is harder to start with wet wood. It has started strong and tall. Carl tries to adjust big logs and collapses the whole fire, putting it out. He rebuilds to teasing. Some guy plays harmonica. Ryan has marshmallows. To bed at 9:00 PM.

Day 4 – Tuesday, August 29

Up at 6:30 AM. Pack up. Breakfast at 7:30 AM: bacon, tortillas, salsa, guacamole, cheese, potatoes, oatmeal, grapes, oranges & coffee.

Break camp at 8:30 AM and hike out. Say our good-bye's at trail head and head home. All had a good time.

Twenty-third Annual Death March

Location: Channel Islands National Park

Dates: September 6-September 8, 2001

Participants: Gerry Herter, Steve and Scott Williams, George DiGaetano, Curtis Williams, Tom Ahling, Marc Richmond, Sheila Ashrafi. Dean Sugiyama, Margie, Brett & Tyler Andrews.

Trail Notes:

Day 1 – Thursday, September 6, 2001

Curtis picked up Gerry at noon, George at 12:30 PM, and headed north. Lunch at 2:00 PM at Sagebrush Cantina in Calabasas. Cajun chicken tacos ($9.95) and margaritas ($16).

Arrived at Santa Barbara at 4:00 PM and checked out boat. Parked on Stearns Wharf and walked into town looking for soap, for George who forgot his, and ATM for money. Meet Dan Dannis who will be on same boat.

Went to Longboard's on wharf for drinks. Steve, Marc and Tom arrived about 7 and we had dinner on 2nd floor outdoor patio. Shark, thresher, slaw, French fries. Others have swordfish, ousters, etc.

Over to boat at 8:00 PM and board. We are assigned the small bunks in center – 3 layers, upper, middle, lower – but the boat is not full, so we move into the larger bunks. The others arrive at 9:00 PM or so. There are 24 on the boat plus crew. Maggie asks where her "cabin" is. She and the boys get a bunk (upper, middle, lower). Andrea Moe is the National Park Service volunteer that will make the trip with us. We relax with beers and sodas and go to bed about 11:00 PM.

Day 2 – Friday, September 7, 2001

At 4:00 AM, the engines start and wake us up. Depart at 4:30 AM. Fairly smooth, but can hear engines, and waves hitting the side. Up at 7:00 AM. Shower. At 8:00 AM a pod of 6-7 blue whales is spotted. They are feeding, so come up sideways, mouth open to catch the food. Breakfast: eggs, bacon, potatoes, pancakes, juice, coffee, toast & bagels, and honeydew melon.

At San Miguel Island at 9:30. Go to island, 6 in a skiff. Hike up from beach about 2-1/2 miles, pass Cabrillo Monument, ranch site, ranger station, and Caliche Forest of petrified trees. Sheila gets soaked on beach landing of skiff. Naturalist gives us history and geology. Chumash Indians for 10,000 years 'til 1800. Through Coreopsis Forest, pink island buckwheat, sage. Snack on granola bars and apples, oranges.

Back to boat at 2:00 PM for lunch: pita sandwiches with turkey, corned beef, lettuce, onions, tomatoes, cheese, curry chicken salad, baked beans, chips, sodas, and chocolate pudding with whipped cream.

In afternoon, go around to point to see sea lion colonies on beach. Then go to other end to Point Bennett and see more harems of sea lions, elephant seals, etc. Also see gray whale. Also pass little island – rock – bird sanctuary – brown pelicans, puffins, etc.

Showers. Then have dinner: tri tip steak, mashed potatoes, mushrooms, salad, warm bread, cherry, apple & pumpkin pie ala mode. Also fresh halibut. Late afternoon, Brett (or Tyler) fishes off the boat and catches a 20 pound halibut – white on one side, bottom colors on other. It took him awhile to bring it in. Captain Dan hooks it and brings into boat. Then he cleans and filets it and barbeques for dinner. Delicious.

After dinner (7:30 PM), boat takes off and goes to Santa Rosa Island. We go to bed about 9:30 PM. Boat arrives later – about 2 hours (9:30-10:00 PM).

Day 3 – Saturday, September 8

Up at 6:30 AM. Breakfast: French toast, Canadian bacon, eggs, potatoes, melon, juice and coffee.

Then boat moves to pier and we disembark for five mile hike along coast. Area is restricted (until 2011?) because of big game hunters – elk, deer. We spot five elk on hillside in distance. See Chumash Indian midden (rubbish heap) filled with shells in layers. Pass Torrey Pine forest. Only area outside of San Diego for this species. Island was once part of that area. See tracks of deer and skunk. At start of trail is ranch. See quail. On bluff above ocean, see orange star fish in tide pool below near a midden.

Hike down to beach with numerous sea caves. Walk along amidst surf. Walk other way and see remnants of sea wreck. On board, Sheila catches several sugar bass. Boat comes to this area. Motorized raft (skiff) comes to pick us up on beach. Waves are a little high. As we are pushing off, large wave breaks over raft, knocking us into water and getting soaked. Get back to ship and change, and dry clothes in dryer. Have lunch: beef & cheese hot sandwiches, watermelon, clam chowder and salad.

After lunch, ship goes to Santa Cruz Island and moves close up to a sea cave. Then take skiffs into cave a quarter mile (1,400'). Dark inside. Put on light at end and see several seals on sandy ledge. Kayakers go in, too.

Back on ship, we head for the mainland and munch on freshly made chocolate chip cookies. Ship has a TV that plays VCR tapes. On way back, some nap, Sheila, Tom, Margie & boys play Rummy-O, like scrabble-chips have a number on them.

Twenty-fourth Annual Death March

Location: Pigeon Point Lighthouse Hostel, California

Dates: August 8-August 11, 2002

Participants: Gerry Herter, Steve and Monica Williams, George and Tom DiGaetano and friend Rich, Carl Greenwood, Curtis Williams, Tom Ahling, Patty and Madison Woolworth, Margie and Tyler Andrews, Karen and Katie Spivey.

Trail Notes:

Day 1 – Thursday, August 8, 2002

Departed at 8:30 AM from Tustin. GH, CW, CG; SW, MW; KS, KS; GD, TD, R (12:30 PM); MA, TA-flew to San Fran; PW, MW. GH group stopped in Santa Cruz to pickup groceries. Arrived at Pigeon Point at 4:45 PM. Checked in. Our building has living room-3 sofas & table/chairs; kitchen w/ 2 refrigerators, stove, sink & table w/chairs; 1 dorm room w/ 6 bunk beds-women; 1 dorm room w/ 6 bunk beds-men; 1 room w/ double bed & bunk Women's dorm has private bath; men's bath across hall. Four buildings like ours and lighthouse and fog signal building. Orientation by Diana at 7:00 PM.

Everyone is on own for dinner. Go into Pescadero-8 miles. Some Mexican. GH group do Duarte's Tavern: cioppino and sea bass, martinis, wine, blueberry pie ala mode.

Sit out by ocean and lots of stars and lighthouse beacon. In bed by 11:00 PM.

Day 2 – Friday, August 9, 2002

Up early-6:00 AM. Take turns with shower. Breakfast: cereals and bagels and fruit. Depart at 8:00 AM. On trail at 8:35 AM.

Big Basin Redwood State Park. From beach uphill through forest with redwoods. 16-1/2 miles total. Three beautiful waterfalls. Temperature not bad at first in woods. Sun filtering through trees. Then gets hot – 100° at peak. Lunch at 1:00 PM at Golden Falls and cool off. Six miles to Berry Creek Falls. Everyone ok. Then we take extra four mile loop. Turns out steep and hot. Everyone struggles. Not enough water. Most had two bottles. Finally out at 4:45 PM.

Redwoods and forest coast very scenic walk. Good trail. Some alongside of mountain. Tommy out first, then Gerry and Carl. Then Steve, Monica, Curtis and Tom. Tommy drives in to pick up stragglers. Patty, Madison, Karen and Katie turned back and went into Santa Cruz. Karen is rear ended.

Back to hostel and showers and rest. Dinner at Duarte's at 7:30 PM. Pepper steak, salmon, halibut, chops, artichoke soup, and olallieberry pie ala mode. Calamari appetizer with martinis in bar. In bed at 10.
Day 3 – Saturday, August 10, 2002

Up at 6:30 AM. Take it easy, showers and breakfast. Off at 9:15 to Ano Nuevo State Park. Friendly docents. Stop in visitor center.

Watch movie. Hike four miles on Point Trail to seal watching area on beach. Male elephant seals lying on beach, molting (4-6 week process). Across the way is an island; former lighthouse. Seals there making a lot of noise we can hear. Docents at viewing area explain elephant seal habits. Breed in winter, migrate to Aleutian Islands.

Stop at Costanoa Luxury Camp. Tents and lodge. Have beer. Drive to Half Moon Bay. Lunch at Distillery, Moss Beach on ocean. Mussels, artichokes, buffalo wings, cheese bread and beer.

Stop at Seal Cove Inn. Back to hostel and shower. Martinis at Duarte's. Charlie- bartender, Stephanie-waitress, Thursday, Lieben-waitress, Friday, Ronny-owner, Kathy-owner-daughter-hostess, Sarah-busboy, Mark-patron at bar-endless search for knowledge. Dinner: pepper steak with mushrooms & onions, blackened Mahi Mahi, mashed potatoes, green beans, and olallieberry pie ala mode.

Sit on point behind lighthouse. To bed at 11:00 PM.

Day 4 – Sunday, August 11, 2002

Up at 6:00 AM. Clean rooms, have breakfast. Check out at 7:30 AM. On road at 7:35 AM.

Highlights: Curtis: getting bottle of water from Steve when he ran out of water. Carl: Golden Falls-after strenuous Sunset Trail hot loop hike, cooled off and had lunch; Gerry: walking through redwood forest with sun filtering through trees; view of Berry Creek Falls in sunlight with sun shining on tree reaching up from top of falls; huge male elephant seal-4-5,000 lbs.; Pigeon Point Lighthouse Hostel; Duarte's.

Twenty-fifth Annual Death March

Location: Yosemite High Sierra Camps – 7 day guided hike

Dates: August 3-August 9, 2003

Participants: Gerry Herter, Steve and Monica Williams, George and Tom DiGaetano, Carl Greenwood.

Trail Notes:

Day 1 – Sunday, August 3, 2003

Met at fire ring behind Tuolumne Meadows Lodge (8,600'). Briefing by ranger Steve Schwartz. He is from Cuyahoga Falls, Ohio. Departed at 9:35 AM. Schwartz's wife, Megan, hikes with us for a short while.

Stopped at Soda Springs-natural-carbonated with iron. Story of Lembert-namesake of Lembert Dome. Caretaker in Valley with wife, Nellie. Talked about Parson's Cabin and looked in McCauley Cabin. Resident showed us the one room cabin where two rangers live.

Hike to river over glacial outcropping and have lunch: turkey sandwich, orange, egg, fig newtons, and apple juice.

Hike to Glen Aulin (total 7 miles). Past two beautiful waterfalls, and another at camp Arrive at 2:35. Thom Dodd, manager, briefs on rules. Lemonade. Carl and I skinny dip bath in river by falls. Tent 6 – Carl, Gerry, Steve and Monica. Tent 7 – George, Tom and Brent. Bent hikes to Waterwheel Falls before nap and read. Dinner: turkey, dressing, mashed potatoes with mushrooms, salad, veggie beef soup and pumpkin pie.

Poem ranger read night before start: "Climb the mountains and get their good tidings. Nature's peace will flow into you as sunshine flows into trees. The winds will blow their own freshness into you, and the storms their energy, while cares will drop away from you like the leaves of Autumn." - John Muir, *Our National Parks*, 1901.

Up to point for sunset and geology talk by Steve. Falls one way – upper & lower. Grand Canyon of the Tuolumne the other way toward sunset. Spectacular orange sun. Mount Coness to right in distance (12,500'), while with clouds in & out – mystic look.

Cooled down fast. Realize how spoiled we are, missing our creature comforts. No blisters, used moleskin. In bed at 9:00 PM. – Start fire in stove.

Day 2 – Monday, August 4, 2003

Up at 6:00 AM. Carl starts fire. Coffee at 7:00 AM. Breakfast at 7:30 AM: scrambled eggs, bacon, raisin scone, cantaloupe and oatmeal. Depart at 8:45 AM after singing song to staff. 8 miles to May Lake. Two tough uphill stretches. Stop for lunch after one at 12:30 PM. Beautiful view on top of granite flow. Passed McGhee Lake, trail junction to Tenaya Lake and Ten Lakes.

Arrive at May Lake Camp at 2:40 PM. (9,350'). Meet camp managers, Sunny and warm. Lake is calm and beautiful. We shower and wash clothes and read. Feet in good shape. No blisters. People in our group: Carol, Linda, Dick & Madge, Sheri & Sean, Brent, ranger & wife, and us, 15 total. Brian Shoor, camp manager – works winters at Badger Pass. Jennifer Riley works with him.

Dinner: chicken breast orange, mushroom soup, salad, brown rice, Chinese cabbage, strawberry cobbler. Sunset up on ridge. Ranger points out mountain peaks and gives history from names of mountains. Follow your dream. Carl makes campfire. To bed at 9:15 PM.

Day 3 – Tuesday, August 5, 2003

Up at 5:30 AM. Make fire. Breakfast: Mexican eggs, bacon, blueberry muffins, fruit salad, and oatmeal. Make up song to sing to staff as we leave. Gary – maintenance man goes camp to camp.

Arrive at Sunrise High Sierra Camp at 2:40 PM. Brent Benson is manager. Shower – great showers – but temperature erratic. Composted johns. Sunny – meadows green and meandering stream. Nap and read.

Got cold fast – very cold.

Dinner: ravioli – beef & Portobello mushroom meat sauce, alfredo sauce, veggie soup, salad, heavy bread, broccoli, chocolate cake with white icing and chocolate chips.

Too cold for ranger talk, so everyone went to cabins, made fire and went to bed at 8:00 PM.

Day 4 – Wednesday, August 6, 2003

Up at 5:50 AM. Carl got up at 1:00 AM and remade fire and again now. Very cold. Breakfast: oatmeal with peach cobbler, scrambled eggs, bacon, cantaloupe, grapes and coffee cake. Sang song: Gold Old Mountain Milk.

Group members: Sheri & Sean Kurita–Bay Area-Oakland?; Brent Williams-Sacramento-computers; Rick & Marge Keller-Pennsylvania-retired; Carol Roberts-Bay area-east of Oakland-guide-cook; Linda Liscan.

Left at 9:00 AM. Downhill ten miles – beautiful day, along Merced River. Arrive at Merced Lake High Sierra Camp– 2:40 PM. Merced Lake manager, Sean Lassiter – 6 years, 5 at Vogelsang. Showers and nap. Four showers plus sinks. Eight toilets – by nightfall all are clogged. Read and talk with lady who is leading two friends. She gives Carl wine and oysters.

Dinner: halibut, spinach salad, veggie soup, mixed veggies on top of rice, corn bread and strawberry shortcake. Campfire – Steve leads a quiz on the National Parks – two sides. To bed at 10:30 PM.

Day 5 – Thursday, August 7, 2003

Up at 6:00 AM. Very cold night. No stoves in tents. Steve & Monica have one tent. We four in another. Coffee at 7:00 AM and breakfast: scrambled eggs with veggies, bacon, scones, apple juice and oatmeal.

Ranger Steve leads tree walk. Breaks group down by personality and then matches us to trees:
    Jeffrey Pine – sun
    White Fir
    Huckleberry Oak – shade, complex
    Juniper – sun, solitary
    Lodgepole Pine
    Quaking Aspen – sun, Type A, active

In depth talk about trees. Steve Schwartz said: "I want you to be able to identify the trees, but also identify with the trees." (Only way to get to know them). "If you introduce yourself to someone, but then walk away, you don't know them."

Dinner menu: homemade focaccia bread, butternut squash soup with summer garden salad, Brazilian roast pork loin with Grandma Jeanne's ratatouille and polenta drizzled in olive oil & bleu cheese, ★ pumpkin spice cake. *

* The cook mentioned an article in PC Magazine on menu boards that said people are more interested if it says i.e. "Grandma's apple pie" than just "apple pie."

After dinner talent show. Some made up songs. Steve S. did a fire baton act. Great fun. To bed at 10.

Day 6 – Friday, August 8, 2003

Up at 5:50 AM. Breakfast: pancakes with strawberries, cream of wheat, eggs with veggies and bacon. Sing song to staff and depart at 8:30 AM. The song we sang had the following lyrics that we as a group composed:

> We thank you Merced staff. O yes we do!
> You made great pork for us, and ratatouille, too!
> If we sound grateful, then it's true!
> Dear Merced staff. We thank you!

Only years later as I input these trail notes did I determine (through Google) that the music to this song was actually a tune from the Broadway musical, *Bye Bye Birdie.* The song was called "We Love You, Conrad." If you change the words "thank you" to "love" and "Merced staff" to "Conrad," and a few other changes, you have the original song.
All uphill – 3,600' elevation gain over Vogelsang Pass and back down to Vogelsang High Sierra Camp at 10,300'. Saw bear on trail about half way. About 3 years old. Watched it meander along side of the mountain for 5 minutes. Lunch in meadow with a deer.

Over Vogelsang Pass into camp at 2:30 PM. Tired. Nap and clean up. Beautiful high meadow setting and rock mountain tops of Fletcher and Vogelsang.

Dinner:Mexican chicken breast and leg, veggies & rice, bread with garlic and pepper, veggie soup with okra, salad, and high Sierra carrot cake.

Steve S has talk on wilderness. "We all care <u>about</u> a lot of things, but we all don't care <u>for</u> many things. Find things to care about."

Final gathering in our cabin. Steve S hands out certificates. We present a card we had all signed. To bed at 10:00 PM.

Up at 1:00 AM to see Mars, closest it will be to Earth in millions of years – a bright, orange star.

Day 7, Saturday, August 9, 2003.

Up at 5:50 AM. Pack up and depart.

A table of impressions I made of the High Sierra Camps:

Camp	Glen Aulin	May Lake	Sunrise	Merced Lake	Vogelsang
Natural	Waterfall	Lake with mountain	Meadow	Lake & river cascades	High country meadow
Toilets	Outhouse – 2	Flush-great-2 & 2?	Compost -2 men, 2 women	8 flush, but stopped up-4 men, 4 women	
Showers	None	1 men, 1 women-	2 men, 2 women-	4 men, 4 women-	None

		hot	erratic temp.	good	
Crew	According to the roles in depth*	Take pride-family	Lay back-late	On their own wave length, but competent	
Tents	OK		Spread out	In line, newer, but no stoves-cold	

* Crew dances out with pots & pans banging to announce dinner & breakfast. Tom has crew tell about volunteer work, what is most challenging, rewarding and interesting. Tom's small daughter, Riley, tells joke: Why doesn't the teddy bear eat dinner? Because he's stuffed.

Twenty-sixth Annual Death March

Location: Zion National Park

Dates: August 14-August 17, 2004

Participants: Gerry Herter, Curtis Williams, Karen Williams, George & Tom DiGaetano, Steve, Sherry, Scott, Monica, Megan & Esther Williams, Marc & Carol Richmond, Patty & Madison Woolworth.

Trail Notes:

Day 1 – Saturday, August 14, 2004

Departed Saturday morning, picked up Karen at Las Vegas airport, arrive at Zion about 4:00 PM. Get permit from ranger. Check in at Zion Lodge. Dinner at Dining Room, three styles of salmon, chicken, steak, pork chops.

Day 2 – Sunday, Aug. 15, 2004

Up at 6:00 AM. Muffins & coffee at window in reception. Shuttle to Narrows entrance at 7. Hike in until 9:30 AM, then turn around. Out by 11:30 AM. Lunch at dining room. Hike to emerald Pools. Dinner at Dining Room. Ranger show on flora & fauna.

Day 3 – Monday, Aug. 16, 2004

Up at 6:00 AM. same routine. Shuttle to trail head for Angels Landing. Hike to Scout Lookout. Madison & Tom go further. Down at noontime. Lunch in Springdale. Bumbleberry pancakes. Afternoon hike to Weeping Rock. Steve and family to Bryce. Dinner in Dining Room. Olympics on TV in waiting area. Men's gymnastics. Ranger talk on his winter sojourn for 18? Days in back country nearly killing himself.

Day 4 - Aug 17. 2004

Up at 6:00 AM. Depart and breakfast on way. Drop Karen at Las Vegas airport, and drive home. Arrive at 3:00 PM.

Twenty-seventh Annual Death March

Location: Grand Canyon – Colorado River Rafting

Dates: August 6-August 11, 2005

Participants: Gerry Herter, Steve Williams and Monica Williams, Jeff and Ryan Hipshman, Jeff and Jarrod Lazerson, Patty and Madison Woolworth, Kelly (Madison's friend), Curtis and Jason Campbell, Scott Shackleton, James (J.T.) Taylor, and Don Cottrell.

Trail Notes:

Day 1 – Saturday, August 6, 2005

Departed at 6:20 AM. Steve picked Gerry up. Arrived at La Quinta Inn in Flagstaff, AZ at 5:00 PM. We had driven to the Grand Canyon first. We met Patty, Madison and Kelly there at 2:30 PM. Patty drove Madison and Kelly to Flagstaff. Steve and Gerry took a shuttle with Route 66 Concierge to Flagstaff, having left our car at the Grand Canyon for pickup at the end of the trip.

At 6:00 PM, we met the others for an orientation by Canyoneers. Curtis and Jason flew in. Scott and James flew from Raleigh, NC. The others drove in.

Dinner at Del Taco, then to bed at 10: PM.

Day 2 – Sunday, August 7.

Up with dry bags, ammo cans, ricksacks and duffels packed and loaded on bus at 6:00 AM. Breakfast and video orientation. Leave Flagstaff at 7:15 AM.

Arrive at Lee's Ferry at 9:15 AM. Meet raft guides, Ben, a high school science teacher in his 50's, has been a guide for 28 years; Toad, about 42 and a free spirit; Jamie, 29. Load gear, don life jackets, and put in at 10 AM. Hot and sunny.

Raft weighs 17,000 lbs. White pontoons. Sit on benches parallel to pontoons. When going through big rapids, sit in center of raft, lower

down. 89 miles to Phantom Ranch. Total river course is 280 miles.
Go about 40 miles today.

Stop for lunch at a sandy beach: cold meats, lettuce, tomatoes, onion,
pickles, peanut butter and jelly.
Several good rapids and stretches of calm water. River muddy olive
green, and later reddish brown. Guide tells stories along the way and
points out geologic formations.

At 4:00 PM, we camp on a sandy beach. Set out tarps and sleeping
bags. We all jump off a ledge into the river for a swim. Guides set up
tables to fix and serve dinner: roast pork, rice, vegetables, salad,
cheese cake, coffee and lemonade.

Hike after dinner to side canyon where nautaloid fossils are found on
the surface of smooth, flat rock floor. Some climbing involved. Ben
helps everyone and stands close by to catch anyone who slips. (He's
a big guy). Along the river today, we see big horn sheep, deer, and
blue heron birds.

In bed by nine. Stars are beautiful. Bats are flying around all night.
The guides set up the "Duke" in a secluded spot. Nearby are green
and red pails and soap to wash hands. Bag of toilet paper there
signifies the Duke is available.

Day 3 – Monday, August 8

Up at 5:00 AM. Coffee. Breakfast at 5:30 AM. : eggs, bacon,
English muffins and juice. Everyone helps pack up raft.

Put in at 7 AM. More exciting rapids today and spectacular canyon
scenery. See beaver and more big horns, heron and deer. Stop at
Saddle (?) canyon for 3 mile (one way) hike to waterfall. Again
some climbing involved. At end of slot canyon, delicate falls and
stream flowing out. Tiny frogs and tadpoles. Wade through stream.

Then lunch: chicken salad pita sandwiches and cookies.

In afternoon, stop at large cave. John Wesley Powell said that 50,000 could fit inside here.

Another 40 miles today. Camp again on a sandy beach. Engine trouble today. They pulled the engine and put in a spare. Looks like possible rain, so we put up tents.

Dinner is halibut with tomatoes, lemon and spices on top, grilled in aluminum foil, broccoli, fettuccini with pesto, salad and fruit cobbler. In bed about 8:30 PM.

Day 4 - Tuesday, August 9

Up at 5:00 AM. Breakfast at 5:30 AM: blueberry pancakes, sausage, melon, pineapple, juice and coffee. At end of breakfast, a large scorpion is spotted entering camp. It's a beauty. We stay a safe distance away.

Pack up camp and put in river at 7 AM. Every day on river we get soaked repeatedly in the rapids. Water is cold 48°, but after the initial shock is refreshing and cools off the heat.

We only go 9 miles today, but hit the best rapids. Arrive at Bright Angel Beach at 9: AM. Unload and say our farewells to our guides. They have been great and friendly. Another group prepares to board to continue down the river.

As we get off, it starts to rain. We get wet on the half mile walk to Phantom Ranch. Check in at 10: AM. Get rooms, some at 11:00 AM, some at 12 Noon. Shaves, have sack lunches we prepared at breakfast: peanut butter and jelly, apple and granola bar. Afternoon relax, hike, nap, and read. Ranger talk at 4:00 PM on geology.

Dinner at 6:30 PM: stew, cornbread, salad, chocolate cake, coffee, ice tea and water. Ranger talk at 7:30 PM, Q & A. Also, wrangler talk on putting mules to bed. To bed at 9:00 PM.

Day 5 – Wednesday, August 10

Wake up call at 4:30 AM. Breakfast at 5:00 AM: scrambled eggs, bacon, pancakes, juice and coffee.

Hit the trail at 5:40 AM. 9-1/2 miles to the rim. Gerry, Steve, Monica, Kelly, Don, Scott, Madison and James (J.T.) hike out at 11:25 AM – 5-3/4 hours. Lite rain for first 2 hours, then cloudy all the way to the top. Kept the temperature from getting hot. Stayed about 80 and rain cooled us. Others got out 2 hours later. All in good shape.

Check in at hotels: El Tovar, Maswik and Yavapai. Dinner at Arizona Room in Bright Angel Lodge at 6 PM (all but Jeff's group and Don).

To bed at 10 PM.

Day 6 – Thursday, August 11

Up at 7:00 AM. Breakfast: polenta corncakes with prickly pear butter and syrup at El Tovar dining room. Check out at 8:30 AM. Pick up Patty, Madison and Kelly at Yavapai and are on the road at 8:45 AM.

All had had a great time and want to do the rest of the canyon in the future.

Twenty-eighth Annual Death March

Location: Mineral King, Sequoia National Park

Dates: August 10-August 13, 2006

Participants: Gerry Herter, Curtis Williams, Dave Kingsbury, Tom Ahling, Steve, Sherry, Megan and Esther Williams, Patty and Madison Woolworth, Sandy, Marc Richmond, Chuck McLucas, George DiGaetano, Rick Reigel, and Don Cottrell..

Trail Notes:

Day 1 – Thursday, August 10, 2006

Departed at 5:00 AM. Arrived at Silver City Resort, Mineral King, Sequoia National Park at noontime. Lunch on burgers. Afternoon hike to Soda Springs. Dinner BBQ steaks, forest razzleberry pie. Employees Kristen, Joel and Lauren. Ranger talk. To bed at 9-9:30 PM.

Day 2 – Friday, August 11

Up at 6:00 AM. Showers. Breakfast at 8:00 AM: bacon and eggs. At 9:00 AM, hike East Fork Grove trail 4 miles. Redwoods and waterfalls. Back at noon. Lunch: salad. Afternoon – some to Soda Springs. Us (Gerry, Curtis, Tom, Mark) to Paradise Ridge – redwoods. Back at 4:00 PM. Showers. Dinner: burgers. Some go to ranger walk at ranger station. In bed at 9:00 PM.

Day 3 – Saturday, August 12

Up at 6:00 AM. On trail at 7:30 AM. Hike to Franklin Lakes. Patty and Sandy to Soda Springs and main part. Lunch at lake. Back at 3:00 PM. Showers. Some play cards. Dinner: fried chicken, mashed potatoes, broccoli, and blueberry, walnut chocolate and caramel apple pie. Some go to ranger talk and show at ranger station. To bed at 9:00 PM.

Day 4 - Sunday, August 13

Up at 5:30 AM. On road at 6:30 AM. Breakfast at "We Three" in Three Rivers. Home at 12:30 PM.

Twenty-ninth Annual Death March

Location: Hetch Hetchy Valley, Yosemite National Park

Dates: July 28-31, 2007

Participants: Gerry Herter, Steve, Sherry, Monica, Megan and Esther Williams, Carl Greenwood, Patty Woolworth, Sandy, Adelle, George and Tom DiGaetano, Rick, Bryce and Shane Reigel, Don Cottrell and wife, Maureen Brooks, Jeff and Ryan Hipshman, David, Clara, Jenna and Lauren Eisenman, Jodi, Joe, Lauren and Nick Ristrom.

Trail Notes:

Day 1 – Saturday, July 28, 2007

Departed home at 6:30 AM. Starbucks coffee. Breakfast at 9:00AM – McDonald's. Lunch-Oakhurst at 11:30 AM – Carl's Jr.

Arrive at Evergreen Lodge at 2:30 PM. Dinner at 6:30 PM – outdoors at restaurant: salmon, ribeye steak, burgers, etc. To bed at 9:30 PM.

Day 2 – Sunday, July 29, 2007

Up at 6:00 AM. Breakfast at 7:00 AM. Off to trailhead at 9:15 AM. On trail at 9:25 AM.

To Lookout Point, 1-3 miles each way. Good trail-uphill 600'. Everyone but George's group. Great views of Hetch Hetchy Valley, Shaughnessy Dam and Wapama Falls.

11:30 lunch at Lodge. On trail at 2:00PM to Carlon Falls through woods, 1-2 miles each way. Beautiful, 3-stage falls, 10-20 feet high with pool beneath each level. We swim in highest one and go under falls. All but George's group and Sandy. Back at 5:00 PM.

Dinner at 6:30: orange roughy, apple pie and tiramisu. In bed at 9:00 PM>

Day 3 – Monday, July 30, 2007

Up at 6:00 AM. Breakfast at 7:00 AM: oatmeal and bran muffins. Meet at 8:20 AM. On trail at 9:00 AM.

We meet Ken Brewer with the Hetch Hetchy Water Supply, who tells us about the dam. Hike across the dam, through tunnel to Wapama Falls. A small flow of water and a pool. Wooden bridge around falls. All but David's family start out. They go to Yosemite Valley. Most only go as far as Wapama Falls.

Jeff & Ryan, Rick, Shane & Bryce, Don, Steve & Monica, and Gerry go on to Rancheria Falls. Carl goes half way. Rancheria Falls a bit like Carlon Falls yesterday. Cascades over rock shelf. Lunch at campsite in shade.

Hike and Valley are spectacular, but very hot and sunny: 90-100°. Arrive at 12:15 PM. Leave at 12:45 PM. Back to dam at 3:10 PM. Drive back to Evergreen Lodge. Showers.

Dinner 6:30 PM: Bison strip steak. HMWC hosted. In bed at 9:00 PM.

Day 4 – Tuesday, July 31, 2007

Up at 6:00 AM. On road at 6:25 AM. Home at 1:50 PM.

Great time had by all.

Thirtieth Annual Death March

Location: Shadow Lake Lodge, Banff National Park, Canada, and Sperry Chalet, Glacier National Park, Montana

Dates: July 27-August 2, 2008

Participants: Gerry Herter, Steve, Sherry, Monica, Megan and Esther Williams, Patty Woolworth, Maureen Brooks, Scott Shackleton, James Taylor (JT), Jeff and Ryan Hipshman, Larry and Aaron Swartz, Jodi, Joe, Lauren and Nick Ristrom, Sandy Wang, and Marc Richmond. Chuck McLucas joins for Montana part.

Trail Notes:

Day 1 – Sunday, July 27, 2008

Participants arrive separately, flying in from various parts of the country. Gerry arrives at Chateau Lake Louise in Banff National Park on July 25, having flown to Seattle and driven across Canada, with stops at Mount Revelsoke, Glacier and Yoho National Parks enroute to Banff. Many fly into Calgary, a 2-1/2 hour drive from Banff.

Up at 6:00 AM. Breakfast at 7:00 AM. One last walk by Lake Louise. Depart at 8:00 AM for Red Earth Creek Trailhead, between Lake Louise and the town of Banff. All hikers converge there at 9:00 AM. Set off on trail at 9:20 AM. Broad trail, generally level, 1,500' elevation gain over 9 miles. Through evergreen forest with numerous streams passing through.

Lead group sets a 3 mile per hour pace. Halfway there it rains for ten minutes, clears, rains again, then sun when arriving at camp 3 hours later at 12:20 PM. Log cabins on edge of broad meadow framed by snowcapped mountains (Ball, Isabelle, Storm). Gerry, Jeff, Ryan, Larry, Aaron and Nick arrive first, followed in fifteen minutes by Scott and JT, and in a half hour by the Williams, Ristroms, Sandy, and Marc. Patty and Maureen arrive two hours later.

Wide array of muffins, coffee cake, banana bread, cookies, cheese and crackers, with coffee, lemonade and ice tea. We check into cabins with Kristen: Storm, Copper, Isabelle, Pilot, Sphinx, Whistling and Red Earth. Kids play in game room. Jeff's group decides to hike out and they leave in an hour. Some hike to Shadow Lake, a mile away. Beautiful lake at base of Mt. Ball.

Rains off and on rest of afternoon and evening. Dinner at 6:15 PM: beef tenderloin with peppercorns, mashed potatoes, butternut squash, Caesar salad, bread, and blackberry crumble pie with whipped cream. To bed at 9:30 PM.

When arriving at Lodge, we enjoy a cup of coffee, which later we discover was just hot water.

Day 2 – Monday, July 28, 2008

Up at 6:00 AM. Breakfast at 8:00 AM: eggs, blueberry pancakes, sausage, juice, bread, oatmeal and fruit.

Depart on hike to Ball Pass at 9:30 AM. Beautiful rainbow this morning. Rained heavily during the night. On trail rained on and off and sun. Five miles to pass. Beautiful view of mountains. Last mile above tree line across rocks to pass at 12:30 PM. Lunch from fixings after breakfast. Sandwiches, fruit, trail mix, cookies and carrots. Hike back about 4:00 PM. Patty and Maureen take shorter hike. Showers and nap.

Dinner at 6:15 PM: salmon, rice, veggies, salad with strawberry vinaigrette dressing, chocolate cheesecake and wine. To bed at 9:30 PM.

Day 3 – Tuesday, July 29, 2008

Up at 6:00 AM. Breakfast at 6:45 AM: oatmeal, fruit and tea.

Depart Shadow Lake Lodge at 7:00 AM. Gerry, Scott and JT hike out to trailhead-Red Earth Creek at 9:25 AM. 9.55 miles per GPS. Drive back to Chateau Lake Louise. Others hike out at own pace. All go separate ways with plan to meet back up on August 1. Gerry and Loretta spend a night at Banff Springs Hotel, then a night at Prince of Wales Hotel in Waterton Lakes National Park. On July 31,drive to Glacier National Park, up and over Logan Pass on the spectacular Going to the Sun Highway, arriving at Lake McDonald Lodge in afternoon.

Day 4 – Friday, August 1, 2008

Up at 6:00 AM. To trailhead for Sperry Chalet at 8:30 AM. Start hike at 9:05 AM. Chuck McLucas joins us, after kidney stone surgery that caused him to miss the first part of the Death March. Hike in, arrive at Sperry Chalet at 12:00 noon (Gerry, Jeff's group, and Nick). Have lemonade and lunch sandwiches. All but Patty and Maureen arrive one hour later. Patty and Maureen arrive at 3:00 PM.

Stone chalet with dining, kitchen, johns and rooms in one big chalet. Gerry, Marc, Jodie and Sandy hike one mile to Lincoln Pass, see views and three mountain goats. Steve, Sherry, Joe, Scott, JT and Megan got flu at last hike. Most better now. Megan stays back with grandparents.

Dinner: roast beef, mashed potatoes, corn, lentil soup, peach with cottage cheese, and pumpkin pie square with crumbles. To bed at 8:30 PM.

Day 5 – Saturday, August 2, 2008

Up at 5:45 AM. Early breakfast: fried egg and ham sandwich. Gerry, Marc and Chuck hike out at 7:00 AM, arriving at trailhead at 9:25 AM. Jeff and group and others have breakfast at 7:00 AM. Hike out at 8:00 AM, out at 10:07 AM. Others later. Shower and check out. All go their separate ways, having had an unforgettable time. Gerry & Loretta, Jeff's group, Patty and Maureen stop off at Many Glacier Hotel on picturesque Swiftcurrent Lake for a night before heading on.

Thirty-first Annual Death March

Location: Sequoia High Sierra Camp, Sequoia National Park

Dates: July 30-August 2, 2009

Participants: Gerry Herter, Steve and Scott Williams, George and Tom DiGaetano, Cassandra, Patty Woolworth, Reberta, Karen Williams, Curtis Williams, Mike Berman, Marc Richmond, Chuck McLucas, and Jim Gilbert.

Trail Notes:

Day 1 – Thursday, July 30, 2009

Departed in five groups: Gerry and Steve's groups at 6:00 AM; others follow George at 8:30 AM. Stop in Bakersfield IHOP for breakfast at 8:30 AM. Arrived at Wuksachi Lodge in Sequoia National Park at 1 PM. Hiked Congress Trail. Checked into Lodge at 4:00 PM.

Dinner at 6:00 PM. Drove to Wolverton Meadow for outdoor bar-b-que of pork ribs, chicken, hamburgers, hot dogs, corn on the cob, baked beans, cole slaw, potato salad, corn bread, apple & boysenberry pie, beer and soda. Curtis brought wine. Back to Campfire talk by lodge about mountain lions. To bed at 10:30 PM.

Day 2 – Friday, July 31, 2009

Up at 6:00 AM. Breakfast at 7:00 AM. Group picture in dining room. Buffet of usual offerings. Pick up box lunches: sandwiches, chips, apple, trail mix, cookies and soda.

Those driving to one mile trailhead about 30 miles north, leave at 7:50 AM to make 8:00 AM opening of road. Construction delays are on the hour. Some stay and do day hikes, i.e. Tokopah Falls and come later. Five do the 12 mile hike to the camp, departing at 8:05 AM: Gerry, Steve, Scott, Tom and Cassandra.

Beautiful, sunny day, cool in morning and hot, 90's in afternoon. In forest and meadows with colored wildflowers, blue, yellow, red, white. We see a big brown bear (black color) with two cubs moving across -Cahoon Meadow about 200 yards away. She looks at us for a moment and moves on.

Lunch at J.O. Pass about seven miles in and 9,400' altitude. Gerry loses trail and goes ½ mile out of way, then backtracks and finds trail. Arrive at camp at 3:30 PM. Long and strenuous, but beautiful mountain and forest views.

We are greeted by the friendly owners, Burr and Suzanne Hughes from Memphis, Tennessee. They bought the 40 acre plot surrounded by the national park ten years ago. Burr says he started the process in 2001. It took three years. Started construction on 2004 and opened in 2006. 36 tent cabins. Sturdy wood columns form dining hall, lounge and kitchen, overlooking valley and view of mountains ion the distance.

Ice water and tea await the arriving hikers, plus bing cherries and cookies. Two Polish young men, Adam and friend, help plus a German girl. We take showers. Hot water and flush toilets in a modern rest room.

Happy hour at 5:30 PM, wine and beer and hors d'oeuvres-melon & prosciutto, cream cheese &. Dinner at 6:30 PM: seared ahi on mix of black beans, pepper, mango and other cut up veggies and asparagus, carrot soup with pieces of celery, tomato with buffalo mozzarella cheese appetizer, home made vanilla ice cream with chocolate mousse cake, coffee and tea.

Too tired for campfire. To bed at 9:00 PM.

Day 3 – Saturday, August 1

Up at 6:00 AM. Coffee at 6:30 AM. Breakfast at 7:30 AM: granola, cereals, blueberries, strawberries, melon, pineapple, blueberry muffins, omelets (ham, cheese, veggies, bacon) made by chef from Iceland, now a photographer in US, and orange juice squeezer- 4 oranges per glass.

Start hike to Mitchell Peak at 9:15 AM. Tom and Cassandra stay back. Patty, Reberta and George go part way. Rest go to Peak, 10,365', at noon with box lunches we made with ciabatta bread, turkey, ham, beef, cheese, tomatoes, greens, raisins, trail mix, and banana bread.

Gorgeous views from Peak of Sierra Nevada Mountains and valley. Rocky boulders last ¼ mile. Gerry, Curtis and Mike make wrong turn going back, extra mile or two and into Kings Canyon National Park. Back at 2:30 PM.

Happy hour – 5:30-6:30 PM: cucumber with sausage slice, Sierra Nevada and Heinekens beer and French wine. Wes, son, tells us stories. Wes is studying for CPA exam. Dinner: ribeye steak on a corn base with pepper and other bits and sauce, tomato soup, burned spinach salad with Gouda cheesecake, pastry shell with blueberries, strawberries and whipped cream. Coffee by the campfire. To bed at 9:00 PM.

Day 4 – Sunday, August 2, 2009

Up at 6:00 AM. Coffee 6:30 AM. Breakfast at 7;30 AM: omelets made by Fridjere, cereals and fruits, bacon, potatoes, and oranges for juice squeezer. Make box lunches again. Meet others from New York and Boston heading to Bearpaw Meadow.

Say our good-byes and depart for home at 8:30 AM. Hike the one mile trail to Marvin Pass Trailhead. At 9:00 AM, drive off. Have box lunches near Bakersfield. Home at 3:30 PM.

A great time had by all. The Sequoia High Sierra Camp is the 5 star of these camps.

Thirty-second Annual Death March

Location: Grand Canyon – Colorado River Rafting

Dates: August 1 - August 8, 2010

Participants: Carl Greenwood, Gerry Herter, Karen Williams, Steve, Esther, Monica & Scott Williams, Patty Woolworth, Maureen Brooks, Curtis Williams, Mike Berman, Jeanie Wooster, Chuck McLucas, Grace Liu, Marc Richmond and Frederick Crawford.

Trail Notes:

Day 1 - Sunday, August 1, 2010

Departed at 6:30 am. Carl and Gerry drove. Curtis and Mike flew to Flagstaff. Jeanie flew in from Atlanta. Karen shuttled from Phoenix. They all shuttled to the South Rim. The rest drove. Steve left Monday.

Arrived at South Rim at 2:30 PM. Pouring rain. Checked in at El Tovar Hotel. Walked rim, drinks and calamari on porch. Dinner in dining room: duck, steak, trout (GH, KW, CG, CW, MB, JW). MR & FC arrived at end of dinner and ate. To bed at 10.

Day 2 – Monday, August 2

Up at 6. Breakfast in dining room: Angus prime rib hash & eggs. Carl forgot his medication. He drove back to Williams to get it. He got back at 12.

Walked the rim trail: Trail of History. Checked out and moved to Maswik Lodge South with all Canyoneers. Lunch at cafeteria: chicken sandwich. Walked to trailhead in PM. Orientation with Drew at 6. To bed at 9 PM.

Day 3 – Tuesday, August 3

Up at 4 AM. Breakfast in Drew's room: muffins, granola, yogurt, orange juice, granola bars, bananas. Coffee in our room.

Drive cars to Parking Lot E. Walk to trailhead and hike down at 5:25 AM. Trail in bad shape because of a lot of rain. Overcast, so not too hot. Lots of ruts and rocks. Water and john at 1-1/2, 3 and 4-1/2 miles marks.

Karen & Gerry start in the lead. Scott & Monica are first down at 10:30. Gerry, Curtis, Steve & Esther down at 11.

Drew stays at rear to assure that all make it. Maureen's knee goes out about 4 miles down. Drew and Patty help and stay with her. Finally, Drew takes their packs and hikes to the "Pipe." He arrives at the boat at about 1 PM. We will depart and pick up Patty and Maureen at "Pipe." While waiting Gerry goes to Phantom Ranch and buys T-shirt. Lunch on beach: sandwiches, chips and cookies.

River is muddy red. Two rafts depart at 2:30, about 3 hours behind schedule. Stop at Pipe. Maureen is using two walking sticks as crutches and finally gets to the raft to applause.
Cloudy, but no rain. We hit several 7-10 class rapids very soon after departure. Hermit is the toughest with a big hole and wall of water high over the raft, pelting everyone mercilessly, as we hold on for dear life. Water up nose and everywhere. Crystal Rapids is hardest for the guides to navigate.

Put in for the night at 6. Guides are great, Carolyn is the leader: 56 years old. Amity is the second boat pilot: 33 years old. Rachel and Drew are about 25 years old.

Set up camp on sand bar. Guides make dinner of roast chicken, mashed potatoes, veggies, salad and carrot cake. To bed at 9: tarp, ½" pad, on top of sleeping bags.

Day 4 – Wednesday, August 4

Up at 5 – coffee. Pack up. Breakfast at 6: French Toast & sausage, o.j.

Depart at 7. Up front: Marc, Chuck, Gerry, Curtis, Scott. Rest in back. All of our group in one raft driven by Amity & Rachel, except Maureen, Grace & Frederick opt for other raft.

Three side hikes today. First is up a narrow canyon to a small waterfall. Second is to Stone Falls, which is like a natural shower. We all go under to cool off & clean off with the fresh clear water. Third is Deer Creek Falls, high & powerful. Pool below to swim in. Some of us hike to upper falls. Climb 500 ft. to dramatic overlook. Scary heights. Then in narrow gorge, with very narrow ledges in places. A couple are only 6" inches wide for stepping, with a hundred foot drop & ledges sticking out at chest level, so very scary for 6 feet or so.

There are painted outlines of hands on wall across 8' chasm that boys had to jump across & paint as initiation to manhood – Anasazi. Only a few left, preserved by overhanging ledge. Upper falls has pools for bathing.

Lunch stop – taco salad in tortilla. Put in at 4. Set up 2 Dukes tonight. Only 1 last night.
Dinner – bratwurst & sauerkraut, cheese burgers, French fries, salad, brownies. To bed at 9.

Day 5 - Thursday, August 5

Up at 5. Breakfast, scrambled eggs w/ mushrooms & other stuff, sausage patty & ham, English muffin. Off at 7.

Side hike at Havasu Creek. Turquoise color water from silt. Cascades & shower rock.
Short hike to lunch stop. On way, see pictographs of corn & rock carved out as grinder. Lunch – sandwiches.
In afternoon, go thru Lava Falls rapids, swiftest in country. Esther is sitting in front of me, "down & in." the force of the wave sends her into my lap. I tell her I've got her & hold on thru the rest of the rapids.

Guides have plenty of stories & explain geology & history as we go, & games & riddles.
Has been very hot & sunny. Anyone who wants gets a "bucket head" of river water to cool off. Also big squirt gun. Plenty of snacks along the way.

Put in at 5 on big beach. Dinner rib eye steak, onions & mushrooms, beans, corn, salad, German chocolate cake. To bed at 8.

Day 6 – Friday, August 5.

Up at 5. Breakfast pancakes & bacon, o.j.

Put in at 7. Generally calmer waters with lighter rapids. Sit on pontoons a lot. Others come up front. A few big rapids. Stop at poison arsenic spring. Looks like pools at Yellowstone.

Lunch sandwiches. Hike to Ladder falls – Elf Chasm. Walk up stream. Tricky climbing upper to falls requires 2 sets of ladders & 2 ropes. Spectacular upper falls & stand under for shower.

On way down second ladder, rappelling, Gerry's foot slips on wet, slippery rock wall, & he slams into wall, twisting & hurting back. – burning stabs of pain. Amity, Rachel & Carolyn check it out & help. I can still move everything, just get stabs of pain in move right upper back. Manage to get back to raft. Marc examines me & determines that spine & shoulder blade are OK. Appears to be bruised muscle between them. Take 3 Advil.

Raft a little further, then put in beyond Separation Canyon, which marks the end of Grand Canyon National Park & start of Lake Mead Recreation Area. Get checked & advice from Marc, Mike, Grace RN said prayer, & Karen. On raft, they broke off a piece of ice to put on back& it took down swelling.

Dinner – chicken fajitas, beans, tamales, strawberry shortcake. We had dry bag for stuff we didn't need during day. Ammo can for daytime items, as well as rucksack. We emptied ammo cans for quick pack in morning. To bed at 9.

Day 7 – Saturday, August 7.

Up at 4:50. Bagels & coffee cake, o.j. Put in at 6:30.

Tied the 2 boats together late yesterday. Smooth all morning. No stops. Land at Pearce Ferry at 10:05. Unload. Say good-byes to our beloved guides. Board our bus at 10:30 & head to South Rim. Box lunch from Subway. CW, MB & JW catch shuttle to Vegas for flight home. CG, GH, KW, and Williams' to El Tovar. MR & FC to Maswik. PW & MB to Yavapai. Dinner at El Tovar.

Day 8 – Sunday, August 8. Drive home.

Thirty-third Annual Death March

Location: Marin Headlands - Golden Gate National Recreation Area

Dates: August 12 - August 15, 2011

Participants: Gerry Herter, Carl Greenwood, Karen Williams, Steve, Sherry, Esther, Megan Williams, Marc Richmond, Don and June Silber, Jodie, Joe, Lauren and Nick Ristrom, Lisa, Mike, Nathan and Garret Young.

Trail Notes:

Day 1 - Friday, August 12, 2011

Departed home at 6:00 AM. Picked up by Carl and met Marc at John Wayne Airport, Orange County, for 8:00 Southwest Airlines flight to San Francisco. Flight delayed to 8:45 am. Arrived at 10:30 AM. Rented car and drove to Marin Headlands, arriving at noon.

Lunch at Cavello Point Resort: crab salad sandwiches. Left luggage at Hostel and went shopping at Trader Joe's and Safeway in Mill Valley. Checked into Hostel at 3:30 PM. We have the Annex, a large old military base officer home. Large living room, soft sofa, love seat, easy chair and fireplace. Dining room with four tables and fireplace. Kitchen entryway with couch. Porch with chairs. One bedroom and one bath on first floor. Five bedrooms and two baths on second floor. Carl, Gerry, Marc and Steve in one bedroom with six bunks. Others in bedrooms. Steve and family arrive soon after.

Gerry, Carl and Marc leave for dinner at Scoma's in Sausalito at 7:00 PM. Karen arrives by taxi at 7:30 PM. Dinner of calamari in red sauce, petrale sole and scallops. Back to Hostel at 9:30 PM.

Jodi and family and Lisa and family arrive in evening. Both drove in on vacation, as did Steve. Orientation and to bed.

Day 2 – Saturday August 13, 2011

Up at 6:00 AM. Make coffee and cereal. On road at 8:30 AM. Arrive at trailhead at Mountain Home Inn at 9:15 AM, outside of Muir Woods National Monument. Start on Panorama Trail at 9:30 AM. Take Ocean View Trail down to Muir Woods. Beautiful moss covered trees and redwoods in thick forest with streams.

After a couple miles, meet main park trail, with lots of tourists. Stop at visitor center. Ranger directs us to Dipsea Trail, but tells us to go right at end of parking lot and detour on road for part of trail that is washed out. We should have gone left. Most of us end up going three miles out of the way and finally turn around. The slower ones find out sooner and turn back, and some (Steve, Carl and Esther) hike out the way we came in, get car and return to pick up those that are worn out (Don, June, Karen, Sherry, Megan, Marc and Joe). Gerry, Jodi, Lisa, Mike, Lauren, Nick, Nathan and Garret go back to parking lot, find right Dipsea Trail and hike to Sun Trail, to Redwoods Trail, back to Panorama Trail and Mountain Home Inn.

The Inn is ready for us and we all arrive about the same time for a delicious lunch of burgers, bratwurst, fish sandwiches, salads, beer, root beer, lemonade and floats. Friendly host, Matt, with tips on places to see.

At 2:30 PM, we drive to top of Mt. Tamalpais and take short hike to top – rocky, steep trail. Spectacular views of San Francisco Bay.

Back to Hostel for showers and nap and drinks. Off to group dinner at Angelino's in Sausalito for pasta, fish and pizza. To bed at 10:00 PM.

Day 3 – Sunday, August 14, 2011

Up at 6:00 AM and make sandwiches for hike. Several stay back: Joe-bad knees, Don and June, Sherry, Esther and Karen.

8:30 AM. Drive to Point Reyes National seashore. To Palomarin Trailhead. Start on trail at 10:00 AM. The Young's go about a mile, then turn around and get their surfboards and hike down to the beach to surf. Later they say it was too scary, isolated, seals present that attract sharks, and cold water.

The rest hike the Coast Trail. Beautiful view of the coastal cliffs and sea.. Four miles to the Alamere Falls Trail junction. .4 miles to falls on unmaintained "dangerous" trail. Carl stays behind. The rest hike to a lookout above the falls. Gerry, Jodi and Nick scramble down the cliff to a level where the stream forms three successive falls. Nick scrambles the rest of the way to the beach to see large falls go over the cliff to the sea. We hike back and stay in a shaded area by Bass Lake that has pretty lily pads. We had also passed scenic Pelican Lake.

After lunch, we hike out to trailhead at 2:00 PM. Drive back and stop at Stinson Beach Market for ice cream and sodas. Back to Marin Headlands for a walk and visit to the Point Bonita Lighthouse, where some of those who stayed back hiked to. Later, families went to dinner. We went to Buckeye's Roadhouse: filet, pork chop, ribeye, key lime tart and parfait. To bed at 10:00 PM.

Day 4 – Monday, August 15, 2011

Up at 6:00 AM. Breakfast and clean up. Check out at 9:00 AM. Head home.

Thirty-fourth Annual Death March

Location: Wawona, Yosemite National Park

Dates: July 28 - July 31, 2012

Participants: Gerry Herter, Carl Greenwood, Curtis Williams, Karen Williams, Steve, Sherry, Esther, Megan and Monica Williams, Scott and Lauren Williams and two children, Mike Berman, George and Tom DiGaetano, Cassandra, Rick Riegel, Marc Richmond, Jodie and Joe Ristrom, Chuck and Vicki McLucas, Don Cottrell, Scott Shackleton, James Taylor (JT), Sandy Wang, Jay and Darlene Wikum.

Trail Notes:

Day 1 - Saturday, July 28, 2012

Departed at 6;30 AM: Carl, Curtis, Mike, Gerry and Karen. Stopped at Starbucks. Stopped in Oakhurst at 11:15 AM. Lunch at

McDonald's. Shop at Raley's for provisions. Arrive at Redwoods in Yosemite at 1:30 PM. Cabins not ready. Drive to Mariposa grove and hike to Grizzly Giant, Faithful Couple and Tunnel Tree.

Back to cabins and check in at 4:00 PM. 92R is beautiful, 48R is large and nice, and 47R is rustic and adequate. Dinner at Wawona Dining Room: trout, mahi mahi, steak, cheeseburgers and salads. To bed by 10:00 PM.

Day 2 – Sunday, July 29, 2012

Up at 6:00 AM. Breakfast: cereal, toast, bananas, o.j. and coffee. Make box lunches. Depart at 8:00 AM for Glacier Point. There by 9:00 AM. Group picture. Hike to Sentinel Dome – spectacular views. On to Taft Point. Sheer drops to the Valley. Lunch at Taft Point. Hike back – 8 miles total. Back to cabins by 3:45 PM and showers and cold drinks.

Prepare bar-b-que with steaks, baked potatoes and salad. Dinner on deck in back of our cabin. Sandy brings pasta to share. Good wines by Carl and Curtis. Watch Olympic swimming and women's gymnastics in London. To bed by 9:00 and 10:00 PM.

Day 3 – Monday, July 30, 2012

Up at 6:00 AM. Breakfast of cantaloupe, cereal, toast, juice and coffee. Depart at 8:00 AM for Chilnualna falls Trail. Beautiful small waterfalls, pools and streams. Dramatic views while hiking around side of mountain. Four miles in and mostly up. Four miles out for eight. Cool going in. Hot coming out. Out at 12:45 PM. Lunch at Wawona Hotel Golf Shop. Deli sandwiches and beer. Carl and Karen hike the Wawona Meadows Trail. Mike and Joe hike the Mariposa Grove to Wawona Point. Shower and relax with Olympics at cabin.

Dinner bar-b-que in Sun room in annex Building above Golf Shop at Wawona Hotel: pork ribs, chicken, corn on the cob, beans, potato salad, pasta salad, brownies, cookies, sodas and coffee. Beautiful setting, indoor/outdoor deck. Discussion, Olympics and to bed at 10:00 PM.

Day 4 – Tuesday, July 31, 2012

Up at 6:00 AM. Clean up. Breakfast: English muffins, watermelon, bananas, toast with peanut butter and jelly, and coffee. Leave at 6:45 AM. Head home.

Great trip! Sunny and warm, mid-80's, mid-50's at night.

Thirty-fifth Annual Death March

Location: Skoki Lodge, Banff National Park, Canada

Dates: August 3 – August 6, 2013

Participants: Gerry Herter, Carl Greenwood, Karen Williams, Steve, Sherry and Esther Williams, Marc Richmond, Chuck and Vicki McLucas..

Trail Notes:

Day 1 - Saturday, August 3, 2013

Gerry and Loretta Herter arrived by train from Santa Ana, CA and rental car from Glacier National Park. Marc, Chuck and Vicki flew to Seattle and by rental car to Lake Louise. Steve, Sherry and Esther flew to Calgary and by rental car from there. Carl and Kathy flew to Spokane and by rental car from there.

Group dinner at Lago in Chateau Lake Louise. All but Marc, Chuck and Vicki. Loretta and Kathy join in. Carl has come down with sinus infection and drops out.

Day 2 – Sunday, August 4, 2013

Group meets at Lake Louise Ski Center, 10 Peaks Lodge at 9:30 AM for check in. We drive up to fish Creek Parking Area and catch a shuttle to Temple Lodge and the trailhead. Partly cloudy with rain expected. But sun shines as we start out at 10:00 AM.

Trail starts up hill and climbs steeply to Boulder Pass and Deception Pass with long, flat sections through alpine meadows in between. Spectacular scenery with pine forest below and mountain faces above the tree line. Karen, Chuck and Marc all have knee, leg or foot problems, but they are troopers. Stop for lunch at Deception Pass about 1:00 PM. All make it to Skoki Lodge between 2:00 and 3:00 PM or so. Chuck and Vicki were in the lead at first, followed by Esther and Gerry. The rest arrived later.

Scones, pumpkin bread, cheese & crackers, cheese cake with blueberries, chips & salsa, lemonade, tea, coffee, beer and wine awaited us at the lodge when we arrived. Chuck and Vicki in Honeymoon Cabin. Steve, Sherry and Esther in Wolverine Cabin. Gerry and Marc in Molar Room. Karen in Silvertip Room.

Tobias in charge of Lodge welcomes us. He is from Australia. Settle in, relax and nap. Steve, Chuck and family play Monopoly. It starts to rain just after all arrive. Rains hard for twenty minutes and then stops. Outhouses with plenty of toilet paper. Everyone is worn out and feels it was a tough hike, 6-3/4 miles.

Dinner at 7:00 PM. Our cook is Teresa. Greek chicken topped with sundried tomatoes, phyllo with eggplant, mushrooms, veggies, corn on the cob, penne with pesto, Caesar salad, chocolate brownie with chocolate frosting, whipped cream and slice of chocolate.

After dinner, manager, Leo Mitzel, of ten years told about Prince William and Princess Kate visit. Entourage of ten. Dinner by themselves by fireplace. William had Alberta beef and two pieces of chocolate cake. Kate had wild halibut.

To bed at 9:00 PM.

Day 3 – Monday, August 5, 2013

Up at 6:00 AM. No one else stirred until 7:00 AM, except staff. Coffee ready about 6:30 AM. Chilly and light rain off and on and cloudy.

Breakfast at 8:00 AM: strata with tomato salsa, cinnamon rolls, mixed fruit, o.j., oatmeal with raisins, coffee and tea. Leo explained the trails. We chose Merlin Lake.

Departed at 10:00 AM. Sunny with clouds. Gorgeous hike across river, through woods, out on rocky slope across boulder field, with emerald lake below. On to pass and down to Merlin Lake – glacial green. Midway starts to rain. We don ponchos. Rains for twenty minutes. Stops and clears. In another twenty minutes we are dry. Along the way, we see marmots and/or badgers and ground squirrels. Wild flowers all over.

Lunch at lake: turkey and cheddar on wheat made at Lodge, carrot and celery sticks, apple, chocolate chip cookies, trail mix and water. Arrive at lake around noon. Leave and head back at 12:30 PM. All make hike except Karen. Back at 3:00 PM. Delicious vegetable soup and goodies set out with tea, lemonade and coffee. Rest and relax. Alternates sun and rain. Sit by fireplace and write notes. Glass of red wine.

Dinner at 7:00 PM: New Zealand lamb, organic rice, quinoa, corn medley, roasted beets, salad, apple caramel cake, tea and coffee. Leo answered more questions about wildlife, supplies by horse weekly-

1.300 pounds, helicopter brings fuel and other heavy stuff as needed. To bed at 9:15 PM.

Day 4 – Tuesday, August 6, 2013

Up at 6:15 AM. Many stars at night and Milky Way. Breakfast: eggs benedict, oatmeal, fruit salad, bacon, muffin and o.j.

Talk with Leo while he makes fire. When first meeting Prince, address him as "Your Royal Highness or Your Majesty." After that, Sir or Madam. One of the entourage is the Chief Inspector for Scotland Yard, a friendly fellow. He said the Prince didn't expect people to show special airs.

Leo is fine with most anyone from anywhere, as long as they have mutual respect. Usually the hike in changes people's perspective. He asked "Why do you come to a place like this?" I say "To be closer to God. I feel closer to God." Leo said his father was Catholic, but not practicing. He wanted to get Leo baptized but priest wouldn't do it, since he didn't go to church. Dad left church as a result. When Leo's child was to be baptized, folks were surprised Leo was casual about it. He didn't mind, but not concerned. They said child may need church later. Leo said when they needed spiritual help, he went to a mountain top and felt god's presence there. He didn't need organized religion for that.

Depart Skoki at 8:45 AM. Leo made us bag lunches: ham and cheese sandwiches, plum, trail mix and cookies. Beautiful sunny day. Vicki and Chuck take alternate route, get a little lost, and catch us at halfway hut. To Temple Lodge trailhead at 12:30 PM. See grizzly bear by ski lift. Shuttle picks us up at 1:00 PM. To cars at 1:15 PM. Back to Chateau at 1:30 PM.

A terrific hike and gracious staff at Skoki Lodge.

Thirty-sixth Annual Death March

Location: Sequoia High Sierra Camp, Sequoia National Park

Dates: July 31 – August 3, 2014

Participants: Gerry Herter, Carl Greenwood, Karen Williams, Steve, Sherry, Esther, Monica and Brooke Williams, Jodi and Joe Ristrom, Mike Berman, Mara, Ben and Samantha, Curtis, Deborah, Christian, Kelly, Jason, Jacob and Austin Campbell, Sheila and Andrew Ashrafi, and Marley Jue..

Trail Notes:

Day 1 - Thursday, July 31, 2014

Gerry, Karen and Carl depart at 6:30 AM. Jodi and Joe at 5:00 AM, others later. Stop for breakfast on the way in Gorman and Bakersfield. Arrive at Wuksachi Lodge at 12:30 PM. Road construction in park slows trip down. Check in and lunch at Lodge. Some go to General Sherman Tree or Morro Rock.

Dinner 5:00-7:00 PM at Wolverton Bar-b-que: ribs, chicken, pulled pork, bratwurst, hot dogs, corn on cob, baked beans, potato salad, coleslaw, greens, corn bread, apple cobbler, strawberry shortcake, pecan pie, lemonade and tea. Talk by woman from Sequoia National Historic Society – book at Beetle Rock. Beautiful weather today, some clouds, sunny, warm, 80's at Lodge. To bed at 10:00 PM.

Day 2 – Friday, August 1, 2014

Up at 6:00 AM. Breakfast at 7:00 AM: scrambled eggs with peppers, onions, pancakes, French toast, muffins, fruit, yogurt, cereal, oatmeal and coffee.

Depart at 8:15 AM. Drive to Marvin Trailhead. Last 2-1/2 miles dirt road, bumpy. 9;30 AM. Beautiful sunny day – 65-70° now, 75 later. Hike one mile to camp. Gerry, Karen and Carl arrive in camp at 10:00 AM. Meet Burr and Suzanne, friendly welcome, water, ice tea and cookies. Relax. Have box lunches. Rest of group arrives at various times, through morning and mid-day. Panoramic view from veranda. Haze in distance from fire in Yosemite.

After lunch, some hike to Rowell Meadow: Curtis and his boys, Ben and Gerry. Carl, Karen, Jodi and Joe make a wrong turn and hike to parking lot. The rest stay in camp. Kids play board games in lounge. Showers.

Hors d'oeuves on veranda at 6:15 PM. Finger sized ham & cheese and spoons of ceviche. Plus wine and beer. Sheila, Marley and Andrew arrive at 6:30 PM. They did cave and Morro Rock today.

Dinner at 7:00 PM. New York strip steak, mashed potatoes, broccoli, Caesar salad, green pepper soup, fruit cobbler, tea and decaf coffee. S'mores later by campfire. Gorgeous sunset over the valley and mountains: blood red. To bed at 9:30 PM.

Day 3 – Saturday, August 2, 2014.

Up at 6:00 AM. Coffee at 6:30 AM. Breakfast at 7:00 AM: made to order omelets: bacon, ham, cheddar and Swiss cheese, onions, peppers, mushrooms, and tomatoes, orange juice, melons, strawberries, blueberries, raspberries, pineapple, banana, granola, yogurt, blueberry muffins and scones. Make box lunches: beef, ham, turkey, cheeses, lettuce, tomato, peppers, avocado, onions, apple, raisins and chocolate bread.

Beautiful sunny day, high in 80's. Depart on hikes at 9:00 AM. Gerry, Steve, Jodi, Joe and Monica hike to Cedar Grove in Kings Canyon and get picked up by two vans at 2:45 PM. Drive through Kings Canyon back to Camp at 4:45 PM. Majestic panoramas, go around Lookout Peak. Lunch at Cedar Grove with sodas from store. Hike mostly downhill about 4,000' over eight miles. Some uphill near end felt good. Carl, Karen, Campbell's, Sheila and Marley hike to Mitchell Peak. Mike and family hike to Rowell Meadow.

Showers. Beer, wine and hors d'oeuvres at 6:30 PM: shrimp on toast squares and mushroom caps with goat cheese. Dinner at 7:00 PM: Mahi Mahi with avocado and pineapple diced cubes, rice, tomato soup, salad with fennel and vinaigrette, pannacotta with berry sauce, sugar cookie and coffee. S'mores by fireplace. Another spectacular sunset. To bed at 10:00 PM.

Day 4 – Sunday, August 3, 2014

Up at 6:00 AM. Coffee at 6:30 AM. Breakfast at 7:00 AM: same as yesterday. Settle bill and depart for home at 8:10 AM. Hike one mile to parking lot. Carl and Karen see bear, Depart parking lot at 8:45 AM. Home at 2:30 PM.

A great time was had by all.

Thirty-seventh Annual Death March

Location: Grand Canyon –Phantom Ranch

Dates: July 10 – 14, 2015

Participants: Gerry Herter, Curtis Williams, Karen Williams, Steve Williams, Monica Williams, Huw and Rachel Christopher, Chuck and Vicki McLucas, Marc Richmond, Peter Scheid, Jodi, Joe, Nick and Lauren Ristrom, Jeff Hipshman, Jeff Lazerson, Michaele Garcia, and Aileen Uy.

Day 1 – Friday, July 10, 2015

Having reached my 70th birthday, I had the desire to hike the Grand Canyon one more time, to experience and absorb the intense, immense grandeur that is found there. When 17 years old, I hiked the canyon for the first time, down the South Kaibab Trail and up the Bright Angel Trail, all in one day, with a brief stop at Phantom Ranch for a dip in the now defunct swimming pool.

This would be my sixth trip to the bottom, prior visits including a hike from north rim to south rim, and raft trips that started or ended near Phantom Ranch. In recent years, I have used the Death March as a gauge on how my body was holding up as it grows older. So far so good.

My friend, Curtis, and I departed at 5:00 AM from Cowan Heights in Orange County, California. Curtis was just coming off knee surgery six months ago, the result of an accident training for last year's Death March. So this will be the supreme test for him. Brave soul! Most of the others left around the same time. Jeff and Jeff will be coming in from Sedona tomorrow. Michaela and Aileen are leaving at 11:00 PM tonight, after work.

Stopping for an eggs & bacon breakfast in Ludlow, we arrive at the El Tovar Hotel on the Grand Canyon rim about 1:30 PM. We check into the Fred Harvey Suite on the second floor, with a spectacular panoramic view of the canyon from its balcony. Our group members join us for a happy hour on our balcony from 5:00-7:00 PM. Then dinner at the El Tovar Dining Room. Good food of sea bass, steak and other good things.

Check in our group for the hike tomorrow at the Bright Angel Transportation Desk. Walk over to the food court at Maswik Lodge to purchase box lunches for the trail tomorrow.

To bed at 10:00 PM.

Day 2 – Saturday, July 11.

Up at 5:00 AM. We breakfast on the balcony with orange juice and part of our foot-long sandwich.

We meet our group at the Bright Angel Trailhead. Michaela and Aileen had arrived at 6:00 AM, and we find them catching a few winks in their car by the trailhead while waiting for us. We chat with a cowboy preparing his guests for the mule ride down the canyon. He tells them "If you are afraid of heights, this will be a very long day." Though the trail is generally wide and safe, the experience can be scary when one is sitting on top of a mule, as it goes around steep switchbacks that have long drop-offs. The cowboy assures them that the mules are surefooted veterans, and there is nothing to worry about as long as guests follow his instructions closely. I am glad to be on my own two feet for the descent.

After a group photo, we start down the trail at 7:10 AM on a beautiful day, with some clouds that offer welcome shade from the sun for a while, and keep the temperature cool, initially. Within an hour the sun comes out and warms things up quickly. The views get more and more spectacular as we descend, with shadows and perspectives constantly changing the lower we get.

Nick and Lauren move out ahead. Jodi and Joe soon go after them and lead the way the full distance to the camp. Steve, Monica, Gerry, and Curtis are together to Indian Garden, and stop for lunch there at 10 AM. Michaela and Aileen catch up there and stay with us until Michaela turns an ankle and slows down. The rest of the group are farther behind.

A rushing stream pours out from springs at Indian Garden and accompanies us for a stretch as we depart on down the trail.

Lauren makes Phantom Ranch speedily at 10:40 AM, with Joe, Jodi and Nick coming in a little while later. Curtis and Gerry arrive about 1:30 PM with Jeff and Jeff not far behind, Steve and Monica at 2 PM, Rachel and Huw at 3:15 PM, Marc, Peter, Chuck and Vicki about 4:30 PM. Karen is last at 5 PM. Lemonade and beer are cold and delicious after the hot, grueling hike. Then showers and naps.

Ranger talk in the ring of benches near the ranch, about condors in the canyon. Dinner at 6:30 PM served family style. The food is on the tables as the dinner bell is rung and we are welcomed and directed to our tables. We dine on beef stew, salad, cornbread, chocolate cake, ice tea, beer and wine.

Another ranger talk at the amphitheater near the campground, about canyon critters. The ranger will follow up after dark with a scorpion walk using a black light. She found four during the walk.

To bed at 9:00 PM.

Day 3 – Sunday, July 12

Up at 5:00 AM. Coffee with Curtis. Breakfast at 6:30 AM. Scrambled eggs, bacon, pancakes, peaches, orange juice and coffee.

At 9 AM, we head out the back of camp on the North Kaibab Trail for a quarter mile to the Clear Creek Trail, which leads a little over a mile up to an overlook high above the ranch. Gerry, Curtis, Steve, Monica, Jodie, Peter, Marc, Chuck and Vicki make the hike, and take in the view of the ranch far below. We are glad to be hiking upward, since different muscles are used, and not our calves which are all sore from yesterday's hike down here. Jodi, Peter and Gerry go a half mile further to a Colorado River overlook and view of both the silver and black bridges. Beautiful sunny day and spectacular views along the way. Bright Angel Creek is running strong.

Back at 11 AM. Jodi goes on to do the River Trail, which Huw and Rachel are doing, also. Karen does the historic Ranch self-guided tour following the descriptive pamphlet.

The hikers convene at the dining hall to indulge in their (plastic) sack lunches, consisting of a bagel, cream cheese, apple, sausage, peanuts, dried cranberries, pretzels, Oreo cookies, and Vitalyte electrolyte powder to mix with water.

After lunch, most are ready for a nap, shower, and then organizing their packs. Many are planning to send out their heavy pack items on a mule tomorrow, to lighten their load for the difficult hike back to the South Rim.

The ranger talk at 4:00 PM is about tips for hiking the canyon, which is helpful as we anticipate tomorrow's trek to the top: plenty of water, salt, electrolytes, eat along the way, dowse head with water, cover up, wear cotton, wet bandanna, hike early and late, avoiding 10:00 AM-4:00 PM hottest period, layover during the heat of the day at Indian Garden.

Dinner is at 5:00 PM. Steak, baked potato, peas, corn, cornbread, salad, and chocolate cake. Delicious.

We finalize our stuff into duffels for sending with the mules. The weight limit is 30 pounds, which we check on the scale at the drop-off point.

13 of our group members decide to leave at 3:00 AM to hike out during the cooler darkness. Gerry, Huw and Rachel decide to stay for breakfast at 5:00 AM, along with Karen who is going out on a mule.

Early hikers are in bed by 8:00 PM, the rest by 9:00 PM.

Day 4 - Monday, July 13

The early group of 13 is up at 2:30 AM, pack up, get sack lunches, and depart at 3:00 AM, to get as far as possible before the hot sun comes up. The remaining four don't sleep much after that, and are up by 4:00 AM. Head over to get coffee, where Gerry meets Brookhart & Familia. They are from Montreaux, Switzerland, though Brookhart is originally from Cologne, Germany. He was here when he was younger. At 4:15 AM on Monday, as we drank coffee and got our sack lunches from the side window at the Dining Hall, Brookhart said "I would prefer to stay for breakfast, but my wife wants to get on the trail now."
Breakfast is at 5:00 AM, but the Swiss couple leaves at 4:30 AM.

I stay for breakfast of scrambled eggs, bacon, pancakes, peaches and orange juice, and am joined by Karen, Huw and Rachel. I depart at 5:10 AM at a fast pace. At the river, I take a wrong turn and add an extra mile going over the black bridge by the South Kaibab Trail. I catch up and pass Huw and Rachel who had left a few minutes after me, but took the right turn. I pass Brookhart and Familia a couple miles up the trail as they rest under some foliage besides the creek.

Daylight had appeared a little before 5:00 AM. The temperature was already in the 70's, but felt almost cool, compared to the 100+ temperatures of the day before. I made good time, taking photos as I go. Hiking without my pack, which went out on a mule, enabled me to move faster than on the way down. Enjoyed the inner canyon, which has its own unique feel with hundred foot walls rising up from the creek in a narrow gorge about 50 feet wide.

I proceeded up the Devils' Corkscrew, a series of switchbacks rising steeply up the inner canyon. I was two-thirds of the way up when the sun penetrated this section of the canyon and accompanied me for the rest of the climb out.

I arrived at Indian Garden about 7:30 AM, and refilled my water bottle, adding Vitalyte electrolyte crystals, while keeping a close eye on an aggressive squirrel looking to get into my fanny pack for food. Before and after Indian Garden, there are some relatively flat stretches. Then as the trail continues to 3-mile-house, it gets steeper again.

Between Indian Garden and 3-mile-house, I catch up with Michaela and Aileen resting on a rock, and I rest with them a couple minutes. Continuing on, I reach 3-mile-house around 8:30 AM, where I catch up with Peter, who is waiting for Marc who is in the restroom. I fill my water bottle again, commune with a blue-colored bird, and then proceed.

From here on, the trail is hot and steep, requiring frequent short stops to regain strength. I keep telling myself "one foot in front of the other," wondering if I have enough left to make it out. By the time I reach 1-1/2 mile house, I am really tired. I catch up with Joe there, and we hike the final stretch out of the canyon together.

We reach the top at about 11:15 AM. Jodi is there to greet us. She finished about 10:45 AM, preceded by Lauren and Nick at 9:45 AM? Jodi and Joe stop in the Kolb Studio right there on the rim. I continue on to the Fountain for a double dip ice cream cone of mocha chip and strawberry. Steve, Monica and Curtis came out at 11:00 AM, preceded by Chuck & Vicki.

Karen left Phantom Ranch at 6:45 AM on a mule named Penelope and with a female guide. She arrives on top via the South Kaibab Trail at 11:45 AM. Karen vows never to take the mule again, as the ride scares her half to death, because of Penelope's tendency to go perilously close to the edges that have steep drop-offs. "She only slipped once," Karen said, "but she caught herself right away."

Huw and Rachel set their own pace, slow and steady, and emerge at the top at 2:20 PM, tired but pleased at their accomplishment.

Gerry and Curtis check in at the El Tovar Suite in the hotel of the same name. The suite is on the third floor, and has a huge balcony overlooking the canyon and the Fred Harvey Suite just below. After settling in, a couple beers help to soothe sore, tired legs, while they take in the panoramic view from padded chairs. A thunderstorm passes though quickly providing a natural show across the skyline.

After a nap, a few of the group come up for happy hour. Then we go down to the dining room at 5:00 PM for a group, celebratory dinner, feasting on prime rib and prickly pear chicken breast, followed by raspberry and blueberry covered cheesecake.

There's a group photo in the dining room and a night cap at the suite. Before long, everyone heads to bed early at 8:00 PM or 9:00 PM, ready for a good long sleep.

Day 5 - Tuesday, July 14

Up around 5:00 AM or so to catch the daybreak on the balcony over the canyon. Clouds make for unusual hues and shadows. Quiet and peaceful out by the rim, with just a couple early birds here and there.

Breakfast of spicy southwestern sausage omelets in the dining room. Steve stops by to wish a farewell, and Karen comes in to join us for breakfast.

Gerry & Curtis check out and are on the road home at 8:00 AM. A quick stop for lunch at Carl's Jr. and we arrive home at 4:15 PM. All make it home safely and have had a good time.

Thirty-eighth Annual Death March aka The Death March That Never Was

Location: Big Sur and Big Bear, California

Dates: July 30 – August 1, 2016

Participants-Big Sur Contingent: Gerry Herter, Carl Greenwood, Curtis Williams, Karen Williams, Jodi and Joe Ristrom, Marc Richmond, Peter Scheid, Marley, Eric, Jenelle, Julia and Sheryl Jue, Kelly and Andy Young, and Paula Novak.

Participants-Big Bear Contingent: Steve, Sherry, Esther and Megan Williams, Laurie, Jaden and Zoey Williams, Scott and Lauren Williams and two children, Monica and Brooke Williams, Scott Wallin, Don and June Silber, Dave Silber and wife and child.

In addition, another 14 individuals who were signed up for the original Death March had to drop out when Big Sur Lodge was closed for the fire.

The Trail Notes are from the Big Sur Contingent.

Day 1 – Friday, July 30, 2016

Carl, Curtis and Gerry departed at 6:45 AM by car on a clear, sunny day, with temperature in the 70's. Pick up Karen at Union Station in Los Angeles, arriving from Arizona on the Southwest Limited at 8:15 AM. Drive to San Luis Obispo. Meet Joe and Jodi for lunch at Luna Red in the center of town. Jodi and Joe did Hearst Castle and will proceed to Santa Barbara for a day trip to Santa Cruz Island of the Channel Islands National Park.

We proceed to Cambria and Hotel Colibri. Walk the boardwalk from hotel to Moonstone Beach and along waterfront for a couple miles and back. Pass Moonstone Landing Hotel where Marc is on balcony reading. Beautiful, sunny day. Surfers catching waves. Beach has scenic rock outcrops. Squirrels aggressively seek food on and under boardwalk.

At 6:00 PM, go to Marc and Peter's hotel room 205, with balcony overlooking beachfront. Wine, hors d'oeuvres and good conversation. Marc and Peter had hiked near Hearst Castle at Hearst State Beach. Also hiked Limekin State Park. Tomorrow they will head back home. We all go to dinner at Robin's in downtown Cambria: lamb curry, steak and other delicious offerings.

Day 2 – Saturday, July 31, 2016

Up at 6:00 AM. Breakfast at hotel. Depart at 8:30 AM for Limekin State Park. Marine layer and patches of sun. Arrive at 9:30 AM.

Hike Hare Creek Trail first. Sunny and beautiful. Ocean surface covered by clouds. Trail through redwood forest along creek. Parts of trail are easy. But several places cross the creek, requiring careful maneuvering across logs and rocks to avoid getting wet. Suns rays cast scenic lighting through the trees and greenery. Trail is about a mile round trip.

On way back, we meet up with Marley and family members, eight in all, along the trail. We take a group selfie. They continue on Hare Creek Trail and we head up the Falls Trail. The falls are about a hundred feet high and form two threads flowing over rock face down to the creek in spectacular fashion, We meet up with Marley again on this trail, also a mile round trip.

Finally, we hike to the lime kilns, four fascinating furnaces built in 1887 to purify lime for use in concrete. They have set idle after limestone ran out in three years.

Lunch two miles north in Lucia, at gorgeous ocean setting of Lucia Lodges and Café: wild sockeye salmon tacos.

Drive back to San Simeon to Hearst State Park and hike beach to bluff for panoramic views of coast and beach in bright sunlight. Back to hotel, clean up and dinner at Moonstone Landing Bar & Grill: sea bass-Delicious. To bed at 10:00 PM.

Day 3 – Sunday, August 1, 2016

Up at 5:30 AM. Depart at 7:00 AM. Breakfast in Cayucas. Then Paula heads north. Drop Karen off at San Luis Obispo Courtyard Inn. Home at 2:30 PM.

Thirty-ninth Annual Death March

Location: Crater Lake National Park

Dates: August 13 – 16, 2017

Participants: Gerry Herter, Carl Greenwood, Curtis Williams, Karen Williams, Marc Richmond, Ray Eggersglus, Marley, Eric, Jenelle, Julia and Sheryl Jue, Kelly and Andy Young, Paula Novak, Steve, Sherry, Esther and Megan Williams, Laurie, Jaden and Zoey Weiner, Monica, Scott and Brooke Wallin, Jeff, Carol, Micah and Noa Richmond, Scott Shackleton, James Taylor (J.T.), Chuck and Vicki McLucas, Robert and Bernie Quiring, Elsie Sodano, and Tristan Harwe.

Day 1 – Sunday, August 13, 2017

Departed home at 6:30 AM. Picked up by Curtis Williams and son. Pick up Carl and go to LAX. American flight at 9:40 AM to

Medford, Oregon. Arrive at 11:40 AM. Drive rental car. Stop in Shady Cove for lunch at Mac's on the Rogue River.

Arrived at Crater Lake National Park about 3:00 PM. Check in to Mazama Village Cabins and take a short hike. Everyone arrives. Steve and family drove in, staying at Morrison's Rogue River Lodge (sight of Death March 19 in 1997) and rafting there. Scott and J.T. fly in from a pre-Death March Alaskan adventure. Karen arrives in Klamath Falls by Amtrak train and takes trolley van to Park. Robert flies in to Medford where he meets his father, Bernie who lives there. The rest drove from California.

Steve's family does the Annie Creek Trail before dinner. The trail was technically closed because of damage during the winter, but they are told not to heed the closed signs, and proceed without incident.

The only travel misfortune was suffered by Paula. Her Uber and taxi failed to arrive and she missed her flight from Chicago. She won't be able to get here until tomorrow night.

Group dinner at Annie Creek Restaurant in Mazama Village: chicken Florentine and mushroom ravioli. Mazama Village is seven miles from the lake.

To bed at 9:00 PM.

Monday, August 14, 2017

Up at 6:00 AM Breakfast at 7:00 AM. Group photo in front of restaurant. All drive to Crater Lake Lodge to pick up box lunches and have another group photo taken overlooking the lake. Ironically, the lake is hidden behind the group. The Lodge is a classic National Park Lodge, perched dramatically on the crater cliff looking out on the lake.

Everyone drove up the East Rim Drive to Plaikni Falls Trailhead and made the one mile hike to the falls. Beautiful, sunny day. Walk through woods. Falls vigorously cascades down the volcanic rock formation. Perfect setting for family pictures.

We hike back and drive further along East Rim Drive to the Mount Scott Trailhead. Have box lunches in picnic area. Gerry, Julia, Marley, Kelly, Andy, Eric, Tristan, Scott S., J.T., Chuck and Vicki hike to the top for a gorgeous 360° view, looking down over Crater Lake. A 2-1/2 mile hike one-way, elevation 8,929', which is 1,200' above the trailhead and 2.756' above the lake surface.

Just a slight haze, possibly from smoke from the nearby Spruce Lake Fire. But no fire or heavy smoke were spotted. Carl, Curtis, Karen, Sheryl, Janelle and Esther hike part way. The others opted for different hikes around the lake.

Returned to Crater Lake Lodge and checked in: the Williams family, Gerry, Karen, Carl, Curtis, J.T., Scott S., Chuck and Vicki. The others remained at Mazama Village Cabins for the duration.

Showers, then relax in rocking chairs on back patio of Lodge with drinks and snacks. Later it got chilly, so moved inside the Lodge.

Dinner at 5:30 PM for the Williams, 6:30 PM for Gerry, Carl, Curtis, Karen, Scott S., and J.T. Shortly thereafter Paula joins us. She flew in from Chicago to Eugene, OR, and drove to the Park. We catch up with each other over salmon, halibut, steak and pasta.

We hear that a boat broke down, so the shuttle we planned to take to Wizard Island has been cancelled. We will be rescheduled to a two hour lake cruise at 9:30 AM.

To bed at 10:00 PM.

Tuesday, August, 15, 2017

Up at 6:00 AM. Coffee at 6:30 AM. Depart at 7:00 AM for
Cleetwood Cove along West rim drive. Sign in for the boat at the
trailhead. Confusion as more people want to go then there is room
for. They can only let 14 of our 18 on the boat. So Scott W., Esther,
Brook and Zoey stay back.

We all hike the one mile steep trail down the side of the crater to the
lake and dock. Sunny, partly cloudy day. Check in again at dock.
More people there who had hoped to get on.

Boat departs at 9:30 AM. Audrey, National Park Ranger, is our
guide for a very fascinating two hour ride to all parts of the lake.
Highlights: Phantom Ship rock, Pumice Castle, waterfalls from snow
pack, stratas from various eruptions, Devil's Backbone, Palisades
where water seeps out from the lake, Wizard Island and others. Great
boat ride! Hike back up trail was tough, since so steep. Marley's
family, Chuck and Vicki take the 11:30 AM boat tour.

We return to the Lodge for lunch of Portobello burgers: mushroom
instead of meat. Showers, then walk along cliff to Rim Village shop.
Carl and Karen had hiked cliff trail instead of the boat ride. Steve's
family does Castle Cregg Wild Flower Trail after boat ride. The
Richmonds, Robert and Bernie, and Tristan do various hikes.

All meet at the Lodge for Happy Hour At 5:30 PM. We have
staggered dinner times in the dining room from 6:15 PM through
7:15 PM. Ribeye steak and citrus chicken are the choices, with
blueberry cobbler for dessert.

To bed at 9:30 PM.

Wednesday, August 16, 2017

Up at 6:00 AM. Coffee at 6:30 AM. Breakfast at 7:30m AM. We say
farewell to Steve's family, as they start the long one day drive home.

Paula joins us for breakfast of omelets, French toast and pancakes. We say farewell to J.T. and Scott, chuck and Vicki.

Gerry, Carl, Curtis and Karen say farewell to Paula, then drive over to Castle Cregg (1/2 mile awat) to hike the ½ mile Wild Flower Trail. Gorgeous with sun's rays through the pine trees, smooth rock path wandering along a brook amongst meadows filled with wildflowers of all colors.

Check out of Lodge at 10:15 AM and head back. Lunch in Medford at Jasmine's gourmet Burgers, recommended by Elsie for their exotic animal burger offerings. I have a Jackaroo Burger, a traditional Australian burger made with kangaroo, bacon, cheese, fried egg and pineapple. I told the waiter the only thing missing from an authentic Australian burger was a slice of beet. Carl and Curtis are not as adventurous and have classic beef burgers. I wash mine down with a white peach milk shake.

Then to Medford Airport for our 4:50 PM flight to Los Angeles. Home at 9:00 PM. A great trip that all enjoyed immensely.

About the Author

Gerald Herter grew up in the suburbs of Chicago, Illinois, graduated from the University of Wisconsin with BBA and MBA degrees in accounting, and achieved the status of Certified Public Accountant. He served in the United States Army as a field artillery officer in Germany and Viet Nam, and then worked for several years at Arthur Andersen & Company in Chicago.

Gerald met and married his wife, Lori, in the Chicago area. They moved to Southern California several decades ago, where he became associated with what would become HMWC CPAs & Business Advisors. He served as Managing Partner for many years, as well as President of the Americas, Asia & Australia Region of Integra International, a world-wide association of accounting firms. He also wrote and edited Integra's Audit & Accounting Alert newsletter for several years, and was a Contributing Editor for Accounting Technology magazine.

Gerald and Lori still live in Southern California with their cat, Jasmine. They are long time members of Tustin Presbyterian Church, where Gerald serves as an elder. He also serves on the Boards of Directors of Family Promise of Orange County, a homeless shelter, and New Theological Seminary of the West.

Gerald and Lori have traveled extensively in the U.S., Canada, Europe, New Zealand, Australia, and Tahiti. Gerald has had travel articles published in the New York Times, Chicago Tribune, Los Angeles Times, and Celtic Life International magazine. His prior book, *My Celtic Journey*, is a series of stories recalling travels to the Celtic lands of the British Isles and glimpses of the Celtic world in North America.